LIVING WITH THINGS

Anthropology Matters : Scholarship on Demand

A new series focusing on significant contributions that demonstrate the scholarship
and depth of the traditional anthropological monograph, perhaps without wide
commercial appeal, but with unquestionable academic merit. It will include important
collections that open up new themes, and will publish research reports that deal with
specific development or policy related issues, and are major interventions in current
affairs and decision-making. All of these exemplify the way 'Anthropology Matters'.

Volume 1: Of Alien Kings and Perpetual King: Contradiction and Ambiguity
in Ruwund (Lunda) Symbolic Thought
Manuela Palmeirim

Volume 2: Living with Things: Ridding, Accommodation, Dwelling
Nicky Gregson

Volume 3: The Potters and Pottery of Miravet: Production, Marketing and
Consumption of Pottery in Catalonia
Rob van Veggel

Volume 4: Sin, Sex and Stigma: A Pacific Response to HIV and AIDS
Lawrence James Hammar

Volume 5: Mutuality and Empathy: Self and Other in the Ethnographic
Encounter
edited by Anne Sigfrid Grønseth and Dona Lee Davis

Volume 6: The Shark Warrior of Alewai: A Phenomenology of Melanesian
Identity
Deborah van Heekeren

Living with Things

✥

Ridding, Accommodation, Dwelling

Nicky Gregson

Anthropology Matters, Volume 2

Sean Kingston Publishing
www.seankingston.co.uk
Wantage

First paperback printing in 2011 by

Sean Kingston Publishing
www.seankingston.co.uk
Wantage

British Library Cataloguing in Publication Data
A catalogue record for this book is available from the British Library.

Printed by Lightning Source

978-1-907774-07-2 paperback

Contents

List of Figures

Acknowledgements

To use a metaphor from climbing, this book only came into being because I wanted to see if 'it would go'. I thought it might, but I couldn't be sure, and putting it all together has only come in the writing. It is a book that started off life as ethnographic stories written at a kitchen table. Eventually it became an unsolicited manuscript, and the sort of manuscript that very few academic publishers nowadays will touch, a place-specific research monograph. That it has become a book and not just a manuscript, then, is very much down to the vision and commitment of Sean Kingston, and Sean Kingston Publishing, to a particular type of social science research output. I also owe a huge debt to the Economic and Social Research Council, who gave me a year out to do the research on which this book is based, and even more so to the friends and colleagues who believed in this (and me) sufficiently to read and comment in detail on various drafts of the manuscript, either wholly or in part; to Alan Metcalfe, Ray Hudson and Peter Jackson, my heartfelt thanks and appreciation; and to Danny Miller, my thanks for both the 'gentle suggestions' and for being a constant source of inspiration.

Chapter 1

From researching ridding to living with things

Beginnings

Like many academic research projects, I suspect, this book's beginnings can be traced to the unfinished business of a string of previous projects. Spanning six years of research in various sites of second-hand exchange in the United Kingdom, including car-boot sales, charity shops and retro and vintage shops, these projects were formulated as a rejoinder to the tendency within the consumption research of that time to locate exchange exclusively within the high street, the mall and the department store (Gregson and Crewe 1997 and 1998; Gregson et al. 1997, 2000 and 2002a; see also Clarke 1998, 1999 and 2000, and Storr 2004). As that research proceeded, however, my sense was that these projects were missing something altogether more important. Although critical to enhancing understandings of how consumer goods are placed back in circulation, the sites and spaces of second-hand exchange actually tell us very little about how and why things are divested and released. This realisation is one that I would ground in the practices that go on in back rooms of charity shops. Working away in various such back rooms through-out 1999: sorting through mountains of seemingly ubiquitous black plastic bin-liners filled with stuff, pricing-up, discarding, separating out and forever making value judgements – usually about worn, used clothing and cloth – I continually imagined. Who had worn this? Why had this bag of things been released? What consumption histories were ingrained in this fur coat? Could it really be – as its cacked and stained materiality suggested – that someone had died in it? Whose wardrobe was this? Had they died? Had they moved into elder-care accommodation? Separated from their previous owner/s, in many instances resonating with loss, the clothes in these charity-shop back rooms fuelled my imagination, as they do for many charity shoppers; they elided to become stories masquerading as objects (Garber 1992). And yet, when they were disclosed, the stories of at least some of these clothes were far more mundane and embedded in routine everyday life than in the instances of loss that I wove into their fabric. They featured divested clothing's connection to mothers' management of their young children's clothing, teenagers' investments in the intricacies of teen fashion, women's management of their wardrobes and vague attempts to make money (Gregson and Crewe 2003). Located in the interstices of those research projects, but never the focus of attention, divestment haunted them; whilst enabling of second-hand exchange, divestment itself remained unexamined.

One of the most fascinating aspects of the entire research process is that it is, of course, full of ghostly presences such as this. Whilst many remain just this, or become things which slipped away, pathways which were never followed or explored because something else got funded and became more pressing instead, in this instance divestment has mutated from ghostly presence to centre stage. That this has occurred here is, I think, about its coincidence with two key moments. One of these pertains to some general tendencies in contemporary research in consumption, the other to the changing regulatory regime of household waste and its management in the United Kingdrom. Both are worthy of comment.

A familiar mantra of the consumption literature through the 1990s was that consumption is more than the act of purchase, and that consumption research has to go beyond the act of purchase (Miller 1987; Jackson and Thrift 1995). Nonetheless, retailing, shopping and consumer cultures remain pervasive presences in the field (see, for example, Miller 2001c; Williams et al. 2001; Entwistle 2002; Dwyer and Jackson 2003; Jackson 1999; Jackson 2004; Jackson et al. 2006). Albeit attention has moved away from the objects of acquisition per se and consumer behaviour – to encompass shopping as a practice (Gregson et al. 2002b), as a means of enacting key social relations as well as identities (Miller et al. 1998) and even as sacrifice (Miller 1998) – our fascination with retail sites and with shopping as acquisition remains. To borrow from Rachel Bowlby's book of the same name, as researchers and not just as consumers, we are 'carried away' with shopping's allure (Bowlby 2000), with the seemingly infinite capacity of retailers to offer us something new to research as well as to buy. Indicative of the continued and pervasive influence of the commodity chain as a conceptual framing device for much consumption research (Gereffi et al. 1994; Hartwick 1998; Hartwick 2000; Leslie and Reimer 1999 and 2003; Hughes 2000; Hughes and Reimer 2003; Raikes et al. 2000), the effect has been to ensure that what consumers actually do with the things they acquire, how they appropriate things and, indeed, divest them, has remained by comparison relatively unconsidered. There are, of course, some notable exceptions to this generalisation, beginning with Gullestad's (1984) pioneering study of Norwegian housewives in Bergen, through Miller's (1988) study of kitchens on a council estate in London, to a number of more recent small-scale studies of key life events in objects, such as Layne's (1999) work on pregnancy loss and Marcoux's (2001) research on older people's movement into sheltered accommodation in Montreal. Such work has been enhanced by the recent flurry of research on home cultures (see for example Madigan and Munro 1996; Birdwell-Pheasant and Lawrence-Zúñiga 1999; Chapman and Hockey 1999; Cieraad 1999; Attfield 2000; Miller 2001b; Painter 2002; Cwerner and Metcalfe 2003; Pink 2004), as well as by research examining a range of kitchen-based consumption practices (Shove and Southerton 2001; Shove 2003). In all this, though, the focus has remained resolutely on appropriation (although see Young 2004) and/or on how ordinary consumers seek to constitute the conditions for re-appropriating things, for example through passing things on to key significant others. What remains invisible, however, is that most consumption, and particularly routine everyday consumption – the sort of activities that just 'go on' – is also about replacing things, about getting rid of other things, about casting them out and abandoning them. Acknowledged and excavated, not un-coincidentally, by a handful of archaeologists of contemporary consumption (Buchli and Lucas 2000 and 2001; Buchli 2002; Lucas 2002; Rathje and Murphy 2001), and by others working on cloth (Norris 2004b), such issues and the trajectories that connect the things that are cast out, replaced and abandoned to the making of rubbish and waste remain woefully under-examined empirically, if not theoretically (Thompson 1979; Bataille 1989; O'Brien 1999; Hawkins 2000; Hawkins and Muecke 2003; Hetherington 2004; Laporte 2002; Scanlan 2004).[1]

At the same time, and paralleling these developments, the connections between consumption and waste generation have assumed greater prominence within United Kingdom policy communities.[2] The primary trigger here has been a raft of European Union (EU) directives aimed at constituting more sustainable forms of consumption. These have focused on specific categories of goods and physical matter, for example paper and packaging, electrical and electronic waste, notably fridges, computers, televisions and mobile phones, and cars, and set clear recycling targets in relation to the manufacture, retailing and 'end-of-life' of certain consumer goods. Allied to this is the EU Landfill Directive (1999). This seeks to reduce dramatically the amount of household waste sent to landfill within the EU, largely by setting recycling targets and a sliding scale of stringent financial penalties for those national governments who fail to meet them. Given the UK's historic reliance on landfill as a means of waste management and its poor recycling rate (at 12% in 2002, the lowest of the then fifteen member states within the EU), both waste management and recycling are firmly on the UK policy agenda. Consequently, for local authorities charged with the task of implementing and attaining these recycling targets – largely through households – waste and its management have become core 'front-line' activities (see, for example, Parfitt et al. 2001; Perrin and Barton 2001; Price 2001; Mee et al. 2004). Moreover, it is through the rolling-out of various local authority kerbside collection services that the formerly exclusively 'green' mantra of 'Reduce–Reuse–Recycle' has come to assume greater prominence and visibility on the streets of Britain. Correspondingly, from being represented as a 'throwaway society' (Cooper 2003), Britain and, in particular, British households find themselves being positioned increasingly within a set of regulatory practices which currently encourage, but which may well yet enforce, that work be done on that that is being discarded, by those who have consumed it as well as by those who have manufactured and retailed it. Typically, matter has to be sorted or graded – some paper, but not all paper; glass jars from their lids. Some matter – notably tins, glass jars and bottles – has to be washed. And other matter has to be separated out for the routine waste collection and placed in wheelie bins or black plastic sacks. Although the norm elsewhere in Europe, and particularly in Northern Europe, such regulatory practices extend notions of consumption in the UK to encompass waste matter and its management, and recast constructs of consumer responsibility to include not just ethical trade (Freidberg 2003 and 2004) but also an ethics of environmental care, and – through their emphasis on doing things to materials and disaggregating objects – begin to focus the consumer's attention on the fact that many consumer goods are manufactured things, composites of fabricated matter and hybrid in their materialities.

Given that research is always a situated practice, it is perhaps not particularly surprising that a project which centred the divestment of things in consumption and which set out to examine how and why people get rid of things got off the ground and was funded.[3] Yet, let me say immediately that this project would probably not have been commissioned as a piece of policy research. Instead, its inspiration and its methodologies are those that have come to typify a material culture approach to consumption (Miller 1998 and 2001b; Buchli 2002). They are then ethnographic (on which more later), and they start not with normative regulatory practices, or even with the detritus and left-overs of consumption, but in homes, with households, and focus on consumer objects. Rather than beginning by presuming to know what is waste matter, the emphasis in this research has been on how and why things come to be discarded in ways that may, or may not, place them in trajectories that connect to waste making. Correspondingly, and to further differentiate this research from the legion of studies that centre on the attitudes of households to recycling and recycling behaviour, as well as from the household waste diaries that periodically surface in the national broadsheets (Freeman 2002), this work explicitly excluded from consideration the matter that can be placed in kerbside collection bins (tins, jars, bottles and certain paper), as well as packaging and left-over food.[4] Like any ring-fencing decision, this had both plus points and downsides. Although it clearly worked to separate the research team from the moral rhetoric and unchallenged normativity of recycling as 'a good thing' (Hawkins 2000) and allowed us to assume a non-judgmental position with respect to what households do with their divested and discarded things – of particular importance when working with households who do not, for whatever reason, participate in recycling schemes (see O'Brien 1999; McDonald and Oates 2003) – undeniably such matter comprises a sizeable proportion of what households identify as rubbish, and of what makes up UK household waste.[5] Moreover, for those who invested heavily in recycling practices, this type of matter was what they felt we as a team really ought to be looking at, rather than more awkward things like consumer objects whose divestment routes often disrupted their owners' largely 'green' self-narratives. Of course, we would disagree: rupture points are altogether more interesting and frequently have far more to tell us. Which brings me to a further set of insistencies which have precipitated the writing of this book.

The broader research project of which this volume is part is interdisciplinary: although located in geography departments, the team includes a sociologist and has been conducted in part in a manner which is identified as the defining methodological business of social anthropology, through a year-long ethnographic investigation of households living primarily in one place in north-east England.[6] Running parallel with, and extending before and after, the ethnographic fieldwork has been a more extensive repeat-interview based study with approximately sixty households living in various areas of Nottingham, a city in the English Midlands. The intent here was to use the repeat interview work, alongside focus groups, to provide an 'anchor' for the ethnography.[7] Without equal as a method to illuminate the particularities of practice and to generate theory through this, the limits of ethnography remain conditioned by its strengths, its labour-intensity and concomitant inability to work with anything other than relatively small metrics. But ethnography is also framed through and limited by its enactor, the situated, embodied ethnographer/s (Coffey 1999). Now, notwithstanding the considerable advances made recently in acknowledging the workings, and indeed limits, of positionality, reflexivity and situated knowledges in social science (Rose 1997), and the ways these encourage working in research teams, it remains the case that the majority of ethnographic work is conducted, as it was here, by the solo ethnographer. This is problematic, particularly for a multi-person research team utilising ethnography. Unable to see the events that unfold in front of and around the ethnographer, and to hear the fullness of talk and the conversations, positioned to know about these only through the filter of the ethnographer's recorded stories about stories, through listening to recorded conversations and through looking at images of objects, rooms and people, those working alongside an ethnographer are positioned (entirely unintentionally) more as audience than within the research as enacted. In its very enactment, then, through its doing, recording and writing, ethnography works to constitute the ethnographer as the witnessing, knowing, authoring subject, as the 'I who was there', and who therefore, somehow, is invested with the authority to know, however much this is acknowledged to be partial and provisional; not because of any desire to be such an I, but as an effect of its practice. I found this foundational, experiential and seemingly incontestable characteristic of ethnography deeply troubling, not least because of the way in which it seems to effect a foreclosing in the capacity of others to offer interpretations and readings of data. Yet, this is a situation which as yet I have no answers to, particularly in a cultural context like the UK, where privacy combines with an intense fear of the stranger to make household-based ethnography difficult in the extreme.[8]

In part then, this book insists that a solo-enacted ethnography be written as a solo-authored monograph. But it is also about the differences between the stories that have emerged from the ethnographic work and the repeat-interview work with households. At the risk of stating the obvious, being able to live in a place, and to work with households in this situated way, exerts a huge influence on the materials collected, on the things we come to know about and on the stories we are told. When we interview households in the UK we are told narratives particular to household members by individual household members, as well as a household narrative. Although the social relations of interviewing households alter through repeat interviewing, the talk and the stories remain household-focused, contained and defined by those who inhabit a particular dwelling structure, be this structure a house or a flat in a tower or apartment block. In contrast, ethnography, through its capacity to work productively with gossip (Gullestad 1984), starts to tell us very different sorts of stories alongside stories of self, household and family. It starts to spill out from the dwelling structure, to refuse its confines, and to admit a relationality of living that is about residing in streets, the socialities of neighbours and neighbourhoods, as well as about households, household members and family. This distinction has, in turn, factored through into the stories we want to re-tell, and indeed the stories we are able to tell in our academic writing of this project.[9]

The mutable character of ethnographic research, however, has been as important in shaping this book. In this instance, what began life as an ethnography centred on what we came to term 'ridding' (Gregson et al. in press) gradually morphed into something more akin to 'living with things'. Rather than constituting ridding – itself a form of divestment – as the defining interest, the ethnography insisted that ridding be conceptualised and understood within a fullness of cohabitations involving human and non-human agencies, and as part of an ongoing flow of appropriation, accommodation and divestment.[10] There will be more on this later, but first to the ethnography, its setting-up and enactment.

The ethnography

As Miller has repeatedly urged over the past few years, for consumption research to develop requires its 'orientation to its primary site of practice', the home (Miller 2001a: 239).[11] Equally, as he comments elsewhere, 'a commitment to the ethnographic study of consumption […leads…] in turn to a commitment to an intrusive form of fieldwork that demands a presence behind closed doors, that is in the midst of the private domain' (Miller 2002a: 239). As both comments imply, homes – and particularly homes in the UK – are far from easy sites for ethnographic fieldwork. Long constituted through phrases such as 'the Englishman's home is his [sic] castle', often surrounded by structures such as walls, fences and gates, and by the type of plant growth that has the capacity to grow tall and thick – typically privet, leylandii and beech hedges, English dwelling structures, and particularly houses, attest to the cultural importance of privacy. Whilst they appear to look outwards, unlike say the courtyard-based dwelling structures of many North African countries, they do so in ways which forge clear boundaries between public and private, the familiar and the strange, self and other. Moreover, at the same time as the walls of many English homes are becoming increasingly porous – particularly to an array of ICTs, including digital and satellite TV, mobile phones, broadband and cable – other tendencies reassert these boundaries with greater vigour. The growing phenomenon of 'stranger danger' for example, particularly in relation to children (Valentine 1997), and the recent expansion in home-based entertainment, both reinforce notions of the safety, comfort, convenience and familiarity of the home and of household members, by counterposing a potentially dangerous outside world of unknown others. Such a culture poses significant barriers to working ethnographically. Moreover, even assuming that we can cross the threshold and are invited in to the home, there are a whole host of other cultural conventions that get in the way of ethnographic working, notably the formalities of visiting and being positioned as the visitor, and the limits these place on movement round, in and through English dwelling structures. Normally visitors to English homes will be offered a tea or a coffee (Miller 1997); they may well be given or offered something 'light' to eat such as a biscuit or cake, and they will be allowed to use a toilet or bathroom (although not en-suite ones); but they would not expect to be shown round or look in all the rooms in the house, particularly the bedrooms and back-zone storage spaces such as garages and lofts (although see Fisher and Shipton 2003). Moreover, they would be treated politely but with reserve; they would be kept at a distance. Yet, their presence would exert its effects, by bringing about a 'stilling' in the household itself; for visiting and being visited suspend the day-to-day activities of the household, as a mark of respect for the visitor. Getting beyond being the visitor is one of the key transitions for ethnographic fieldwork in an English setting: indeed, unless we can do this with at least some of our research participants, we have to acknowledge that what purports to be ethnographic research is little different in its social relations to other qualitative methodologies, notably depth interviewing.

Setting-up

Like others attempting to work ethnographically in this cultural context, my efforts to circumvent cultural impediments to research focused on trying to work productively with the culture, rather than against it. Correspondingly, in late 2002 I took the decision to take up an academic friend of mine's offer of her house as a base from which to begin the ethnographic work for this research, scheduled to take place from January to December 2003. 'Janet' had organised six months working in the US for the first half of 2003; she did not want to leave her house empty, but neither did she want the hassle of renting it out on a short term let.[12] The arrangement we came to was of mutual benefit: Janet got a temporary house-sitter and I had a means of living amongst others rather than just visiting others, albeit that I did not live in this house permanently. Rather, I stayed there for extensive periods of time at varying times of the day and into the evenings during the longer summer days, for living there was a constant accommodation to my significant others – to partner, pets, family and friends – and their lives. It was therefore, a continual reminder of classic ethnography's presumptions that the ethnographer has no social ties, can suspend these at will and/or can move all the significant others with them to the ethnographic site (Macdonald 1997; Aull Davis 1999; Amit 2000).[13]

Janet's house, like all our houses, says much about her and her value systems, but she is not a research participant here. Her house, however, turned out to exert a not inconsiderable agency on the research. Janet's house is located in what was formerly a coal-mining village in County Durham, 'South Hightown'.[14] Her house is one of a number of terraced 'miners' cottages' which together comprise a long street in this village. These houses all have long front gardens, many of them formerly vegetable gardens, and

Figure 1.1: Terraced 'miners' cottages

a small backyard which abuts onto a back lane. Some of the houses have outbuildings and a few have DIY-built garages, again at some remove from the dwelling structure. Consisting typically of two bedrooms and of two bedrooms, a bathroom and two downstairs rooms, including a kitchen/diner, such dwelling structures, built at the end of the nineteenth century at the height of the expansion of coal mining across the county, are a major part of the built fabric of County Durham villages (Figure 1.1).

In South Hightown, as in many of the Durham villages, these housing structures attract particular social groups. They are where the 'greenies', the 'lefties' and general non-conformists co-exist with the 'left-behinds'.

'Alternative Terrace', then, is a place where academics, youth workers, social workers, psychiatric nurses and artists live side-by-side with older, often widowed, men and women; where gay and straight identities, along with nonnormative ways of living, are co-present; and where everyday life is enacted through the street as well as the home. For me, Janet's place was a home-from-home; far from strange, although somewhere that had to be 'made strange'. As I made myself and the research known about on this street, there was no shortage of households here who were keen to participate in the ethnography. Rather, my difficulty was more one of having to restrict numbers (in the end to five households), to forestall the research turning into an ethnography of only one street. Instead, and in order to capture diversities in everyday life in South Hightown, I wanted the ethnography to be embedded in different areas of the village.[15]

Like all the Durham coal-mining villages, South Hightown displays its history in and through its various areas of housing and its housing structures. With well over 2,000 dwelling structures, the 'village' expanded dramatically through the twentieth century, but it did so in distinctive ways at different times, and in ways that show that it does not have the problems of second-home ownership that characterise other villages in other areas of the UK (see also Bennett et al. 2000). Following the 1951 County Development Plan, a large area of back-to-back terraced housing was demolished and replaced by a considerable expanse of low-rise local authority housing.[16] This included a range of houses designed for family occupation, as well as single-storey one-bedroom bungalows intended for older residents with no dependents. The estate, referred to here as 'The Rivers', mixes bungalows with two-, three- and four-bedroom houses in a semi-detached and terraced patchwork (Figure 1.2).

All the houses and bungalows have sizeable front and back gardens, and there are large expanses of open, grassed space between the various streets. None of the houses have garages, but a sizeable number of the houses, unlike the bungalows, have been purchased by tenants under the Right-to-Buy scheme.[17] Following the sale in the 1960s of what had been farmland, another estate was built by private-sector developers. This was aimed at the family market, and comprised of three- and four-bedroom semi-detached houses with garages and front and back gardens. The development of this estate changed the character of South Hightown dramatically. From being a village striated by class (Williamson 1982), in which the key social distinctions contrasted large numbers of council tenants with small numbers of the professional middle classes (the doctor, the teacher and the vicar) and the bourgeoisie (a few shop owners and local traders) – all of whom lived in the stone-built large detached houses in the village (Figure 1.3) – South Hightown started to become, in part at least, a commuter settlement.[18]

This trend continued through the 1990s, during which large swathes of suburban-style estate housing, comprising both 'starter homes' and 'mid-price family dwellings', were built on the cul-de-sac design (Figure 1.4).[19] A further significant expansion is also in the offing, this time of 'executive homes'. To call South Hightown a village, then, is something of a euphemism: to be sure there are still villages *within* South Hightown with their legacy in North-east

Figure 1.2: Post war council housing

Figure 1.3: Stone detached housing

coal mining, on which more below, but increasingly – inexorably – parts of this village have been transformed in appearance into the urban fringe, virtually indistinguishable from the suburban estates against which villages such as this one have long defined themselves.[20]

Having worked an entrée into South Hightown through Alternative Terrace, I wanted to be able to work intensively with a similar number of households in other areas in this place, and to do so in ways which, as with Alternative Terrace, allowed households to opt-in to the research.[21] Whilst this was possible in some areas of the village, other areas remained resolutely resistant to the ethnography. I followed multiple pathways and sites of research simultaneously, including leafleting the entirety of the areas of private-sector estate housing and participating in various village-based activities. These activities included acting as an observer at monthly parish council meetings, doing a research presentation at a local Environment Day in the village hall, volunteering within a village environmental group, taking part in litter-picking events, participating in table-top sales, church second-hand sales and school 'fayres', hanging-out at the post office and the hairdressers, and going to community coffee mornings. The one social institution that I did not use as a means to potential recruitment is the village pub. Although I spent time drinking in these pubs with residents, I found them difficult sites to work, for two principal reasons. Firstly, these are predominantly masculine spaces, which during the day time are constituted as sites for all-day drinking

Figure 1.4: Estate housing

by a core of unemployed men in the village, most of them from the Rivers estate. At night the pubs are given over to entertainment, mainly karaoke and darts matches, neither of which is particularly conducive to disclosing what households do with their things. Secondly, and more significantly, the pubs are key nodes in the village 'informal' economy. As I quickly came to learn, some of the core activities within this economy are casual building and repair work, gardening and landscaping and 'rubbish' removal, all of which have clear connections to the things households get rid of. At the time the ethnography began, increased taxes on landfill had recently been introduced through the annual government budget. These placed a charge on builders and traders taking matter to civic amenity sites, and impinged directly on self-employed builders' and traders' already tight profit margins. At the same time, fly-tipping – the dumping of rubbish by roadsides, in fields and by field gates, in lay-bys and on open ground – was in the throes of being re-cast as an instance of 'anti-social behaviour'.[22] As my activities within South Hightown's environmental group quickly revealed, the environs of the village were the sites of repeated fly-tipping. Disclosing what I felt would inevitably be interpreted as an unduly suspicious interest in such activities seemed to me to invite a not particularly positive response, either personally or against Janet's property. Correspondingly, I took the decision relatively early on in the fieldwork to allow any such activities to disclose themselves through the activities of the study households, rather than to go looking for them directly.[23]

The research 'presentation' at the Environment Day consisted of a looped PowerPoint slide show of provocative images of discarded and abandoned consumer objects, including fridges, burnt-out cars, discarded mattresses, 'fly-tipping' and some things exiting from our house. It also included a short questionnaire. This was set up as a self-directed activity for people to become as involved in as they wished. Through this I recruited three more households to the study, and elicited over fifty questionnaire returns, which provided some much needed background information on the routes indi- viduals used to dispose of their unwanted things. Participation at the parish- council meetings led to contacts with the elected councillors for the village, and through them a Tenants and Residents' Group on the Rivers estate. In the course of a series of informal discussions with the officers and commit- tee of this group it became clear that one street on this estate was shortly to undergo a wholesale modernisation and improvement programme. Given the obvious connections this had to this research project, this street – known here as Wear Road – became the focus for another zone of ethnographic working, with four households living there participating in the research. These four households were effectively selected for me through the Tenants and Residents' Group: although I suggested to them that I wanted to include a strong degree of social diversity within the participating households, and to work with households of older and younger people, with young, teenage and adult children, in and out of work, with and without pets, it is undeni- able that their identification of appropriate households for me to get to know was indicative of their understandings of and aspirations for this particular street. As I quickly came to realise, I was not pointed in the direction of those households and families that are radically othered within this street and the Rivers estate, those who are labelled by the self-declared 'respectables' as 'smackheads, thieves and rogues'.

There are two sets of points that I want to make about this here, one to do with the fieldwork itself and the other to do with this development per se. Throughout the fieldwork I agonised about the way that I was told stories about these others by those who live amongst them. These second- hand stories were ones of widespread drug, substance and alcohol abuse and its effects; of a local economy increasingly run through drug-related crime; of fraud; of bricks being hurled through people's windows; of intergenera- tional unemployment and of intergenerational teenage pregnancy; and of an increasingly out-of-control teenage 'youth', excluded from secondary education, who spent their days riding motorbikes on the open areas of grass, sniffing glue, engaging in petty crime and appropriating public space aggressively. I was also told stories of National Front activism, of sleeper cells, and of explicitly racist attacks on people and property. Like all stories they may have been elaborated and have assumed a power of their own in the telling, but undoubtedly the events they tell of were and are grounded in the everyday life of the Rivers estate. For those with whom I worked, the effect of living amongst this, with this sort of everyday life going on all around them, was to produce a complex mix of fear, alienation, retreat, despair, resilience, pride and determination, as people strove to differentiate themselves from these others, to protect themselves, their family and their property from these others, and – more rarely – to attempt to do something by getting involved in community politics. In coming to know and work with these households, I felt that I had to accept their lives' capacity to shape this part of the ethnography. To try to do otherwise would have been to contest the key socialities of the street. Moreover, it would have failed to recognise how my presence in their lives was itself mobilised, as yet another marker of their respectability.[24]

The second point I would make about this is that this area of South Hightown is far from unique among the former coal-mining villages of County Durham. As my 'off-the-record' conversations with community police officers, social workers and youth outreach workers working in the village indicated, in its key social problems this estate is much like any other similar estate in the former coal-mining villages of the county. With the collapse of the coal-mining industry, many living on estates such as this one have turned to the informal and benefit-dependent economies, and increasingly the drug and criminal economies, to 'get by'. Moreover, compounded by their relative geographical isolation, by the vestiges of a fierce community-based pride and insularity that are one legacy of the coal-mining industry, and by the conservatism of some of the older residents, such places have come to be identified as potential vote-winners for far right political parties, notably the British National Party (BNP). Their targets are the alienated youth, whom old and New Labour policies are seen to have failed, and the more reactionary of their elders, for whom racist talk was and is a taken-for-granted mode of everyday speech. As anti-asylum-seeker fly posters appeared on telegraph posts through the summer of 2003 on this estate (and were removed), as racist graffiti were daubed on the walls of public space (and were removed), and as the St George's flag appeared on various upstairs windows,[25] I was continually reminded of the ways in which many academic representations of North-east England remain defined by the historical coal-mining industry rather than being located in the now (Bulmer 1978; Beynon 1984; Hudson 1994; Armstrong 2000; Bennett et al. 2000; Atkinson 2001; Clark 2002; although see Nayak 2003 for discussions which have more affinities with the points raised above). A consequence, undeniably, is that a subsidiary objective of this volume is to provide a rather different and more contemporary set of narratives of everyday life in North-east England than that of 'coal is our life'. [26]

Altogether, the various recruitment pathways described above yielded a total of thirteen study households: six from the Rivers Estate, including four from Wear Road, five from Alternative Terrace and two from the historic core of older properties. The notable absence here is households from the areas of relatively newly built private-sector estate housing. Notwithstanding a range of recruitment strategies, including 100% leafleting, these areas remained impenetrable and their residents seemingly uninterested in investing in the project. In time I came to interpret this response as a manifestation of lives in which the key socialities are forged through the workplace, the home and the homes of known others. For the residents of Wear Road and Alternative Terrace, however, and members of the parish council, this pattern of response – once disclosed – attracted considerable critical comment. In turn, this disclosed further lines of othering in South Hightown. Seen as indicative of a lack of embeddedness in the village, this pattern of non-participation was connected up to, and made sense of through, a narrative that counterposed those whose lives were enacted in the village to those who merely slept in it and drove out of it. Its key markers, predictably, were the village primary school, the post office, the shop and the local economy.[27] This left the ethnography with a gap that had to be filled however, to satisfy the requirements of the funding body. Moreover, to filter out households living in what are regarded as quintessential suburban 'boxland' neighbourhoods would have been to write-out of the research one of the characteristic modes of everyday life in the UK. Consequently, I drew on existing personal social networks to recruit three further households into the study, all of them living in suburban estate-housing on one large housing estate on the edge of the Newcastle conurbation.[28] Although not living in South Hightown, these households do exhibit many of the socialities attributed by the South Hightown study households to those who live in such housing in South Hightown itself. Their lives do indeed revolve around family and the workplace; their friendship networks map into these sites and their connections to those who live immediately around them are largely shallow, semi-detached, particularly when compared with the gossip that characterises Wear Road and, to a lesser degree, Alternative Terrace.

Doing the research

Working with these 16 households and their 38 members (Appendix) over a period of twelve months was both a privilege and an exercise in cultural ingenuity. As mentioned above, the framing of the unknown stranger through the cultural conventions of visiting is one of the biggest hurdles facing ethnographic fieldwork in English homes, and impinged strongly on this research. Although visiting, and the talk that characterizes it, are clearly part of everyday life in English homes, to talk with household members about what has been done with and to their things is not the same thing as observing and participating in what is done with and to these things. Instead, such talk is about the constitution and telling of stories, about things and the connections they weave. Moreover, we have no way of knowing whether these stories actually do correspond with what actually happened to these things. Attempting to find ways through the limitations posed by visiting to discover what people actually did with and to the things they were getting rid of was a major methodological preoccupation as well as a core empirical research question. How I worked at this merits further discussion.

The first point to make here is that attempting to find out what people do with their things when they get rid of them turns one into a very peculiar sort of visitor indeed. To focus on, talk about and photograph what people say they no longer want and have no future use for, the things that have broken, which are old and cannot be repaired, is not what most visitors do. Moreover, when we have visitors ourselves, we are unlikely to talk about the things we are getting rid of, unless we think that some of these may be of potential value to the visitor/s. Instead, we are more likely to show off our new acquisitions. In conducting this research, then, I had to get used, initially at least, to being a rather odd visitor, and to finding ways to disclose the things that households were or might be going to get rid of. To assist in this, at least initially, I used a 'disposal diary', which we gave to all the households participating in the research, and not just to the participants in the ethnography. Household members used these diaries (or not) to record the things that left their possession, the routes they went and any stories they wanted to record about them; we used them as prompts for further questioning and story telling, as a polite means of being impolite.

For the duration of the fieldwork my encounters with the three households living in the Newcastle conurbation were little more than extended periods of such visiting, oriented around diary-talk and taking pictures of particular objects. However, in South Hightown, at least with certain households, things were very different. Using Janet's house as a base, I was able to be amongst the participating households on Alternative Terrace, able to observe and to hear the various goings-on of their everyday lives. Moreover, when my car was there these participants knew that they could shout over the hedges to attract my attention, bang on the door or just pop round to let me know what they were up to and/or to come and visit me should they wish. They knew too that, as part of the research, I would appear to them as the intensely 'nosey-neighbour'; someone who appeared if workmen's vans turned up, who would chat to them if they were out and about on the street; who took a particularly obsessive interest in them during periods of room decoration; but who could also be asked to help out in various activities. Over the course of the fieldwork these activities included sawing up and dismantling a garden table, clearing out some outbuildings, heaving wood up the street and cutting hedges, as well as minding and playing with children, walking dogs and doing the occasional bit of shopping. In short, through living temporarily on Alternative Terrace, I became a participant in some of the doings of these households, whilst at the same time being able to be an acute observer of many of their goings-on. It probably says a lot about this street that such instances of reciprocal practice appeared not only routine and taken-for-granted by the residents, but was understood to be normative. In framing the research as enacted through the favours of gift exchange, my practices certainly helped reproduce this normative. At the same time, though, it enabled me to be a far fuller participant in the everyday lives of these households than could be achieved through visiting alone.

On the Rivers estate things were rather different, not least because I never lived on Wear Road. For three of the six households living on the Rivers, I never really got beyond the social conventions of visiting. Here, though I visited frequently – usually at least once a fortnight – I would be given a mug of tea and a biscuit and sat in the living room or, as in one household, kept in the kitchen, because the living room there is always kept spotlessly clean, reserved only for family visitors and evening TV viewing. With the other three households – all of whom lived on Wear Road – although we began like this, things changed as the fieldwork progressed. That they did owes much to the effects of the Wear Road modernisation programme. As we will see in Chapter 3, this work was a huge upheaval for all the households and provided a massive disruption to the routines of everyday life, including the norms of conventional visiting. But what it provided me with was a way of transcending the subject position of the visitor, as I ripped wallpaper off walls, assisted in redecorating and acted as a general sounding-off board for tenants frustrated at the mess, delays and general uncertainties of modernisation. Again, it is through participating in and helping out in moments of households' everyday life that the ethnography moved from being purely talk about things and people (gossip) to encompass doings with people and their things.

There are two methodological points that I want to make about this transition. For a household-based ethnography such as this one, in which a core objective was to access practice (and not just talk about practice), it seems to me essential that we find ways of positioning ourselves as researchers in the enactment of doings.[29] Achieving this requires firstly that we bear witness to these doings and, secondly, that we take seriously the body as a research tool. Of course, bearing witness can be achieved through a combination of observation and talk about these observations, but when, as here, the emphasis is on household practices that are located in the flow of everyday life, then it seems to me that we need to position ourselves at least partially within the flow of these enactments, whilst at the same time being ever mindful of our capacities to affect, disrupt and challenge these enactments, through presence alone or active participation. Households comprise possibly the most difficult sites in which to assume such a position: they have routine, habitual, often unarticulated ways of doing things with and to things, which could equally be consensual or the source of considerable animosities, tensions and conflict. To take just one example, hanging wallpaper is a learnt and situated practice, one that is enacted in different ways in different households, even if the stylistic effect may look much the same. To participate in doing the decorating as a researcher requires simultaneously observing and absorbing immediately the intricacies of who does what and when, suppressing any tendency to assert ways of doing the task to hand, and establishing a means to being able to assist as well, whilst monitoring all those gestural moves that might signal a dissatisfaction or disagreement – the tut, the raised eyebrow, the pause for a cigarette break and a sideways glance. This is not easy. And yet the flow of everyday life is the means through which many things are routinely rid. To continue with the decorating example, stripping wallpaper off walls frequently connects seamlessly and in a non-discursive way with the placement of the detritus in black plastic bags, which in turn are routinely deposited within the household rubbish, out in wheelie bins or in black refuse-collection bags. Or changing a baby's disposable nappy is followed immediately by the noise of the wheelie bin lid opening and shutting. Or think of how the practices of cooking and tidying-up the house result in similar trajectories, as packaging and left-overs, as well as used-up things like paper hankies, are all cast from household interior bins in the direction of the wheelie bin with nothing by way of articulated explanation. So, if we are to come to know how households constitute trajectories in things, then we need at the minimum to work in ways which enable us to bear witness to their enactment. This requires either that we be there, as physical co-presences, or the development of virtual methodologies of the type discussed above (note 8).

Yet I would argue that bearing witness is not quite enough. When I think back to the examples of ridding work in which households involved me as a participant, and not just as an observer, the majority of them involved a perceived need for extra, additional or substitute bodily capacities. They were about doing things with and to things, for example moving excessive amounts of matter from one place to another, shifting heavy and/or bulky things, persuading stubborn things to come apart, helping to attack and/or destroy inanimate things or helping people to burn things (usually garden waste); or doing things that other, usually elderly or unwell, bodies found hard to do by themselves, or impossible to do alone. That these actions frequently, though not exclusively, involved households comprising elderly people or women living without a live-in male partner is no coincidence; it discloses that for some of these households I was perceived to be a fit, able-bodied and readily available extra pair of hands. More generally still, it testifies to the way in which the body itself is a research tool, through its capacity to enact doings. I can honestly say that it is only through my own embodied actions in the fieldwork that I came fully to appreciate just how much the inertia in certain things can be a manifestation of individual corporealities and capacities, and how in certain circumstances ridding can be just too much to enact. I only learnt this through doing; through using my body in relation to excessive things, and through this coming to know how other co-present human bodies were relating to variously bulky, heavy and seemingly immovable things confronting them, and us, and through their presence exceeding us.

Positioning myself amongst participating households, helping household members do certain activities, as well as observing what they did with and to their things, constituted some of the key ways in which the ethnography was enacted. At the same time, however, much of it was also about getting to know households and their various members, talking with them about their lives, their hopes, their fears, their aspirations, their goings-on, their homes, their previous homes, about past lives and present ones and about many of their things. Inevitably, some were more reserved and chose to disclose less than others, but others were so forthcoming that I felt there was little I didn't know about them by the end of the year, and vice versa. And it was a similar story with the things. In getting to know these households I very quickly dispensed with diary talk. Instead, I talked a lot with them, and on numerous occasions, about their rooms in things – about furniture and furnishings, decorating styles, about pictures, ornaments, displayed photographs and photographs in photograph albums, about TVs and music systems, video recorders and DVD players, books, CDs, music and musical instruments, toys, games, kitchen appliances, clothes, flooring; in short about the world of consumer objects in their houses and what was happening to these things. Inevitably, the talk spilled over to encompass other living presences – gardens and pets – as well as consumer objects that transcend the home, for example cars, motorbikes, skateboards, roller blades and bicycles.

As this talk proceeded, it became increasingly apparent that all these households, and most household members, drew a key critical distinction: between things in everyday use in consumption and those objects, some of which may previously have been in everyday use, which had been memorialised, made sacred and reconstituted as memory devices. One of the clearest instances of this in action in the fieldwork was the prevalence of the memory box amongst the mothers of young children. Other instances encountered included holiday mementos, family inheritances such as china, antiques and paintings, key items of clothing, notably wedding dresses and bridesmaid dresses, and objects with a particular symbolic resonance, such as a first performance-standard guitar, a first racing bike or a Masters dissertation. What connects all of these things, and their owners, is that none of these things can ever be thrown away; they are kept because their value in narrating a life, and in being able to tell stories about that life, is just too great (Csikszentmihalyi and Rochberg-Halton 1981; Hoskins 1998; Mara 1998; Kwint et al. 1999). Frequently, it is these very same things that pass between the generations, and which are used by families to constitute the inalienability of the family (Weiner 1992). Such matter has been a particular preoccupation within material culture studies for some years. Rather less interest has been shown, however, in the matter that never assumes the memorial state, which remains in everyday use or storage and which is eventually cast out, for whatever reason (Young 2001; Colloredo-Mansfeld 2003). It is precisely these sorts of things that were the primary empirical concerns of this research and which figure centrally in this book.

About this book

Notwithstanding that the research on which this volume is based began with a focus on ridding, this book has a rather different orientation, with its primary intent being to further the development of an account of consumption in terms of dwelling (see also Dant 1999). The shift from ridding to dwelling occurred relatively late in the ethnographic research, and is clearly an effect of ethnography's capacity to engage with practice. In the ethnography then, and in marked distinction to the household interview work, ridding events emerged as thoroughly embedded in the intricacies of both routine and exceptional everyday life in the domestic realm (de Certeau et al. 1998). As we shall see in the following chapters, they occurred in the midst of, and as part of, a whole range of mundane activities such as tidying-up children's toys, doing the laundry, doing the gardening and living with pets, as well as in the course of more exceptional events such as moving in and being modernised, redecoration and having a new kitchen installed. Ridding events, then, were disclosed not as discrete events marking key moments in the social lives of things, their passage from one value regime to another. Rather, they occurred as part of a seamless flow of appropriation and divestment, storing, keeping and holding, involving an array of things in the domestic sphere. To paraphrase Tim Ingold, 'they did not begin here or end there, but (were) always (just) going on' (2000: 172).

It would be difficult to exaggerate the potential effects of such thinking on consumption research. For the most part, consumption research continues to be positioned, framed and understood in a way that connects consumption to production. Its emphasis may be the commodity chain, or commodity fetishism, objectification and the work of appropriation; or it may take its inspiration from accounts that emphasise the extended social and geographical lives of things, as they move in and out of the commodity phase, in so doing constituting networks of global exchange and consumption (see, for example, Appadurai 1986; Kopytoff 1986; Miller 1987; Thomas 1991 ; Tranberg Hansen 2000; Norris 2004a). What connects all these approaches, however, is their continued indebtedness to the ghosts of Hegel and Marx. Specifically, they rest on an identification of an object world that is distinct from human life, yet which is continually appropriated and re-appropriated within human life; which is not only distinct from but fabricated by people and which is used to constitute social relations and identities, as well as relations of unequal exchange and dependency.

Now, whilst I continue to find such an approach a not inconsiderable aid to understanding a consumption that is positioned in relation to production and which is fundamentally a matter of exchange, I am less convinced of its capacity to illuminate home-based consumption. Indeed, much of this volume is devoted to demonstrating that when we make this radical shift in location, acts of consumption elide from being purely acts of appropriation to encompass acts of sorting, holding and keeping, and ridding as well. They become, then, more about ways of living with certain things, and about ways of making other things physically absent, not just about acts which move things from the commodity phase of their lives into domestic culture and out again. Where this takes us is in the direction of approaches which refuse a separation between the human and the non-human and which insist on the object-ions and object-edness of things, but which position such cohabitations within the dwelling structure itself. Where this takes us, in turn, is to a very different tradition of continental European philosophy from that of Hegel and Marx, which is to Heidegger and phenomenology, and to thinking in terms of being at home with things as well as people, with the things we have to hand around us, in cupboards, drawers, wardrobes and boxes, as well as in interior rooms and external outbuildings such as sheds and garages.

Let me say immediately that I remain firmly of the view that there is little merit in framing acts and practices of consumption as purely an illustration of either metaphysical or ontological questions. Instead, and as will be apparent, I prefer to emphasise the specificities of time and place, and to ground generalisations, rather than to impose them. Correspondingly, although I begin this section by outlining Heidegger's critical essay on dwelling – 'Building, dwelling, thinking' (BDT) – I argue, on the basis of this ethnography, that dwelling encompasses far more than building and cultivation. Rather, and drawing on Miller (2002b), I argue that contemporary dwelling is best thought about in terms of inhabitation, cohabitation and the practices of habitation, and that it is fundamentally and simultaneously about accommodation and accommodating. Dwelling is oriented around the dwelling structure as home and, as critically, around the things, the people and the non-human animate presences that move through it and stay within it, or not, over temporalities which range from the everyday through decades. In this sense, dwelling is achieved through an ongoing flow of appropriation and divestment; through acquisition, holding, keeping, storing and indeed ridding.

In BDT Heidegger advances a key proposition, that building is not a means to achieve dwelling but is rather indicative of a prior state of dwelling. We build because we are dwellers, and not as a means to an end:

> The way in which you are and I am, the manner in which we
> humans are on the earth is *bauen*, dwelling. To be a human
> being means to be on the earth as a mortal. It means to dwell.
> (M. Heidegger 1978 [1954]: 349)

This understanding of dwelling is not simply a matter of occupancy, but is thoroughly immersed in the intricacies of the German *'wohnen'*, 'to live', and its connections to *'bauen'*, 'to build'. Dwelling here connotes an enduring sense of residing, a staying, but it also carries associations with being at peace, content. It is about growing accustomed to and feeling at home in a place, and is achieved notably through acts of construction and cultivation. Building then is a manifestation of dwelling. Furthermore, dwelling in this reading is also about a staying with things; about preserving them and caring for them. In BDT Heidegger connects such states to metaphysics and specifically to his complex notion of the fourfold, to divinities, mortals, earth and sky. We can see these at work in his exemplar of building/dwelling, the Black Forest farmhouse, in which the things he highlights – the child's bed and the coffin – have intense connections to the phenomenological sense of being, and to birth and death:

> Let us think for a while of a farmhouse in the Black Forest, which
> was built some two hundred years ago by the dwelling of peasants.
> Here the self-sufficiency of the power to let earth and sky, divinities
> and mortals enter in simple oneness into things ordered the house.
> It placed the farm on the wind-sheltered mountain slope, looking
> south, among the meadows close to the spring. It gave it the wide
> overhanging shingle roof whose proper slope bears up under the
> burden of snow, and that, reaching deep down, shields the chambers
> against the storms of the long winter nights. It did not forget the

altar corner behind the community table; it made room in its chamber for the hallowed places of childbed and the 'tree of the dead' – for that is what they call a coffin there: the Totenbaum – and in this way it designed for the different generations under one roof the character of their journey through time. A craft that, itself sprung from dwelling, still uses its tools and its gears as things, built from the farmhouse. ((M. Heidegger 1978 [1954]: 361–2).

Earlier in BDT, Heidegger questions if the same state of dwelling can be achieved in 'contemporary housing', stating:

Today's houses may [...] be well planned, easy to keep, attractively cheap, open to air, light and sun, but – do the houses in themselves hold any guarantee that dwelling occurs in them. (p. 348)

Contrasted tacitly to a more authentic, rural, indeed peasant way of dwelling/building, encapsulated by the Black Forest farmhouse and the things contained within it, it is evident that Heidegger regards many of modernity's buildings as, at best, lacking the capacity to dwell within them (and see too his remarks on factories and railway stations in the same essay). Restless, transient, constantly moving and un-enduring, for Heidegger we seem to have lost the capacity to be at home and at peace in our homes, in part because we no longer stay or reside in what we have built through generations, but instead pass through the constructions of others, continually moving along.

Outlined thus, it is not difficult to see why such arguments have failed to attract much attention within contemporary research on consumption and the home. Not only do they valorise and romanticise an imagined rural past over an inauthentic contemporary urban life, but they run counter to a huge amount of empirical evidence that points to just how central contemporary homes are in achieving the state of being at home (Wardhaugh 1999). Indeed, although Heidegger's arguments in BDT have attracted recent attention, notably in Tim Ingold's reworking of people–environment relations through phenomenology (Ingold 2000), it is only in Tim Dant's (1999) *Material Culture in the Social World* that aspects of these arguments have been revisited in relation to material culture and consumption. However, the emphasis here, when it is not on the house as a container of cultural meaning, is more on what Dant terms 'the activities of dwelling' (1999: 70) – house maintenance, repair, refurbishment, decoration, gardening and so on. Conjoining a sense of making-do from de Certeau with the Heideggerian notion of using things that are to hand to accomplish particular tasks, Dant argues that activities of dwelling have been recast through sets of scientific and technical discourses of doing repairs properly, and as such that they are usually commodified. The implication, although this is not spelt out, is that we have lost the capacity to dwell, merely occupying buildings that others fabricate for us.

Undeniably, there is something in Dant's argument. Indeed, the recent buoyancy of the housing market in the UK could be argued to have fuelled still further housing's position as a commodity, witness both the strong growth in the buy-to-let market and in re-mortgaging as a means to finance other consumer purchases. Yet, to see the 'activities of dwelling' as largely commodified is to miss that much of this work is actually enacted by do-it-yourself (DIY) labour, that is by householders (Mintel 2003).[30] Indeed, in the course of the ethnography, whilst I did encounter a few households who relied on professional labour to do either major repairs or wallpapering, and even supervised the installation of a new bathroom in Janet's house whilst she went to work, there were many more who seemingly turned their hand to anything. These included a loft conversion, kitchen and bathroom fitting, plumbing, electrical repairs, re-flooring and outbuilding repair and renovation, as well as redecoration. Albeit that those concerned relied on tools and materials purchased from retail outlets to do this work, their approach was consistently to draw on stocks of practical knowledge – their own and those of known and socially related others – to work out how to accomplish these tasks. Taken in conjunction with the array of literature which testifies to the ways in which home interiors are continually made and remade through consumer objects and through practices of decoration (see, for example, Gullestad 1984 and 1993; Madigan and Munro 1996; Clarke 2001 and 2002; Painter 2002), this suggests that it is the locus of dwelling that has shifted in contemporary life, not the ontological state of dwelling. Although the vast majority of people living in the UK no longer build dwelling structures or live in 'family' homes, or indeed cultivate the land to produce food, but instead buy, sell and live in housing produced as a commodity, most do engage in sets of activities that are about seeking to constitute these dwelling structures as appropriate sites of habitation for them. It is precisely for these reasons that I want to persist with Heidegger, specifically by reworking his arguments about dwelling through the twin concepts of accommodation and accommodating.

In a recent essay, Miller (2002b) points to the importance of a sense of accommodation to any study of home-based consumption. Drawing on the extensive semantic purchase of this term, he identifies three critical facets to accommodation: as accommodation, the structure in which we live and where we feel at home; as the appropriation of the home by its inhabitants and of the inhabitants by the home; and as an agreement to compromise. Immediately, we can see here how the Heideggerian sense of dwelling is tied primarily to the first two of these meanings. Yet, as Miller shows, using as exemplars several key studies of home decoration, the state of feeling at home is achieved principally through acts of appropriation, through which accommodation is transformed into the accommodating.

Drawing on the work of Marianne Gullestad (1984), whose research on Norwegian housewives first highlighted the significance of home decoration (see also Gullestad 1993), Miller emphasises how appropriate decoration not only works to make visitors feel at home, but provides the frame for forms of socialisation that are key to the constitution of normativity (Miller 2002b: 119). Similarly, but this time utilising Pauline Garvey's (2001) research on home decoration in another Norwegian town, he highlights how home decoration is far from simply expressive of self, but is a practice through which we explore and narrate the complexities of self, biographical and multiple, or indeed idealised (see also Clarke 2001). Whether we accomplish this through apparently innocuous activities such as moving things around within a room (Garvey), or through the kind of routine redecoration and refurbishment discussed by Gullestad, we use home furnishings both to accommodate ourselves and others, be they actual visitors or imagined projections. However, as Miller also argues, we frequently also find ourselves having to accommodate to the accommodation that is the dwelling structure we live within. Using as his primary example the case of older property, Miller examines how such houses seem to require of their occupants particular styles of home decoration and the acquisition of particular sorts of furnishings, ones in keeping with the period of the house – wooden sash-window frames, period chairs, the authentic fireplace. Accommodating, then, is portrayed by Miller as a constant reciprocal process of accommodation, involving houses, people and the things within them. Moreover, it is a process which occurs across several temporal registers simultaneously, spanning the relative frequency of moving things around in a room, through more infrequent phases of periodic refurbishment, to the relative infrequency of moving (house) itself (Marcoux 2001).

In the chapters that follow I focus on a number of practices of inhabitation which span the temporal and spatial registers of the domestic and which elucidate the various meanings of, and interplay between, accommodation and accommodating. All these practices, however, disclose that getting rid of things, along with sorting, holding and keeping them, and not just acquisition, is fundamental to our everyday lives with things and to making dwelling structures accommodating accommodations. Furthermore, they establish that divestment, and not just appropriation, is fundamental to making accommodations accommodating and to achieving the state of being at home.[31] I begin at one temporal extreme, with two chapters which highlight relatively exceptional dwelling events, and the processes of accommodating that accompany these. In Chapter 2 the emphasis is on three instances of moving in, as a process of fabricating an accommodation, a dwelling structure, into a place that is accommodating to its inhabitants and to others, yet which simultaneously is about an accommodation to the 'estate agency' of the structure itself. In Chapter 3, attention shifts to the process of being modernised. Here local authority tenants are shown to have to accommodate their lives to a programme of works, yet are shown too to use the very same process to come to new accommodations with their homes in things in order to recast them as accommodating. The events of moving in and modernisation foreground moments when the state of being at home is ruptured, through the acts of moving house and re-fabricating a dwelling structure, respectively. Furthermore, they highlight how the state of being at home is re-established, through what happens to and what is done with and to certain things. In contrast, the remaining four chapters address some of the more mundane and repetitive forms of accommodation and accommodating that occur within the dwelling structure. All, however, are critical to achieving the state of being at home and all, as with the exceptional, involve simultaneous acts of appropriation and divestment.

In Chapter 4, I focus on the connection between the state of being at home and sleeping (well). I argue that, in order to be accommodating of us, our homes have to accommodate the human need to sleep well. This however is something that has to be fabricated, using the dwelling structure as well as the material culture of sleep itself, beds, bedding and so on. Focusing on three instances in which the sleeping patterns within households are disrupted, the chapter shows how new sleep accommodations are forged, in homes and in things. Chapter 5 addresses consumer objects that are more familiar within the consumption literature than beds and bedding, collections, children's clothing and toys. It argues that both enduringness and transience are key temporalities in the state of being at home. To be accommodating of us, then, our homes have to be able to hold safely those things that we use to weave some of our most powerful and enduring narratives, of self and of biography. But they must also allow us to accommodate changing identities by allowing the release of troublesome and/or no longer wanted things. The chapter shows how holding and releasing things are themselves bound up in mundane practices, in this case, of collecting, laundering and tidying-up. It shows too how practices are central to fabricating continual accommodations with things. In Chapter 6 the focus is on kitchen appliances. Integral to contemporary ways of caring for clothing, to storing, preparing and cooking food, and to clearing up after eating, kitchen appliances make our homes accommodating environments in which to live, by virtue of what they do for us. They also live parallel, largely taken-for-granted lives, in our kitchens, until that is they start behaving badly. The chapter focuses on a number of such moments, highlighting the connections between appliance failures and wasting. It also emphasises how such moments work to rupture the accommodating state, making homes mere accommodations. Appliance failure makes it difficult to cook, to wash clothes, to store food ... and therefore to live in the ways to which we have become accustomed. For our homes to be reconstituted as accommodating places requires that these capacities be replaced. In Chapter 7 the emphasis is on two different yet quintessentially English home presences: gardens and pets. Seen by many to define an English home, gardens and pets nonetheless have the capacity to make homes seem less than accommodating, particularly to others. Although classic instances of the domesticated in the domestic, plant growth and animal habitation have the constant potential to constitute excess. Correspondingly, living with plant growth and with companion animals is argued to be a matter of constant vigilance and projection. It also involves plenty of acts of 'getting rid', as those who live with living things struggle to accommodate nature's constant capacity to exceed culture.

Taken together, these four chapters show that the temporalities and practices of the mundane are as critical as relatively exceptional dwelling events, such as moving in and modernisation, to achieving the state of being at home. Moreover, with the mundane this state is achieved through appropriations and divestments that do indeed just go on, all day and everyday, simultaneously in the vast majority of lived-in dwelling structures. Yet the various activities highlighted here as part of the mundane are also vital to the disclosure of contemporary dwelling. Far from being arbitrary selections, or indeed what the ethnography disclosed (although, of course, it did just that), I would argue that these activities constitute the state of being at home. Together, sleep, collecting, laundering, tidying-up, cooking food, storing food, raising children and domesticating nature, define inhabitation. These very ordinary activities, then, are the very stuff of ordinary life; they are what just goes-on, all day, everyday, habitually, simultaneously, in the course of lives being lived. Indeed, I would argue that we do these very activities because we continue to be dwellers, and because doing these very activities in particular dwelling structures is what fabricates them, transforming them from accommodations into accommodating homes. As will become clear, however, these chapters, although ordered through academic intent, are largely unfettered by the tropes of academic writing. Instead, and as with Hoskins (1998), the emphasis is on some of the key stories that emerged in the ethnographic fieldwork and through this, on people living in households, their various day-to-day activities, on their homes, the things in them, their doings with things, and the things they got rid of. This is deliberate. It reflects on my part, firstly, a desire to write accessibly (Macdonald 2002) and, secondly, to find a way to accommodate non-academic audiences within a single academic output, rather than being displaced to another product. Moreover, it is also indicative of the incorporation of a number of the ethnography's research participants within the process of drafting itself. Indeed, some of these households have read and commented on these empirical chapters in their entirety, whilst others have read only 'their stories'.[32] For me this is important. It shows that ethnography can be, at least in part, a co-production, in its writing as well as its doing, and that writing too is a process of accommodation, in this case to the thoughts and responses of others. At the same time however, and as well as establishing the foundations for a very different set of arguments, these chapters do engage with some of the core debates in the contemporary literature on home consumption and material culture.

Chapters 2 and 3 are located in the housing studies–consumption–material culture interface, and engage particularly with the recent work of Miller (1988 and 2002), Dant (1999), Shove (2003) and Skeggs (1997). Together they span the key housing distinction in the UK, owner occupation (Chapter 2) and living as a council tenant (Chapter 3). Both chapters are concerned with advancing an account of consumption that pays due attention to the importance of the built fabric of the dwelling structure and utilities alongside an emphasis on aesthetic and surface appearance. In Chapter 2 I provide a theorisation of moving in which goes beyond contractual agreements and decorative change to encompass practices of inhabitation and accommodating that are, in turn, suggestive of contemporary forms of dwelling. The emphasis here is on 'estate agency' and on the material traces of previous habitation and occupation. In Chapter 3 I revisit and rework Miller's earlier take on appropriating the state on a council estate (Miller, 1988), showing that the state too has to do the work of appropriation. I also entwine this with Bev Skeggs' work on respectability and working-class femininities, arguing that the wrecking of ideal homes consequent upon being modernised brings about widespread related practices of ridding, wasting and acquisition, as women, in particular, attempt to remake their ideal homes through new interiors, in things and decoration.

In Chapters 4 to 7 the focus switches to everyday practices of inhabitation in dwelling structures. The emphasis in Chapter 4 on the accommodation of sleep provides a contribution to the literature on the moral economies of mothers (Clarke 2000; Gregson and Crewe 1998), an extension to my previous work on clothing, divestment and the body (Gregson et al. 2000; Gregson and Beale 2004), and the first of several explorations of the effects of the normative. I show here how accommodating children's growing bodies in sleep provides further evidence for Clarke's arguments about the traffic in the material culture of childhood, as cots and children's beds circulate between mothers and make moral economies between mothers. And I show too how these practices of circulation are being modified by regulatory discourses of risk, as cot mattresses in particular have been identified as unsuitable things to hand around. As a consequence, cot mattresses are more likely to be wasted in their ridding. The chapter also demonstrates how the material culture of sleep far exceeds beds and bedding, extending, through its connections between the sleeping and waking body, to include clothing and its storage in wardrobes and chests of drawers. The chapter shows how changes to the accommodation of sleep frequently involve not just the ridding of beds and bedding but clothing too. As such it shows how clothing comes to be released to charity shops and charity doorstep collections, in practices of inhabitation.

Chapter 5 engages with a similar range of literatures, conjoining work on collections (Belk 1995; Pearce 1995 and 1998; Ellis and Haywood 2004) and on collections in the domestic sphere (Gregson and Crewe 2003) with the above literature on mothers' management of the material culture of children through a focus on children's clothing and toys. Through its emphasis on the accommodation of these things within dwelling structures, the chapter extends existing work on collections to examine the practices of their holding within the domestic. Collections, then, are rarely rid. Instead, they stay with us. Such stayings contrast markedly with children's clothing and toys, where ridding is far more commonplace. Unlike collections, the practices of managing and caring for children's clothing and toys highlight the importance of the mobility of certain things within practices of inhabitation and, as such, connect with Hetherington's (2004) portrayal of the house as conduit. As I show though, the mobility of things in the domestic is critical to understanding their ridding.

Chapter 6 focuses on kitchen appliances and can be read primarily with and against Elizabeth Shove's recent work on invisible consumption and the technological production of environments in the domestic (Shove 2003: although see also Cowan 1983; Cockburn 1985; Hirsch 1992; Cooper and Mayers 2000; Livingstone 1992). The chapter accords with Shove's arguments in several respects, notably in demonstrating the importance of convenience in contemporary practices of inhabitation. Appliances are valued for their capacity to do certain practices of consumption such as laundering clothes, food storage and preparation, and washing and cleaning utensils and dishes. And they are valued too for the way in which doing these tasks enables household members – often mothers – to do other things simultaneously (Gershuny 1978). But appliances can and do fail, and as a consequence they make apparent how certain domestic environments have become dependent upon them. The chapter focuses on some of the key instances of appliance failure occurring during the ethnographic fieldwork. It demonstrates conclusively that appliances are ambivalent accommodations within the domestic; they are valued for what they do but are also hated and feared for their capacities to not do what they were manufactured to do. As such, getting rid of these failed things almost invariably places them in trajectories which connect to their wasting. Moreover, the chapter shows how living with appliances is not just a matter of manufactured convenience but fundamentally about the social relations of cohabitation in dwelling structures.

Chapter 7 continues the emphasis on living with the capacities of non-human things. It provides a contribution to the emerging literatures on domesticated 'nature' (Miller et al. 1998; Anderson 2003), albeit a contribution located firmly in dwelling structures and the domestic. The chapter examines practices of gardening, highlighting particularly many households' struggles to accommodate plant growth and manage excess. In this respect, the chapter provides a different take on gardens and gardening to the emphasis thus far within the emerging literature on gardens and home culture (Chevalier 1998; Bhatti and Church 2001; Brook 2003; Hitchings 2003; Milligan et al. 2004). The chapter also extends these arguments to living with companion animals and their effects. In both instances, the chapter demonstrates conclusively the power of the normative to effect ridding through wasting.

This chapter, however, has served a rather different purpose. And in Chapter 8 I return once more to the conventions of academic narrative. A core facet of my argument in this volume is that we are constantly doing things with and to things (Dant 1999), placing them and displacing them, acquiring them and appropriating them, sorting them, holding on to them, keeping them, storing them, discarding them and releasing them, maybe via routes that connect to the waste stream, but maybe via others that enable their re-contextualisation and revaluation. In all these instances, what we do with things is always simultaneously a social activity, a way of making and reconstituting key socialities, identities and subjectivities. In the final chapter I draw the various strands of this argument together into a synthetic position statement. I argue that the various practices of habitation that characterise our inhabiting of dwelling structures and that work to make them accommodating accommodations not only move things around across several temporal registers, but constitute what I term a 'gap in accommodation'. This gap moves things from the physical state of co-presence to the representational state. Constituted by the movement and handling of things in practices of inhabitation, the gap provides the temporal interval and the spatial displacement necessary for the effects of the representational outside to permeate the walls of the dwelling structure. It therefore opens up the potential for ridding, for making physically absent that which is representationally troublesome (Douglas 1966). But equally, it allows for the release of things that most closely map into the self we wish to be seen to be. At the same time, the 'gap in accommodation' is shown to be fundamentally about the accommodations of cohabitation, of people living together in households. What is rid, that is displaced, moved along and indeed wasted through the 'gap in accommodation', is shown frequently to be a means of using physical absences in things to make present the social relations of love, care and devotion that sustain living in proximity, together, under one roof. I end the chapter by turning finally to the connections between accommodation and dwelling, highlighting their relation to the dwelling structure as a conduit. Focusing on birth and death events, I show how both events have the capacity to disclose forms of contemporary inhabitation that are about dwelling, and accommodation, before closing the volume by insisting on the continued importance of a dwelling perspective for research on consumption and the material culture of the home.

NOTES

1 The exception to this generalisation is Strasser's history of trash in the United States (Strasser 2000), although this is based on documentary analysis rather than on a direct examination of household practices (see also Chappells and Shove 1999). In addition, and for historical comparison, see the pioneering research being conducted at St Andrew's and Stirling (http://www.cehp.stir.ac.uk).

2 The increasing prominence of waste management within UK policy circles is charted by a succession of papers (DoE 1990; DoE and Welsh Office 1995; DoE, Transport and the Regions 2000; MORI 2002; Strategy Unit 2002). Of these, only *Waste Strategy 2000* set statutory targets, with 25% of household waste to be either recycled or composted by 2005/6. The Number 10 Strategy Unit document *Waste Not Want Not* (2002) admits that this target is highly unlikely to be met, and sets out a strategy for developing an economic and regulatory framework for establishing a sustainable waste management system for England by 2020.

3 The project was funded by the Economic and Social Research Council (R000239972) from 2003 to 2005, and had the title, Disposal, devaluation and consumerism: or how and why things come not to matter. End of award materials are available via http://www.esrc.ac.uk. Further details of the project are available at http://www.shef.ac.uk/disposal-and-consumerism/index.html.

4 See, for example: Boldero 1995; Dahab et al. 1995; Barr et al. 2001; Emery et al. 2003; Barr 2004; McDonald and Ball 1998; Obara 2006; Tonglet et al. (2004), Tonglet et al. (2004).

5 Although notoriously difficult to quantify accurately, existing figures suggest that household waste accounts for approximately 90% (25 million tonnes) of municipal waste per annum, and shows that this is made up of a wide range of materials (Strategy Unit 2002: 2.2). Percentage weight figures are as follows: garden waste (20%), paper and board (18%), putrescible, including kitchen, waste (17%), glass (7%), miscellaneous non-combustible (5%), dense plastics (4%) and textiles (3%). These figures are used normally to support claims that over 50% of household waste by weight is open to recycling. However, and notwithstanding that they are based on definitions used within the waste management industry rather than on categories of consumer goods, the same figures also suggest that much exits households besides matter suitable for recycling.

6 The full research team comprised Nicky Gregson, Louise Crewe and Alan Metcalfe.

7 The in-depth interview work was carried out by Alan Metcalfe, and the focus-group work was by Alan Metcalfe, Jenny Carton and Louise Crewe.

8 Whilst it is certainly the case that the majority of qualitative methodologies rely on data collection procedures that juxtapose single researchers, working either alone or as part of research teams, with research subjects, the recording of ethnographic data makes it a unique way of working. With the majority of qualitative methods, research interactions are recorded simultaneously in the moments of their enactment, be this through audio or visual technologies. They are then translated into another medium prior to their analysis and interpretation. Usually this form is textual, typically a transcript of conversation; a move which, whilst it has its problems, renders it

(and the conversation) open to both the scrutiny and the interpretations of other co-researchers. Whilst the recorded conversations and/or visual materials collected as part of an ethnographic piece of research undoubtedly can be subjected to the same procedures, ethnographic encounters vastly exceed such forms of data collection. Indeed it is often the unspoken, an action or a glance for example, which proves critical to developing interpretations. Recorded in field notes, such data is already cast as an ethnographic story when it is offered, as it was here, to others to read. It can be further interpreted, as text, but the bases for at least some of these interpretations remain opaque to those who were not co-present in their enactment, and interpretations are consequently harder, seemingly, to subject to potential counter-readings. Although the use of visual technologies *in situ*, notably web cameras, offers a means round this difficulty – in that they make 'raw' data available to all researchers simultaneously – their use raises a further set of questions regarding technologically mediated research subjectivities, performances and ethics. An alternative is to enact ethnography through a multi-person research team. Although this appears to circumvent several of the difficulties discussed here, it does so by making heavy research investments in a particular place, which may or may not be justifiable to funding bodies. I would add that, whilst I have utilised multi-person ethnographic methods in previous projects, I remain less than convinced of the appropriateness of such strategies in situations where the research subjects are a small number of households. Aside from its not inconsiderable practical difficulties, living alongside, working within and with households over a lengthy period of time is already possibly the most intrusive and demanding of fieldwork relations for all participants. To substitute a team for a person seems to me to have the potential to ratchet the level of scrutiny up still further, and – at least in the context of the United Kingdom – to invite comparison with some problematic cultural parallels, for example with the professional practices of social work and policing, or indeed with the litany of 'reality TV' programmes, notably *Big Brother*.

9 One of these stories, albeit one that cannot be fully developed here, is that this particular ethnography has, at least in part, refused to comply with the script of alienated, household-centred yet intensely mobile life that characterises so many theoretical accounts of the contemporary moment. The social-science literature is replete with numerous theoretical accounts of mobility and its relation to time-space compression (Harvey 1989), modernity (Bauman 2002), globalisation (Held et al. 1999), travel (Clifford 1997) and connection, distance and proximity (Urry 2002 and 2004); although see also Highmore (2002) and Hubbard and Lilley (2004). Although highly influential, such accounts lack grounding in the actualities of practice, in what people actually do in their quotidian lives. Moreover, they present an account of social life characterised more by the metaphor of the 'Business Traveller' than by the lives of those who clean airport terminals or whose annual encounter with 'liquid modernity' is a delayed charter flight to Palma (Massey 1993). That quotidian lives are perhaps not quite as mobile as they are imagined to be is apparent from the pages that follow.

10 In contrast, the depth interview work, by virtue of its temporalities and distanciated mode of enactment, remained at the level of narratives, of households and of the particular ridding events that occurred within them.

11 Whether the home is indeed the primary site of consumption, and particularly a consumption of practice, is more debateable than Miller's assertion here suggests. Acts of consumption occur in multiple sites, including not just homes but schools and hospitals, court rooms and restaurants, clubs, bars and stadiums, for example. Furthermore, if – as Warde (2005) argues – consumption is but a moment of practice, then the home is not the primary site of consumption but a site for multiple moments of practice (cooking, eating, ironing, washing, playing…), all of which entail consumption in some form or another. That the home does indeed conjoin (simultaneously) these moments is what works to differentiate it as a site of consumption from many other sites, where practice, albeit internally differentiated, appears to be rather more singular.

12 All names in this book are pseudonyms. In addition, and in order to protect confidentiality, any potentially identifying characteristics of research participants have been altered.

13 Although there is now a huge literature devoted to acknowledging the effect of the researcher on research subjects (see, for example, Aull Davis, 1999; Bell et al, 1993; James et al, 1997), and some attendance to the relations between ethnography and autobiography (Okely and

Callaway, 1992; Okely, 1996), it remains the case that the ethnographic self is represented primarily as a self constituted in relation to a research 'field' (Amit, 2000; Gupta and Ferguson, 1997). All too commonly, only marginal reference is made to a wider 'field', encompassing the key social relations and social identities inhabited by the researcher (although see Pink, 2000). Not only do these coexist alongside and within the ethnography, shaping it and both foreclosing and opening up its possibilities, but they are affected by it too, hence my use of the term accommodation above. Rather than look upon ethnographic field work as a period in which normal life is suspended, I prefer to regard it as characterised by co-present accommodations.

14 Much as Janet's house exerted effects, so did its location in South Hightown. The most significant of these is the overwhelming whiteness of this place. Not to be white British here is to stand out. Moreover, for the handful of non-white households living in South Hightown, racism is a key facet of their lives in this place. South Hightown is also a pseudonym. As with people, any identifying characteristics of this place have either been altered or modified.

15 The research design here has clear parallels with Miller and Clarke's ethnographic work in North London in the mid 1990s (Miller 1998; Clarke 2000 and 2002), in which one street – 'Jay Road' – provided a geographical base from which to spiral out. Unlike Jay Road, however, and whilst heterogeneous in many respects, in South Hightown Alternative Terrace's very diversity sets it apart. Indeed, as I found out in the course of the fieldwork, the street had another name in other areas of the village, 'Nutters' Row'. To generalise from it to South Hightown, as Jay Road is made to stand for North London, would be misplaced, as will be obvious from the remaining discussion in this section.

16 The 1951 County Development Plan is critical to both UK planning history and to understanding the post Second World War history of the County Durham villages (Pattison 2004; Hudson 1989). Intimately linked to the future of the coal-mining industry in the North-east and in the UK, it was notable for its 'Category D' policy which condemned 114 (of 357) settlements by denying them future investment and development. Whilst a few Category D villages did indeed disappear, bulldozed and razed, and whilst others were partially demolished (to become, typically, industrial estates), many more settlements were reprieved as a result of concerted campaigns by local activists and politicians.

17 The 'Right to Buy' was introduced by the Thatcher government in the 1980s and proved immensely popular with many council tenants. A consequence, however, and a source of much intergenerational tension on the Rivers estate, is that teenage mothers with young babies are primarily housed in poorly maintained council-owned one-bedroom bungalows, whilst older residents who have bought their properties live out their lives, often alone, in the more spacious housing previously intended for families.

18 At this time commuting was mostly a male phenomenon, with men travelling out of the village to work, by and large in the East Durham coal field. Women and younger children, typically, at this time remained in the village, at home and at school.

19 By the 1990s commuting involved both men and women, travelling to work in the primary urban centres within the North-east region, i.e. Newcastle and Teesside. As a consequence, the day-time life of South Hightown predominantly involves older, largely retired people, the unemployed and/or benefit dependent, mothers at home with young children, and older teenagers who, for varying reasons, do not attend school.

20 Current house valuations place properties on Alternative Terrace in the £130000 – £150000+ bracket; on the Rivers Estate, £36000 – £100000; in the old core, up to £500000; and on the suburban-style estates, £150000 – £300000+. Estate-agent marketing represents South Hightown as within easy reach by road of major regional employment centres, including Durham City, Derwentside, Newcastle and Darlington/Teesside, and is indicative of the degree to which speed has shrunk distance regionally, not just globally.

21 Opting-in was an important part of the research protocol for the ethnography. With the research requiring a commitment to a long period of intensive and intrusive scrutiny, lasting potentially well beyond the twelve months of timetabled fieldwork, I felt it vital to avoid putting households in a position in which they felt compelled to participate in the research. So, rather than approaching households directly, through, for example, knocking on doors or

deliberately trying to recruit the few ethnic minority households living in South Hightown, I adopted the classic ethnographic tactic of allowing households to come to know about the research's presence in their midst, and to become as (un)involved in it as they wanted to be.

22 UK readers will be familiar with the Blair government's use of Anti-social Behaviour Orders (or ASBOs) as a key plank in attempts to regulate behaviour in public space. Aimed primarily at disciplining 'youth', the same approach has been extended to encompass dumping and abandoning things in public space.

23 I should mention here as an aside that there is a strong tradition of informal policing in South Hightown that works to protect the informal economy against informants.

24 With attention focused on a rights and risk-based approach to research ethics, the capacity of research to afford social capital is frequently overlooked. In the UK context, such capacities are particularly important in areas such as Wear Road, or the Rivers estate more generally, where gossip about known of others is intense, and where stocks of social capital are not particularly high. In such circumstances, quite who gets the opportunity to be an academic research subject can itself be a matter of social value and a way of making and re-inscribing social distinctions. Whilst subverting such social relations is a possibility, its effects have to be carefully thought through, as well as weighed up against research resources. To be sure, I could have attempted to recruit households drawn from these 'others', but – leaving aside the question of resources – to do so would have been to disrupt the protocol of opting-in, and to contest the stocks of social knowledge of the Tenants and Residents Group. An additional consideration is what effects such inclusions may have had on the data generated. My suspicion – it is of course no more than that – is that they would have introduced degrees of self-censorship and diminished research depth. Wear Road is an instance where the merit of teams over individual ethnographic researchers is apparent.

25 Although the St George's flag is not synonymous with support for the BNP, as the fieldwork progressed I became increasingly aware of the ambiguity surrounding its display in South Hightown. At times this coincided with key sporting events, notably England football games and the Rugby World Cup of 2003. But the display went beyond such temporalities, resonating in some instances with support for British troops in Iraq, but in others with a more generally felt xenophobia that coalesced around the figure of the asylum-seeker. A similar degree of ambivalence surrounding the St George's flag emerged in the Nottingham-based interview work.

26 I would also argue that it is vital that we pay attention to places such as the Rivers estate in South Hightown, precisely because of the ways radically intolerant, acquisitive, violent, abusive and disrespectful socialities feature in social life in such places (see also Sennett 2003). These are socialities which few societies can continue to ignore, and which – for those who live amidst and in juxtaposition to them – work to define their everyday lives in terms of the others whom they struggle against.

27 Chief amongst the perceived negative effects raised in discussion were: depressing the performance potential of the village primary school by enrolling primary-school-aged children in schools elsewhere in the region with better performance indicators than South Hightown's; creating excessive school-related traffic flows in and out of the village; not using the few village services, including the post office and remaining shops; and not employing village labour in the domestic economy.

28 This research tactic is indicative of a preoccupation that has impinged on all phases of this research project, one which we have come to term 'searching for the other'. At key junctures, then, we have found ourselves compelled to go looking for particular categories of household, either, as here, to satisfy both the conditions of the funding body and a vaguely-felt anxiety about representativeness, or – as in the depth interview work – because certain household types living in particular types of neighbourhood can be imagined to display particular types of disposition toward things, hoarding and chucking being prime examples.

29 It will be evident from this emphasis on doings that I take very seriously, and accord with, recent attempts to rethink consumption in relation to theories of practice (Warde 2005; see also Gregson et al. 2002b). Indeed, at one level this book can be read as highlighting how a

whole series of interrelated home-based practices involve moments of consumption (although see note 31).

30 Mintel (2003) report that approximately two-thirds of consumers in the UK engage in DIY activities; that 28% of consumers enjoy these tasks, compared to 43% who describe themselves as reluctant participants; and that, whilst 18% claim to do no DIY activities, only 11% hire professional help for such tasks. The DIY sector is shown to be growing at 7–8% per annum, fuelled by both a buoyant housing market and the increased value attached to home improvement and enhancement.

31 In emphasising practices of inhabitation and their connection to acts of acquisition, holding, sorting and ridding, it will be clear that I draw a distinction between types of practices that is about more than dispersion and integration (Warde 2005). Indeed, acquisition, holding, sorting and ridding emerge in this volume as meta-practices; ones that go on in relation to and as part of other forms of routine behaviour, doings and sayings, and know-how with things. In this way, I would argue, consumption is not just a moment in all practices but also a conjunction of meta-practices entailing not just appropriation but also divestment.

32 A central part of the research protocol here was to locate research ethics within research practice, rather than to reduce these considerations to the prior and predictive effects of a discourse of contractual rights (Thrift 2003). Consequently, ethnographic encounters extended beyond the period of fieldwork to encompass discussions of both the process and the products of writing. Indeed, they have in some instances exceeded the period of research funding, as I have returned to South Hightown in the two years since the fieldwork was completed, both to visit Janet and to visit some of the households living on Alternative Terrace and Wear Road. All the participating households were encouraged to play as active a role in the reading and commenting process as they wished. However, in practice this varied considerably. Whilst roughly half of the adult members in these households wanted to discuss interpretations, and whilst around a quarter of the adult research participants chose to read and comment to varying degrees on drafts of the manuscript, others opted to leave such issues entirely to me, professing that they either trusted me to write whatever I wanted or that they really didn't care what I chose to write about. To a degree these differing responses were exactly that, a matter of degrees and the value of 'the book' for participating households. Households with strong investments in education, and particularly in higher education, were far more likely to read, comment, and to make suggestions and alterations to the draft text than those without such stocks of social and cultural capital. This leaves me with a sense of profound unease about even the most sophisticated of contemporary discussions of research ethics, in which the capacity of research participants actively to resist our efforts at best practice have been overlooked in favour of representations which homogenise participants as co-producers.

Chapter 2

Moving in

In this first chapter to feature key ethnographic stories, my concern is with what happens to things when households move in to a dwelling structure. Together with its counterpart moving out, moving in constitutes one of the most significant events for domestic things. Moving house requires that things be sorted. But in their sorting things are also kept and discarded. Moving house requires too that things be packed-up and physically transported. It is, then, a moment of profound instability in the ordering and placement of things. The things that accompany us as we cross the threshold may – if we are ordered and methodical about our enactment of this process – be specified as to be placed in a particular room, the kitchen, bathroom or living room for example, but their precise location in the new dwelling structure is, almost certainly, uncertain. We may have an idea about where to position particular consumer objects – pieces of furniture, appliances and consumer electricals for instance – but this is frequently highly provisional and may change. And we can never anticipate just what matter might confront us, what might have been left behind by the previous occupants or what state the vacated property might be in, and what implications this might have for doing things to things, other people's things.

What concerns me here, however, is not the moment of moving in, the day itself, but moving in as a practice of inhabitation, of moving into a dwelling structure, and its effects on things. As I show, moving in is a much more stretched out temporal process than the contractual moment of passage-in (as owner, mortgagee or tenant), and one which I argue is better understood through the lens of accommodating. Indeed, the term accommodating readily captures the way in which we attempt to fabricate a building structure into an abode, that is, make a dwelling structure accommodating to us, a place we feel at home in through what we have to hand around us. But it also conveys a sense of the limits to the possible in that this accommodation, literally the material fabric that constitutes it and its spatial fixity, exerts effects on what we can do with it, place in it and on how it is possible to live in it and for what duration, particularly as our social relations change, as we age, (choose to) have children or not, keep animals or not and so on. Accommodating too suggests an ongoing temporality, an open-ended flow of action. It is this sense that I find particularly potent as an aid to understanding the moving-in stories encountered in the ethnography. For, in a sense, what this implies is that moving in is never finished or complete, but rather is an ongoing state of inhabitation, a process of accommodating to material configurations through habitation.

The chapter examines at some length the moving-in practices of three households, and focuses on what happens to things in this process. At the beginning of the fieldwork, none of the households had been living in these particular dwelling structures for longer than six months.[1] All three live on Alternative Terrace in South Hightown.[2] As will become clear, the three households exhibit considerable social differences and all disclosed highly divergent practices of moving in. These differences have considerable implications for what happens to things. In the first part of this chapter I narrate and interpret the three moving-in stories. I then proceed to draw out the more general observations that emerge from these stories, focusing on moving in and its relation to the other, before ending the chapter with three broader theoretical points about moving in and accommodating, about moving in and others, and about moving in as a practice of inhabitation.

Moving-in stories[3]

Jo-Anne's story

In beginning with Jo-Anne's story, I am starting deliberately with the type of household which features strongly in the imaginaries that underpin much of the consumption literature. This is a household which displays strong positive investments in contemporary consumer culture, particularly in fashion, shopping, clothes and cars. In this sense, then, it could easily be an ideal type. As will become clear, however, Jo-Anne's moving-in story has more depth than might initially appear.

Jo-Anne is in her early thirties, has lived in the North-east all her life and has recently separated from her husband of thirteen years. She and their five-year-old son Mark live on Alternative Terrace, in a property Jo-Anne purchased after their separation with her share of the financial settlement. Jo-Anne is in full time employment, working in sales for a national distribution company. Her mother – who does not work but who lives a short ten-minute drive away – does most of the before- and after-school care for Mark. Mark continues to see his dad, who also lives relatively nearby, on a weekly basis, usually at weekends, whilst Jo-Anne attempts to juggle being his mum with a new long-distance, 'on-off' relationship.

Having taken possession of her new house on Alternative Terrace, Jo-Anne did not move in for approximately six months. Instead, she and Mark lived with her parents whilst her dad and brother took on some major DIY projects, including re-plastering the whole of the downstairs, knocking out the fireplace and re-flooring the kitchen. The house had previously been rented to students, but before then had been lived in by the previous owner and – according to the immediate neighbours – was decorated in keeping with the age of the property. Apparently it had featured a cast iron bath, and a specially sourced toilet and washbasin. Jo-Anne, however, was not so enamoured by these authentic things. Before she and Mark moved in, both the bathroom and the kitchen were gutted and replaced. In the following passage of recorded conversation, Jo-Anne narrates her motivations for doing the kitchen:

Jo-Anne: When I first saw the house, although I loved it very much, you know the sitting room, the bathroom, the bedrooms, it all sold the house, but the kitchen – although it was live-able – and I knew I could live with it, it didn't suit us at all.

Nicky: What was wrong with it?

Jo-Anne: It was a fair kitchen, and it was clean, but it wasn't my style. It wasn't my style. The kitchen units wasn't my style.

Nicky: What was it like?

Jo-Anne: It was a wall-to-wall fitted kitchen – there was an oven in that corner, you can see where that's been. Where the fridge is, can you see, and then there was a hob here and benches here which was a bit scruffy, old. If you know what I mean; they needed changing. But the rest of it was wall to wall cabinets, really clean, right across the walls, was in lovely condition. I could've passed them on if somebody would've had it because it was in good con, nick. But it just wasn't my style. I could have lived with it if I knew I couldn't have afforded, but I knew I could afford a brand new one.

Nicky: Was that the most important thing for you to do then?

Jo-Anne: Yeah, yeah.

Nicky: What do you think that's about? Why's the kitchen so

Jo-Anne: Cos it's a woman's pride [N: mmm] the kitchen is the heart of the home I think. I know people say the fire and the living room is the heart of the home, but the kitchen's the heart of the home in my eye.

Nicky: So it really mattered to put your imprint on it?

Jo-Anne: Yeah – and I knew that if I put in a nice kitchen it would put a little bit of profit into the house as well.

Nicky: But that wasn't the main?

Jo-Anne: It wasn't the main thing because I knew I wasn't going to be moving out of here that quickly.

Nicky: So did you have an idea of what sort of style you wanted to do?

Jo-Anne: I had an idea of all the modern kitchens that were kicking about cos I had the magazines, and I just looked around. IKEA was

Figure 2.1: Jo-Anne's kitchen

my main area, MFI and the rest of them. They were all gorgeous. But the magazines – I had a good look through them. I didn't buy them. It was all just stuff that I picked up from the stores – from MFI, from B&Q and from IKEA. And I saw a lot of fitted kitchens that I liked, but I liked the idea of this free standing thing.

Nicky: What was that about?

Jo-Anne: It was all about hygiene [N: uhuh] cos you can get underneath, you can get underneath with the mop [...] But like at the same time as well I'm a fashion victim and I knew the free standing units were quite fashionable. So I like the style. I liked the chrome. [Figure 2.1]

Nicky: So this is all from one place?

Jo-Anne: IKEA – it's all an IKEA one.

Nicky: So you like that sort of style.

Jo-Anne: Yes, yes.

Nicky: What does it say to you?

Jo-Anne: It says to me like clean for starters. Professional. And Nice Taste. So if I sort of got some nice guy that I could invite along he'd think 'God this woman's got some taste!' – laughter – And he might like us a little bit.

Complemented by new lighting, cutlery, shelving, bowls, dishes, plates, cooks' knives, wooden chopping-board, pans, a range of pasta jars, and a table and chairs – all from IKEA – plus a new tiled floor, microwave, toaster and espresso-maker, the things that constitute Jo-Anne's new kitchen are seen (and known) by her to be 'fashionable' and 'contemporary'; to encode her 'contemporary' style; to satisfy her demands for easy-care hygiene, and – perhaps – to constitute her as the tasteful desirable other to an as yet unknown taste-conscious male. It would be difficult indeed to envisage how such a conjunction of desired meanings might be seen by Jo-Anne to be achieved through the declared to be 'not my style' accumulation of unfashionable yet functional things previously located in this house's kitchen. Yet, of perhaps greater significance is that Jo-Anne budgeted for her house purchase to allow her to make these purchases. So, not only is she not having to live with an arrangement of things dictated by a previous owner/occupant, but she is also able to 'start again', in this case by immediately filling the room that she regards as having the most symbolic power to constitute 'home' with clean-slate purchases, with things with no histories of previous consumption – hers or others.

Except, this kitchen is not quite the clean slate. For one, the slate is an IKEA one, manufactured and retailed to appeal – as it does so successfully here – to a particular consumer identity. But, more potently, elsewhere in the kitchen and outside the house – in zones of storage – are traces of other presences. In the kitchen stands a fridge: a white plastic one, not the chrome one that Jo-Anne would really like in its place but which she cannot afford to buy:

Jo-Anne: Me mam gave me that fridge because I couldn't afford a brand new one […] what happened was, when my granddad died, she inherited his freezer or his fridge – I can't remember, but it wasn't an all-in-one. So she bought another single fridge and she gave me hers.

However, when Jo-Anne bought the house, it came with the in-situ kitchen appliances:

Jo-Anne: The cooker and the hob […] they were pretty minging. I'd have been as fat as a pig living off that Chinese [takeaway] cos I could not have eaten anything out of that cooker.

Nicky: What was the matter with it?

Jo-Anne: Minging – grease. It was minging.

Nicky: How long do you reckon it'd been in here then?

Jo-Anne: Oh a hundred years definitely! […]

Nicky: And there wasn't a fridge?

Jo-Anne: There was a fridge in there but that was minging as well, so when me mam said that she was going to give us that, me dad found this guy who was living on his own who didn't have a fridge, so he said he could have it if he took it away, so he helped himself. So it wasn't thrown away.

The narrations that map the movement of the various fridges weave stories of intergenerational familial inheritance and gifting – from the dead father to the daughter, who in turn releases another fridge to another daughter whose hygiene/cleanliness thresholds declare the fridge in the house she has purchased to be unacceptable, yet whose budget for purchasing the new has finally run out. Here we see how Jo-Anne's declared to be 'minging' fridge, inherited from the vendor, is replaced by another discard, yet one from a known – imputed to be safer and cleaner – source, her mother. However, the narrations also feature stories of charitable acts of reclamation and gifting between men. Indeed, it is hard not to see the actions of Jo-Anne's father – who rescues the 'minging' fridge for someone else (not un-coincidentally another man) whose capacity to overcome (or tolerance of) the traces of the food storage of unknown others is presumably somewhat greater than Jo-Anne's – as a form of partial resistance to his daughter's jettisoning of things and investments in the new, and his wife's complicity in this. The remainder of the old kitchen appliances however – the cooker and the hob – together with the kitchen units and cupboards, and the old lino flooring, remain stashed away in an outbuilding on Alternative Terrace; behind a closed door out of sight, out of the inhabited living space if not entirely out of Jo-Anne's mind.

It is a similar story with the bathroom toilet, which is currently residing in another outside shed on Alternative Terrace:

Figure 2.2: Jo-Anne's 'pebble-dashed, old' toilet

Jo-Anne: I was never happy with that toilet. [Figure 2.2]

Nicky: Why?

Jo-Anne: Although it was very natural looking – I probably could have had it made to look a bit fresher but I felt it had been well used, and I'm funny about that – a few pebble-dashes in its time. I didn't like it. It just said 'germs'. I just saw 'germs' wrote all over it. Even if I couldn't have afforded to do the bathroom I'd have done the toilet. That would've definitely gone!

The rest of the bathroom makeover, however, is a rather more anxiety-laden affair:

Nicky: Tell me the story about what you decided to do with the bathroom.

Jo-Anne: I was happy with it actually – when I bought the house it was one of the things that attracted me to it, it had loads of character and I was prepared to leave it like that but one day I just visited MFI[36] – out of curiosity really. I popped in there and I saw this really 'contemporary' sink [laughs] and I thought 'God I love that', and although I thought at the time that that would not really suit a cottage I still had to have it.

Nicky: What was that about then?

Jo-Anne: Well I just liked the new style – because I think in the olden days they used to get bathed in little tin baths and washed in little glass bowls and I just thought 'it's all going to come back'. And this thing was like a duplicate of what probably was like years ago sort of thing. So that's what tempted me to go for it. But I kept the old bath

Nicky: Was that a cast iron one?

Jo-Anne: Yeah – I think it is – yeah – with the legs on and stuff. But because the sink and the toilet was going to be sort of extra modern I thought, 'Well I could do something with the bath that was originally in there to make it a bit more modern than it looked with the old style legs and stuff. So I bought the wood that matched the sink and the toilet unit and surrounded the back and that for it all to match.

Nicky: Are you happy with it?

Jo-Anne: Oh yes. The only thing that I was a bit unhappy with was the colour of it 'cos I chose that colour because of the floor, the wooden floor that's in there, and I thought it would go with that; I thought it would be the same colour as that [...] that it would all mingle in. But the wood on the floor is so old, old pine, and the wood that's been built in the bathroom is so modern, it just clashes so much. So that's the only bit I'm a bit disappointed with, but it's grown on us, it's not that bad

Figure 2.3: Jo-Anne's bathroom

Nicky: So you're not going to do anything about it then?

Jo-Anne: Not yet. I might in the future. I wouldn't change the floor – maybe I'll consider sanding it down, taking the stain off it. Maybes having a more sort of natural look that would maybes match the units. But that's going to take money so that'll be some time. It might just never happen. It might just stay there forever. I'll live with it. [Figure 2.3]

As this passage suggests, going shopping – as in just looking, browsing around – is an activity that Jo-Anne finds immensely pleasurable, as well as something she does frequently, to keep up with what is 'fashionable' and 'contemporary'. It is, nonetheless, not without risks, for browsing carries with it the possibility of seduction and acquisition. And – as Jo-Anne tells it – the story of the bathroom makeover is almost one of 'I bought a new bathroom because I loved a bowl I saw and had to have it'. As Jo-Anne narrates this, we see how the seduction of the MFI bowl is allowed to overcome her initial awareness that this bowl was somehow not suitable stylistically; how Jo-Anne weaves an imaginary tale entwining pastiche, the copy and nostalgia to connect this contemporary bowl with the imagined practice of bathing in a miner's cottage in the nineteenth century, and how this tale legitimates the MFI bowl's purchase. But what we also see is the agency of this bowl, and for that matter a classic instance of the Diderot effect.[37] Having purchased a bowl and accompanying modern wood surround, Jo-Anne is compelled to carry on with her intended (again hygiene-risk related) act of bathroom disposal – getting rid of the old toilet and replacing it with a modern unit – and to complete the transformation by covering-up the cast-iron bath with a modern wood surround. As she reveals in her talk, Jo-Anne is anxious about the visual effects of this, particularly about the juxtaposition of old and modern wood – surfaces, textures and colours that she acknowledges do not really 'go'.[38] For a woman who takes a not inconsiderable pride in the 'matched-ness' of her interior aesthetic and her ability to put together a particular look through the mass market, this is a difficult and expensive mistake to negotiate. Not only does it suggest that her design skills are not quite what she might like them to be – that she can make mistakes, particularly when deviating from the visual securities offered by package-buying of the IKEA kitchen variety – but the uncertainties of the modern–old juxtaposition work to destabilise her confidence in what she sees as her project of doing the contemporary look in a cottage. Jo-Anne's financial circumstances are currently such that she will have to do with the bathroom what she didn't want to do with her kitchen, namely 'live with it'. But it is instructive to see how she ends up reflecting that any change might never happen, and that the current arrangement of things 'might stay forever'.

Elsewhere, in the sitting room, Jo-Anne's moving-in transformations have been more restricted (Figure 2.4).

A chrome surround and hearth now mark the open fire, where previously there was a stone surround and wall-plinth – in a deliberate echo of the chrome splashback behind the hob in the kitchen – and there are two new leather sofas purchased from DFS,[4] which almost didn't fit through the door. There is also a widescreen TV, DVD player and music system, all bought from either Comet or Currys.[5] The walls – as elsewhere – are all white-painted plaster. And here, as in all other rooms, the windows have been fitted with wooden shutter-blinds, for security, privacy and to reduce the noise. Interestingly, and what marks Jo-Anne's moving-in practices as different from other moving-in stories in the ethnography, she has not undertaken any core structural work beyond re-plastering the downstairs and renewing the kitchen floor. She says: 'I did have plans' (for the windows), which she acknowledges to be old and so rotten that they cannot be opened. But then she goes on to say: 'But then I was told how much they were, what I was looking at. Then I thought, "Well I might as well just leave them and get a new car!"'

Moving in as enacted by Jo-Anne is an event practised almost exclusively through the immediate acquisition of a vast array of consumer goods; new purchases bought precisely because of their assumed clean-slate properties and because of their imputed style connotations, meanings which Jo-Anne invests heavily in and which are central to her identity. But, although Jo-Anne makes selections from the vast array of possibilities offered by the mass market, it is IKEA, MFI, DFS, Comet and Currys who provide the assemblages of objects and rooms that constitute her understanding of moving in. It is of critical significance, however, that the moment of moving in itself is deferred until the point at which these rooms have been configured through particular acquisitions, purchased and put together to constitute distinctive finished 'looks'. Moving in is choreographed in this instance as a relatively compressed temporal event, with a definite end-point marked by inhabiting the dwelling structure. The house then has been fabricated to accommodate, produced to be a place that is accommodating for Jo-Anne (and Mark) to live

Figure 2.4: Jo-Anne's living room

in. On becoming lived in it is telling that no further work has since been done to it, and that very few things have been bought for it.

And yet this fabrication is not something produced solely through the commodity form. As Jo-Anne makes so abundantly clear in her talk, accommodating her and Mark is also about ridding the house of others' material presences. Rather than locating these presences in a general sense throughout the house, Jo-Anne seems to attach them to particular object forms – in this case the 'not-my-style' kitchen units and fireplace and a small number of named objects identified explicitly with hygiene risks (the cooker, hob, fridge and toilet). As will become increasingly clear in the following chapters, the 'not-me' stylistic appraisal is particularly important to understanding many instances of ridding, and is possibly at its most potent on occasions such as house purchase, where the tastes of others frequently collide and where redecoration has become a normative practice. Indeed, capitalising on the disruption of moving house, many UK kitchen and bathroom retailers are marketing moving as the ideal moment to install 'your dream kitchen or bathroom'. By contrast, Jo-Anne's aversion to inherited objects associated with food preparation and storage and the passage of bodily waste appears to border on the phobic: intriguingly, whilst she cleans her new kitchen and bathroom on a daily basis and polishes the chrome hob splashback with baby oil every night, cleaning these specific things – with their imagined consumption histories – was apparently not an option. Instead, their 'minging-ness' and 'pebble-dashed-ness' – negative qualities both – were sufficient reason to expel them. Over-used and unclean, these things exceeded Jo-Anne's personal dirt tolerance thresholds. Nonetheless, it is questionable whether, even if cleaned, these things could have had a place within Jo-Anne's clean-slate script: perhaps indeed, their very difference from 'contemporary', in shape, materials, colour and texture, would have precipitated their ridding?

Before leaving Jo-Anne's moving-in story, it is important to emphasise the trajectories of those things that were ripped out and replaced. With the exception of the fridge, all this matter was placed, by Jo-Anne's dad and brother, in some of the outbuildings on Alternative Terrace. At the end of the fieldwork it had been there for over a year. At various junctures in the field-work I ventured to talk explicitly with Jo-Anne about this lingering, on each occasion hoping fervently that our talk would not exert effects. Fortunately it didn't, even though on one occasion the talk precipitated the opening of one of these outbuilding doors – at which point Jo-Anne shuddered, exclaimed 'Urghhh, spiders!!' and shut it quickly! When Jo-Anne talked with me about this stuff she made it very plain that she didn't care about it per se, but she also talked more speculatively about what she might or might not do with it. She talked vaguely about hiring a skip, but then couldn't work out where to put it. The tip was equally problematic, 'Because it won't go in my car and I haven't got a man in my life who'll do it for me.' Similarly, although she knows that there is someone in South Hightown who might take the stuff away for cash, she doesn't know how to get in contact with him.[6] 'And any-way', she says, 'it's out of sight and out of mind' – at least until my talk, or even my appearance on Alternative Terrace, reminds her of its presence.

There is a sense in which this partially expelled matter both exceeds Jo-Anne's capacities to deal any further with it and, simultaneously, marks out the relatively constrained socialites of her life in South Hightown. A relative newcomer, with no immediate family living in the village, in full-time employment, and a woman, she has no points of easy access into the predominantly male informal economy, and her relationship with her new partner is not at a point where she feels that asking him to take what she regards as 'filthy old rubbish' to the tip is a possibility. But what both the talk and bodily reactions to this stuff also suggest is the degree of Jo-Anne's lack of identification with this matter, which to me seemed to be about her refusal to come into bodily contact with this stuff, through its touch and removal. Instead, what Jo-Anne wanted was for others to move it for her. But the limits of available (familial) others had been reached with the passage of the matter to the outbuildings. To displace the stuff still further – to move it to a skip or to take it to the tip – required Jo-Anne to make investments in its removal, investments which, throughout the ethnography, she was unwilling to make. Ultimately then, Jo-Anne actually just didn't care enough about any of this matter to do anything with it or find ways of getting others to do something with it, and the outbuildings' capacity to store it all invisibly – away from the scrutiny of others – enabled the matter to linger on. Still *in situ*, displaced but only partially so, declared to be 'rubbish' but not carried-away, it is tempting to speculate that the traces of others' inhabitation and consumption practices that Jo-Anne was so anxious to remove as part of her fabrication of moving in will still be there whenever/if ever she comes to move on, as a trace of her own living there.[7]

Andrew and Mel's story

Andrew and Mel are in their early 30s and late 20s, respectively, engaged and planning their wedding, to occur in a village Andrew describes as 'another country!' in Northern Ireland, Mel's place of birth. This is their first house purchase together, though they have lived together in rented accommodation for some years, also in the North-east region. Andrew was born in the North-east; his family – who are from London – live relatively nearby, while his sister attends one of the region's universities. Andrew himself spent several years 'on the road' playing in a rock band and travelling widely; years he now describes as his 'wild, idealistic, rambling youth!' He is now employed as a professional youth worker. Mel has recently embarked on a radical career change. After several years in pub/bar management, and midway through the fieldwork, she began studying for a nursing qualification. Notwithstanding the sizeable reduction in their joint income, and its effects on what can be done to the house, the couple narrate this change of direction as liberation. 'Free' of the time-scheduling demands of bar management, this couple are able now to spend their time off together rather than apart.

Janet's house (see Chapter 1) is next door to Andrew and Mel's house. This means that I was able easily to observe and talk with them on a routine basis, in the throes of events being enacted, rather than talk about these events retrospectively, as with Jo-Anne. As we will see, however, most of this moving-in story is about Andrew and enacted by him. For the most part, throughout the period of fieldwork, Mel was either working or, latterly, studying. Two extracts from my field notes serve to open the couple's moving-in story:

It's a beautiful sunny morning and I'm sitting on the garden step reading a book when Andrew comes out and starts talking. He's got a lieu day off and is stripping wallpaper off the bedrooms. He says: 'The only trouble is, the more I take off the more gets revealed, as do all the cracks'. He is also going to attempt to get round to filling in the wood frames on the windows. 'Downstairs they're not too bad but up there [he points to the bedroom window] they're shot through'. (May 2003)

Another conversation with Andrew – he got rid of an old carpet from the hall over the weekend – taken to the tip. This was part of the future project of 'expose the floorboards, sand and varnish'. At the same time he discovered that the entirety of the hall floor and some of the joists have a severe case of woodworm – to which the previous occupants' solution appears to have been to nail-over various offcuts of wood. The banister also has woodworm; it disintegrates to the touch. Andrew has got his dad to come over to look over the newly discovered level of trouble and to confirm what he thought. Andrew says, 'So I think the priorities might have changed a bit!!' and glances skywards with an exasperated stare – 'God can it get any worse' he says. (June 2003)

Figure 2.5: Andrew & Mel's interior doors

Changing priorities is a recurrent thread to Andrew and Mel's moving-in story. When I began the ethnography and first met Andrew in early 2003 he was lovingly planing down some 'Victorian' wooden interior doors that he had sourced from a second-hand furniture outlet. [Figure 2.5]

He told me then about the grand design plans that they had for the house: to demolish the kitchen and build a new double-storey extension with solar panels on it. He also wanted to demolish the 'jerry-built' garage. Later that same month, Andrew had discovered that demolishing this garage was going to be more problematic than he had assumed, for it contained asbestos panelling. For some months Andrew struggled to get someone from the council to advise him on how to go about getting rid of the garage. Eventually he gave up on this and started asking around the village informal economy, where it appeared progress was to be made: 'Apparently there's some guy who'll use it for his pigeon cree – "What's a bit of asbestos", they said!!', says Andrew. Twelve months on, however, and the garage is still *in situ*; Andrew is now trying to coerce a friend into helping him to demolish it. Throughout this time Andrew and Mel live in one 'living room' which houses almost all their, largely second-hand, furniture, whilst the rest of the house is in various states of DIY repair and renovation. The kitchen and bathroom remain as they were when they took possession, with a 1970s bathroom suite in avocado green and the appliances inherited at possession. Some of their appliances are still

Figure 2.6: Andrew & Mel's floor project

in the garage and the extension remains a dream: in January 2004 Andrew shows me the architect's elevation plans that he has had drawn up. 'I got these done for free', he says, 'like between friends. They're going to be kind of nice to look at, as a reminder of The Dream, a memento'. At an estimated cost of £16,000, and with their drastically reduced household income, these plans are currently seen to have no possibility of being enacted.

Andrew and Mel have a 'Plan' of sorts, of that there is no doubt. But what is particularly fascinating about this plan is its multifarious quality – part dream/fantasy and part multiple ongoing projects – and its mutability. These qualities are related. As the second extract above demonstrates, the Plan keeps unravelling, generating a momentum all of its own: in this instance, what had begun as an assumed-to-be straightforward act of decorating-related removal, ridding and disposal – taking up a carpet and taking it to the tip – had exposed another set of major difficulties (the woodworm), evidently ignored by the previous occupants. As well as effecting a wholesale reorientation in ongoing actions, this revelation has exerted not inconsiderable effects on decorative practices, specifically on the project to expose the original floorboards. What it meant was that Andrew (and his dad) not only had to remove and burn the infested wood and treat the rest, but that they had to replace almost the entirety of the hall floor with new wood. As a consequence, Andrew is currently attempting to use varnish to overcome the visual problems posed by the spatial juxtaposition of contrasting wooden materialities (cf. Jo-Anne above). Somewhat ironically then, a project that centres archaeological practices (uncovering, excavating and sanding down) and the restoration of period authenticity, and which valorises age in materials, has ended up being derailed into a work of material and temporal fusion instead (Figure 2.6).

Listening to Andrew talk about their house over the course of a year is instructive too for the way in which the continued presence of the previous occupants of this house becomes increasingly central for him. When they purchased the house, Andrew and Mel had known that it had been lived in for many years by one family, and that it had been empty for approximately a year following the death of 'the old lady'. They knew too – at least in the abstract – this meant that renovation and improvement were going to feature as major motifs in their moving-in experience. As Andrew, in particular, began to work on renovation and improvement, his talk about this began to be peppered with references to 'bodgery' – 'When I look at it, all I see is bodgery', he says recurrently, with a mixture of exclamation and despair. But, as the work progresses, and as the archaeological practice proceeds, the 'bodgery' comes to be revealed as integral to the very fabric of this housing structure, indeed as a limiting factor on the possible. So, the covering over of the woodworm at some point in the past renders the hall floorboards defunct; the insertion of a wooden window frame into the roof at some point previously is declared by builders and architects to mean that this cannot be rectified without altering both the entire roof and the wall (declared to be a financial impossibility); and the garage remains – a testimony to the difficulties of its disposal, which in turn are entirely about its asbestos content; a structure which Andrew now imagines as 'bodged-together' from various leftovers from the pit. Together, the practice of excavation and the Plan (both key components of Andrew and Mel's enactment of moving in) are uncovering the degree to which the former occupants are co-present in their house, as effects and in the traces of their inhabitation, living on after their deaths in the very fabric of the building. And, as this co-presence has become increasingly visible, Andrew, in particular, has become increasingly fascinated by 'the old man', whose practices of repair and upkeep have been such a source of exasperation to him. He wants to know more about this old man who lived for so long in this house. At one point towards the end of the fieldwork period Janet tells me that he asked her what she knows about him, saying to her: 'You know, in a funny kind of way, I'd love to be able to meet him.'

A rather different confirmation of the potency of this type of material trace is provided by one further excavation. One weekend in the late summer of 2003, at a time when the demolition of the garage seemed imminent, Andrew was clearing out stuff left in the garage by the vendors. I had driven over to Janet's house, although by this time she had returned to live there and I was spending most of my time in South Hightown on Wear Road:

I drive up the back lane [...] Andrew greets me and starts talking.
He tells me that he's sorting out stuff prior to the ordering of a skip;

he's going through the garage. Janet comes out. Andrew lowers his voice and asks her whether the 'old couple' had grandchildren. Janet tells him what she knows. 'No' says Andrew, 'that can't be right. Someone called [name]. He seems to be the dad'. He goes on to explain: 'I've found some stuff in there – personal stuff. At first I thought it was just stuff like cards, birthday cards, and there were a few poems, silly stuff you know, kids' stuff, but I read one of the poems and it was odd, to someone called [name], who was going away and couldn't be a proper daddy sort of thing. Kind of cute but kind of odd. I wondered whether it was someone doing time. And there's birth details, not a birth certificate but birth weights. It was all in an old suitcase, underneath a load of old men's clothes. I'd say almost hidden you know. And there's other stuff – what I'm sure is an umbilical cord stuffed in an envelope. What the fuck do I do with it? We can't keep it – no way. I was going to toss it when it was just the cards, but then I found all the rest – you can't toss that, it's way too personal and it's someone who's really sentimental. It's someone's kid. But who the hell is it?' Janet goes on to speculate about who it might be. There are possibilities. And we try to make suggestions as to what Andrew might do with this stuff, in a way that doesn't cause any pain or trouble. (August 2003)

Much later on, in January 2004, I asked Andrew directly about what he'd done with this suitcase: 'Well one day when they[8] were over there doing some painting – obviously trying to tart the house up a bit – I tried to approach him, but he blanked me completely. So I thought, "Bugger you mate". I chucked it in the wheelie bin. Mind it took me a long time to do it. I didn't do it till the autumn, November time. And I felt guilty about it – well a little bit.'

This chain of events began by looking as if it would be a story in which excavation uncovered matter which could not be thrown away, precisely because of its memorialising a birth and a child's love for a parent. But it ends up as a story in which this matter is cast in a trajectory that connects the wheelie bin to landfill. The mementos are made waste, because they have become separated from their owner/possessor and because this stuff is far too potent for Andrew to have lingering around, even in their garage. Although the story of the umbilical cord continues to weave its effects in its telling and lives on in its telling, adding value and a degree of exoticism to the narration of the house as a historic dwelling structure, the matter itself has been expelled by Andrew, jettisoned in a way that has not been possible with the fabric of the dwelling structure. Furthermore, its power to haunt has lessened through its ridding.

Lesley and Ginny's story

Lesley and Ginny are in their 40s, considerably older than Andrew and Mel. When they 'got together' Lesley sold her house and moved-in with Ginny while they searched for another, more appropriate, property. This property turned out to be two properties knocked together on Alternative Terrace. Ginny, who is from the North-east, works in an estate agent's office but her passion is horses. She owns, cares for and rides a three-quarter bred hunter, liveried nearby on a DIY basis. Lesley works in local government and is a keen hill-walker and environmental volunteer. As well as the horse, which is strictly Ginny's, this couple have three cats and regularly act as dog-sitters for friends.

Like Andrew and Mel, the property which Lesley and Ginny have taken possession of is a late-nineteenth-century terraced house. Like Andrew and Mel's house, this was occupied by the vendors for a considerable number of years (if not the 50+ years of Andrew and Mel's, nearer 20 years than 10). Working in an estate agent's, Ginny was well aware of the potential effects of this duration of occupancy. Indeed, she recounts how she came to view the house twice just to work out how much it was going to cost to 'put it right', whereas Lesley had virtually dismissed it out-of-hand as 'too much work'. Ginny's feelings about the house – that it was worth it and right for them, being in a quiet location that wasn't going to be redeveloped in any way, and on a, self-evidently to them, 'alternative street' – prevailed and they went ahead with the purchase. Like Andrew and Mel, this couple have a 'Plan', but unlike Andrew and Mel, theirs is a plan of mostly sequentially choreographed projects. The first thing they did, 'After cleaning the house for a month – did That Woman ever clean? I have never been through so many rubber gloves in my life!!' (Lesley), was to have gas installed. Then they had a combi-boiler put in, followed by a new central-heating system. The old one – taken away by the heating engineers – was described by Ginny as 'a cock and bull system that somehow fed the living room off the bathroom radiator!' The next project was to remove the solid fuel Aga stove – 'sold through the paper to someone who was still on solid fuel' – and replace it with a gas-powered range cooker. Through the spring, summer and early autumn the couple's attention switched to the gardens, and particularly to the constant demands of vegetable cultivation, but they also removed and replaced the bathroom and kitchen tiling during this time (taken to the tip). With Christmas and New Year gone, in early January 2004 they had the uPVC windows and doors ripped-out, replacing these with ones to their taste, again in uPVC.

Unlike Andrew and Mel, who – eventually after eight months – finally let me across their threshold to see and photograph 'Our tip', Ginny and Lesley assiduously kept me on the outside of their property throughout the ethnographic fieldwork. Indeed, Ginny repeatedly said: 'You can't come in, it's a fucking TIP!!' – a feeling I had to respect. Our talk therefore was all conducted outside their house, around where they sit out, in their vegetable gardens and by their cars. Compared with Andrew and Mel and Jo-Anne, then, it lacks a degree of depth and certainly visuality. Nonetheless, their talk does convey a sense of their practice and intentionality. Ginny and Lesley portray their actions repeatedly as improvement talk, as 'putting right' what the previous owners had done wrong. In this they share Andrew and Mel's commitment to rectifying 'bodgery' appropriately. But their moving-in practices have little affinity with Andrew and Mel's commitment to excavation, archaeology and authenticity. Instead, Lesley and Ginny's prioritise the installation of largely invisible consumption services and the appliances and systems that supply these – gas, a good boiler, a 'proper heating system'. The comfort and convenience of a manufactured domestic environment is what is being valued here. So, rather than keep an original Aga they rip it out and replace it with a gas copy; and rather than opt for wooden windows they go for the easy-maintenance, 'non-warping' counterpart in plastic. Furthermore, they tackle this comfort and convenience version of improvement practice in a strictly ordered, sequential manner, and narrate this with a strong sense that they know the right order in which to do the things that they are doing. Doing the decorating and the purchasing of a vast array of consumer goods are the last things on their agenda.[9]

Parallels and convergences

Taking place in relatively close proximity, Jo-Anne's, Andrew and Mel's and Lesley and Ginny's stories provide three different moving-in stories. They feature room makeovers through the simultaneous purchase of a vast array of new consumer goods (Jo-Anne), archaeological excavation and the valorisation of authenticity (Andrew and Mel), and the installation of comfort and convenience (Lesley and Ginny). The differences in these stories are indicative of the differences between their authoring subjects: they all attach greater or lesser significance to surface appearances and structural fabric; they display strongly contrasting investments in the mass market and its imperatives; and their enactments have variable temporalities, from the tightly choreographed 'beginning-middle-end' orchestrated by Jo-Anne to the much more drawn-out, continually ongoing flows of Lesley and Ginny's and Andrew and Mel's projects. Yet what brings these three stories together, are the ways in which ridding features within moving in and the connections the stories display between ridding and the previous inhabitations of these houses.

In starting this chapter with Jo-Anne's tale, I was deliberately beginning with the prevailing understanding of moving in, as the elimination, through ridding, of the other. This is what Jo-Anne does through rejecting and replacing some of the things residing in her kitchen and bathroom when she took possession. And, to a degree at least, this is what Lesley and Ginny embarked on when they set about cleaning their new home for a month, a virtual decontamination process. But beyond this, their enactments began to alter and – as with Andrew and Mel – ridding started to become more an effect of improvement-related removal and replacement than a matter of taste judgements and personal dirt thresholds. This seems to imply a rather different positioning of the other. Indeed, in Andrew and Mel's case we can see an increasing accommodation to, even fascination with, the other, who mutates from the locus of exasperation to a haunting co-present ghostly figure. By contrast, Lesley and Ginny position themselves as correcting presences, methodically working through and making good the errors of their othered predecessors and, in the process, eliminating the trace of their presence. Although, of course, their trace remains in the trail of improvements enacted, so even here it is possible to think about the ridding of moving in as part of a more general process of accommodating.

I will make some more general observations on this by way of conclu-
sion to this chapter, but for the moment it is important to emphasise that,
unlike Jo-Anne, Ginny and Lesley and Andrew and Mel actually did get rid
of virtually all the matter that was excavated and or torn out from the fabric
of their homes and replaced, and they did so in distinctive ways. Most of
this stuff was carried away, displaced not to the zones of storage of the house
– although these are available to both households – but taken (or assumed
to be taken) by these householders and/or their agents (builders/installers) to
the tip. This was the trajectory of Andrew and Mel's leaking cast iron gutter-
ing, the old carpet left by the vendors, and of Ginny and Lesley's inherited
heating system, tiles and windows. The exceptions to this trajectory are the
woodworm-infested wood (burnt in Andrew and Mel's garden), the suitcase
of mementos (placed in the wheelie bin) and the Aga (sold to an unknown
other via the local paper). Not only do these ways of dealing with ripped-out
matter suggest that both Ginny and Lesley and Andrew and Mel care rather
more about what happens to this stuff and its placement than Jo-Anne, and
that they are prepared to invest the time and work required to deal with
these things' displacement beyond the immediate confines of the house, but
it suggests too that it matters to them that they do ridding appropriately.
Moreover, quite definite routes appear to be being travelled here by matter
that is adjudged to have particular material properties and qualities. Old, rotten building fabric, faulty and/or damaged appliances, and goods for which
a use can no longer be envisaged were designated by both couples as things
destined for and to be taken to the tip. In comparison, that which is seen
to be of potential re-use was placed in a location that made its availability
known to others – in this case through advertising, something which Jo-Anne
conspicuously did not identify as a possibility for her unwanted kitchen
units. Finally, we should note that risky matter is either burnt (eliminated as
a particular configuration of form and matter) or, as with Andrew and Mel's
garage and Jo-Anne's old oven and toilet, left *in situ*. Although very different
in their motivations towards and investments in contemporary consumer
culture, both these households continue to retain large, bulky and/or dirty
things. By comparison, matter that is too potent a presence, too troublesome
to leave *in situ*, and which can be easily handled is made rid through the
medium of the regular household waste-collection service.

Accommodating, others and inhabitation

The portrayal of moving in as a consumption event, at least in the popular
media, tends to emphasise the practice of redecoration, representing this
as an instance of expressive agency, as an explicit assertion of the currently
habiting self/selves and as the elimination of the assumed taste preferences
of the frequently othered previous occupant/s. By comparison, the account
of moving in that emerges from this ethnography construes moving in
more as an ongoing process of accommodating to the presence in material
trace of these others. That it does so may, of course, be a manifestation of
'estate agency', specifically of the age of these three dwelling structures on
Alternative Terrace and their histories of occupancy. Indeed, it would be illu-

minating to compare these moving-in stories to those attached to newly built homes without such histories of occupation. Nonetheless, there are three general points that I want to make by way of ending this chapter.

Firstly, as is demonstrated repeatedly by the three case studies, the presence in trace of previous occupants is not something that is located exclusively in decorative schemes but is present too in those objects that have been left behind (cookers, fridges, toilets for example) and the state they are in. Critically, it is also located in the bricks and mortar, wood and glass which constitute the fabric of the dwelling structure and in the technical systems that fabricate the dwelling structure as a particular environment fit for habitation – in heating systems, cooking systems and roofing systems, for example. Moreover, the traces of previous occupants, through practices of upkeep, repair, care and maintenance, are as felt in these technical systems and fabrications as they are in the surface appearance of decoration. Such findings further testify to the importance of thinking in terms of less visible, even invisible, consumption (Shove 2003) alongside more conventional narratives of surface appearance.

Secondly, however, as two of the case studies show in particular, these traces of previous occupancy frequently place greater limits on the possibilities for action of new occupants than do decorative schemes. Whilst decoration can be readily stripped off, ripped up and covered over, both technical systems and configurations of building materials are, by comparison, relatively durable and integral to the conditions for habitation, as well as costly to rip out, replace and/or re-build. Consequently, and as we see here, new occupants frequently have to accommodate to these traces, either living with them (Andrew and Mel) or having to accommodate their living to building work (Lesley and Ginny). As a result, I would argue that moving in is best thought about in terms of inhabitation. It is a way of living in and inhabiting a dwelling structure, which in turn becomes incorporated into the very fabric of that dwelling structure, and which successive inhabitants have to accommodate themselves to, as well as be accommodated by. A corollary is that moving out is never complete. Rather, what remains is a trace of having lived in, inhabited, and even dwelt in a building.

The third point builds from this. What we see from this chapter is how 'estate agency' works. This is not just about the capacity of a dwelling structure's fabric, materials and age to suggest what might/might not be done to it (Miller 2001a), but about how sequential inhabitation is woven into the very fabric of a dwelling structure, combining people with the non human over generations. The effect, again as we have seen, is that the dwelling structure does not merely exert agency with respect to the current occupants. Instead, we are talking about an extended temporality of estate agency; a chronology, but one that enfolds those who live now in a place with those who have previously lived here. More telling still, at least theoretically, is that this form of estate agency is itself suggestive of dwelling. This, however, is a dwelling that is located in the fabric of buildings, and one that binds together a sequence of unrelated occupants; to be sure, it is not the rooted, intergenerational form of dwelling disclosed by the Black Forest farmhouse. But that it is a form of dwelling seems assured. That this is so is made clear when we look closely at the various ripping-out and related ridding activities (actual and projected) that accompany the moving-in events described above. What these are all about is inhabitation and accommodation. In accommodating in these ways to previous occupants' ways of living in and inhabiting a dwelling structure, we are still – in the early part of the twenty-first century – building, and building because known of and imagined others, whose presence remains, and who have inhabited, that is, dwelt, before us.

NOTES

1 It would, of course, have been instructive to have followed the moving-out events that preceded these moving-ins. For varying reasons however, this proved impossible. Two of these properties were vacant possessions. One was sold following the death of the previous owner and had been unoccupied for approximately twelve months prior to its purchase. The other had been rented out to students and had been put on the market once their tenancy agreements came to an end. When I began the ethnographic fieldwork one of these houses had just been moved into and the other was being done-up. The third property followed the more conventional exchange procedure, in which the vendors moved out the day prior to the moving-in of the new occupants. This type of moving out, however, turned out to be less amenable to investigation. What I was looking for, when introducing myself to the residents of Alternative Terrace, were a number of households willing to participate in the study for a full year. Consequently, the one household in the throes of selling-up had no reason to invest in the project.

2 Although unfortunate, in that this means that we are talking about similar dwelling structures in all three instances, this is an inevitable effect of the workings of the housing market at the time of the fieldwork. Alternative Terrace is pitched by estate agents as offering desirable housing in reach of the finances of first-time buyers, although see Chapter 1, note 20. That three properties changed hands around the time of the fieldwork is evidence of the general upturn in the North-east housing market at the time of the research. A similar degree of movement in the housing market was discernible in a swathe of starter-homes built in the 1990s. As discussed in Chapter 1, however, and notwithstanding various tactics of recruitment, this area proved consistently resistant to ethnographic research. By contrast, on Wear Road, through the same fieldwork period, none of the tenancy arrangements changed and none of the owner-occupiers moved out, a reflection of the general durability of inhabitation on this street.

3 As will become clear, different temporalities (and tenses) infuse the telling of these moving-in stories. On the one hand, there is the temporality of the fieldwork, an ongoing flow of activity over a period of twelve months, which I both cast and re-tell as a present tense narrative entwining people and things. On the other, there is a set of more distanciated observations, grounded either in post-fieldwork analysis or in knowledge gleaned from subsequent return visits to South Hightown. These two temporalities characterise all the chapters detailing ethnographic stories. Narrative primacy however is afforded to the former, rather than the latter – an inversion of the normal academic narrative conventions. Privileging the former is, of course, a means to finding ways to writing the becoming of things.

4 MFI is a mid-price UK retailer, specialising in fitted kitchens, bathrooms and bedrooms.

5 The Diderot Effect refers to a tale narrated by the Enlightenment philosopher of the same name. On being given a new red dressing gown as a gift, Diderot gets rid of his old one. But things do not stop there, and he relates how the presence of the new gown works both to eject various furnishings, tapestries, chairs, desks and bookshelves, and their replacement with things that conformed with the look initiated by the new dressing gown. As McCracken (1988: 118 – 30) notes, the Diderot Effect has a ratcheting effect on consumption and on consumer expenditure. Indeed, potentially it can work through all one's possessions.

6 Further evidence for Jo-Anne's anxieties over this was provided by her looking to me to comment on these juxtapositions. In my initial talk with Jo-Anne I assiduously avoided being drawn into making any such value judgements. Later conversations, however, over bottles of wine in her kitchen, fuelled both by alcohol and by the presence of some of Jo-Anne's friends

– for whom such comments are normative – meant that I too had to agree: the old and the new do not 'go' together in this bathroom.

7 DFS is a mass-market UK furniture and furnishings retailer.

8 Comet and Currys are major UK electrical retailers. Although distinct as retailers, consumers frequently blur the two together, as Jo-Anne does here.

9 Jo-Anne knows this because I told her, having learnt of this individual myself through other households participating in the ethnography. One key dilemma in the fieldwork was whether to tell her any more. Although I did not come to know how to contact this individual directly, I did know people who knew how to get in touch with 'Frank'. If I had passed more information on to Jo-Anne, then, I could undoubtedly have facilitated moving along Jo-Anne's unwanted matter, but I would also have exerted undue effects on the trajectories of things. Reasoning as a researcher that I wished to minimise my effects on what people did with their things, I kept quiet about potential ways of getting in touch with Frank, and the things remained in situ. On the other hand, keeping quiet had social effects. In not passing this information on to Jo-Anne I both reinforced her lack of embeddedness within the street and felt guilty about this. Ethnographic fieldwork is full of dilemmas such as this. What matters is making such dilemmas explicit rather than feeling one has made the 'right' decision.

10 As a postscript to this story, when I returned to South Hightown in Easter 2005, I was told that Jo-Anne had sold up and moved on. The outbuildings, however, still contained the old kitchen and bathroom fixtures and fittings, which had now become the problem of the new owners of this house.

11 The 'they' referred to here connects to the speculation in talk referred to in the diary extract above.

12 On a return visit to Alternative Terrace in summer 2004, Ginny recounted how this was a point of some considerable tension between herself and Lesley. The improvement work was still ongoing but Ginny felt that this did not preclude painting the interior walls as an interim measure. She pronounced to me that she was just fed up with living with plaster and the place 'STILL being a fucking TIP!!' In contrast, Lesley regards decoration as the final part of the work, and refuses to decorate until they have got the place finished. The effect of this lack of decoration remains, as in the ethnography, to keep visitors, even well-known ones, on the outside of the dwelling structure. It was with some amazement therefore that in Easter 2005 I was finally allowed across the threshold, to be shown round the full extent of this dwelling structure.

Chapter 3

Being modernised

In this chapter the emphasis is on another relatively exceptional inhabitation event, in which the relations of living with things in a dwelling structure are again radically ruptured or suspended. This is the process of being modernised as a council tenant.[1] The focus of action in South Hightown therefore switches from Alternative Terrace to Wear Road. As with moving in, modernisation is a process which has huge effects on things. In being modernised, council tenants have to accommodate to a local authority programme of works. The timing of modernisation, the choices available in certain things, and even its occurrence, are events over which tenants have little control. Yet, as with moving house, being modernised requires tenants to disassemble their homes in things, to pack them away, store them, and then – once completed – to unpack them and reconstitute their homes through things. As we will see, getting rid of certain things is an integral part of this process. It is fundamental to the making of key social relations and identities. But getting rid is critical to councils too. So, and in a slight twist to 'appropriating the state' on a council estate (Miller 1988), the chapter shows how in modernisation it is councils – and not just tenants – who are doing the work of appropriation and divestment. Again, as we shall see, ridding and wasting are as integral to the process of modernisation as they are to moving in.

This chapter proceeds, similarly to the previous one, by juxtaposing socially contrasting households. The four households featured here include older and younger couples, couples with children and those with grown-up offspring; and they live in a range of dwelling structures, from a four-bedroom house to a one-bedroom bungalow. The households were recruited through a long set-up phase and via a housing action group, and incorporate a diversity of social categories (see Chapter 1).

The chapter begins by outlining the modernisation programme. It then details the four study households, before examining the practice of modernisation through two sections, anticipatory preparations and being modernised. I close the chapter by making some more general observations on modernisation, and the making of key socialities through the ridding and wasting of certain things.

Modernising Wear Road

In common with other modernisation programmes being rolled out in the County Durham villages during the fieldwork, the programme affecting Wear Road entailed radical structural and aesthetic change.[1] Built-in coal stores – the legacy of heating systems dependent on solid fuel – were demolished and gas was installed to the few remaining dwellings without it; wooden exterior doors and window frames, together with their single-pane glass, were ripped out and replaced with uPVC 'modern designs'; twenty-year-old wiring systems were torn out and replaced with new electrical wiring systems, complete with the latest safety devices; lofts were insulated; and kitchens and bathrooms were gutted and re-fitted to a small range of available designs. Some of these changes – those affecting the fuel supply, windows and doors and electricity supply – were compulsory, so modernisation is a process which impinged on the lives of all the tenants on Wear Road regardless. But choice was also an integral part of the programme. Tenants were allocated a notional 800 points to 'spend' on what they liked from an itemised list. Some opted to plough virtually all their points into a downstairs bay window and/or patio doors, whilst others opted for a combination of improvements including new kitchen units, a new fireplace, kitchen and bathroom floor coverings and tiling, and extra electrical sockets.

As is readily apparent from the foregoing, in part the work of modernisation is invisible on completion. It was about installing the sorts of consumption services and utilities that provide safe, instantaneous environments for inhabitation (Shove 2003) that are more convenient for the temporal rhythms of everyday life in the early twenty-first century than solid fuel, for example, with its requirement to be kept-in and reliance on a constant (usually female) presence (McDowell and Massey 1984). But what this modernisation programme also offered, in particular through bay windows and patio doors, was the opportunity to transform the external aesthetic of the dwelling structure in specific ways. As several commentators have acknowledged, one of the most immediate effects of selling off council housing in Britain in the 1980s was the radical change enacted to house exteriors by the new owner occupiers, usually through the medium of uPVC doors and windows. Interpreted as an effect of being able to do something to house exteriors, this, along with the installation of a satellite dish, was a way of indicating advancement and social differentiation from the neighbours, both powerful facets of living on a low-rise council estate in the UK.[2] Correspondingly, and in a delicious irony, whereas those tenants who bought in the 1980s paid themselves to install new uPVC windows and doors, to mark their freedom from the constraints of living as council tenants and to mark their social difference from their neighbours, this council modernisation programme allowed council tenants to achieve the desired and socially accordant aesthetic at no cost to them. Indeed, for many the intention was to buy their homes, having had the council bear the cost of modernisation.[3]

Having provided the context for the Wear Road modernisation programme, I focus in the remainder of this chapter on the programme as an unfolding event, emphasising in particular its effects on things. To write in this way requires a constant vigilance. It is tempting – very tempting – to represent the modernisation story as one with a definite temporality, with a beginning, middle and end framed by the first mooting of the work and the final disappearance of the council work lorries. But this would suggest that modernisation is a finished business, and – as with the previous chapter – part of my argument here is that living with things is always an unfinished business, with constant effects on the possible trajectories of things. Furthermore, the period of time available for ethnographic fieldwork came to an end when the modernisation work was still incomplete. Far from being a disadvantage, this has positively enabled writing the practice of modernisation. What follows then is two lengthy sections: 'anticipatory preparations', in which I discuss the various practices and occurrences that preceded the onset of modernisation work in specific dwelling structures, and 'being modernised', where I focus on modernisation work in progress. In both cases the emphasis is on what happens to people's things in the throes of events happening around them. To make matters more manageable, the sections are broken down into events occurring within the individual study households and the generalisations these suggest. First, though, I provide some situational and positional material on the households themselves.

The households

Peggy and Harry

Peggy and Harry are in their early 60s and early 70s, respectively. They have been together for over thirty-five years and they live in a one-bedroom council owned bungalow, which they have been in for approximately seven years. Prior to this they owned their own home, also on Wear Road. They lived in that house for approximately 30 years. Harry is 'born and bred' in South Hightown. Although born in one of the County Durham villages, Peggy only moved to South Hightown when she and Harry got together. This is the second marriage for both of them. Harry's first wife died; and Peggy walked out on her first husband, having 'had enough of the whacking'. She had been pregnant at 15, was married at 16, and had four kids by the time she was in her mid twenties.[4]

Both Peggy and Harry have been in paid employment almost all their lives. Harry, relatively unusually for a man of his age and social class in the North-east, was able to avoid going down the pit. Initially he'd worked for a butcher, but then he worked for many years in a factory on the outskirts of Durham City. Peggy worked in a sewing factory once she became a single parent, living initially with her parents and then with her first husband. Later on, once her parents became increasingly dependent, and when she and Harry were married, she moved them from the village where they lived to South Hightown – 'for love and duty: with me dad it was love, but with me mother it was duty'. She then cared for both her parents through two terminal illnesses, nursing her mother in their house for several years. As a long-term carer, Peggy's opportunities for employment were increasingly confined to South Hightown: throughout this time therefore she worked behind the bar in the working-men's club and as a domestic cleaner ('to get out of the house – Harry minded her while I was out and when he'd got back in from work'). Once her mother died, Peggy could no longer bear the associations of living in the house; in a very real sense it was haunted by the presence of caring for her mother and the work of getting her up and down the stairs. At Peggy's instigation the couple sold-up and moved into a council bungalow.[5] Harry, who has always been a keen gardener, continues to work on a casual basis as a gardener for a few households in South Hightown, although not on Wear Road or elsewhere on the Rivers estate. Peggy has had several strokes in recent years and has severe arthritis. She has 'good days and bad days' and is in receipt of the maximum disability allowance. Peggy and Harry's four adult children all live relatively nearby, for the most part within a twenty-minute to half-hour drive away. The bungalow therefore is a frequent popping-in zone, for the adult children and the large number of grandchildren. Peggy and Harry also go shopping frequently – just to get out of the bungalow – and Peggy in particular participates in several of the village social events, notably the bingo. However, like many other 'elderly couples' in South Hightown (their designation), they spend a lot of time in the house, watching old films and now DVDs of old films on the TV.

Carol and John

Carol and John live in a four-bedroom council house with three of their children. Carol and John are in their early 40s and this is the second marriage for both of them. Previously they'd been living in another (smaller) council house on another street in South Hightown, but they swapped with another couple and moved to this (larger) one about eleven years ago.[6] Carol, who is from South Hightown and who has lived here all her life, has two children from her previous marriage, one of whom recently became a father. The other child from her first marriage, Zoe, is 16. She lives with Carol and John, and is in full-time education. Also living in this house are Carol and John's two children, Natalie (7) and Amie (5), Zuki – a Yorkshire Terrier dog – and a Netherland Dwarf rabbit. John works in the construction industry. For the period of the fieldwork Carol was not in paid employment and had not been so for twenty years. Right at the end of the fieldwork, though, she began to talk about returning to paid work and successfully applied for a post as a mobile night-care worker, but 'putting the tea on the table for John and the bairns' is a key personal priority for her.

Christine and Malcolm

Living nearby to Carol and John, and to Peggy and Harry, are Christine, Malcolm and Kylie. They live in a two-bedroom council house, which they have been in for sixteen years. Both Christine and Malcolm are from South Hightown and are in their mid 30s. Malcolm's mother still lives on Wear Road, as do two of his brothers and Christine's sister. Christine's dad also lives in the village, though her mother does not. Malcolm works as an electrician, a job that causes him considerable health problems; not only does he have permanent back and knee problems, but he is also asthmatic. Christine has a few domestic cleaning jobs in and out of the village and also cleans for her mother. She also spends two full days a week cleaning her own house, which is always immaculate. Kylie is 14 and attends the local comprehensive. Although Christine and Malcolm would like to buy their house, they feel that financially this would be too risky for them, particularly given Malcolm's increasing health problems.

Claire and Nathan

Also living on this street are Claire and Nathan and their daughter Abigail, who is 5. Their house has three bedrooms. Claire and Nathan are in their late 20s. Nathan is from Manchester, but his family moved to the North-east when he was still at school. He now works in a car-component factory. Claire's mother and father also live on Wear Road, in a house they bought from the council in the 1980s. They have lived in South Hightown all their lives. Claire's sister lives in another of the Durham villages: 'We don't go far', Claire tells me. When she became pregnant, Claire and Nathan were housed in a one-bedroom council bungalow in South Hightown of the type lived in by Peggy and Harry. At the time her grandmother lived in what was to become their house. Before her grandmother died, however, they swapped tenancies, so the couple now live in this house and have done so for nearly four years. Their aim is to buy it. Claire works part time as a dental reception-ist. Like Natalie and Amie, Abigail attends the village primary school.

✳

As is immediately evident from the above, and unlike the households that featured in the previous chapter, these households – and those of their relatives – are characterised by the immense stability of living in a particular place, often on the same street. Wear Road, and the Rivers estate, is somewhere where families and extended families continue to live in close proximity, and where specific houses are exchanged across generations.[7] The social relations of cohabitation, however, are relatively fluid, as couples form, have children, separate and have more children. Indeed, the longevity of Peggy and Harry's marriage marks them as unusual on this street, where having grandchildren living with their grandmothers for reasons of separation is not uncommon. The other point that marks these four households out is that they all have adult members who are either in paid employment in the formal economy or who are retired. Another important group of households on Wear Road claim benefit and/or engage in various activities in the informal and criminal economies (see Chapter 1). As will become clear, these distinctions mattered profoundly to the process and course of modernisation on Wear Road.

Anticipatory preparations

'We're being modernised' was one of the recurrent phrases uttered on Wear Road during the early phases of the fieldwork. Mooted for eighteen months previously and campaigned for by a local village-based housing action group, at this juncture modernisation was widely regarded as something to be proud about, and as doing something – at last – about the decaying internal and external fabric of tenants' dwelling structures. When I began working on

Wear Road, the future promise of modernisation had led many to adopt a tactic of deferring any house decoration plans till after the event. Carol's sentiments were felt by many:

> I was going to decorate in the summer but it would've been pointless.
> So you let everything run right down and it looks a mess. You've got
> paint peeling off, paper ripped off – you know it's just an eyesore.
> So you just leave it because you know it's going to be even more of
> an eyesore, because they'll come in and they'll just wreck it. (August
> 2003)

A few months later, however, this talk was increasingly being couched in terms of 'I'll believe it when I see it': although all the tenants had received letters from the council informing them of an anticipated start month for the work, that month had come and gone with no sign of any work commencing. This was widely interpreted on the street as yet another instance of the council's indifference and lack of care toward tenants, and is indicative of the degree of alienation felt by many living in these housing tenure relations. It transpired later that there were reasons for these delays, ones bound up in the difficulties encountered in modernisation work going on simultaneously in other villages in the county. But for the tenants on Wear Road this was just another excuse for incompetence: as Carol said, 'Folk have been sitting around with their things packed up for weeks now waiting for them to start, and where are they? It's not good enough!' Eventually, some months on, the tenants all received letters with a definite start date. This mailing was read as a mixed blessing: although, on a positive note, it was clear that something was going to start happening, it was also clear that the work was going to occur through the colder, wetter winter months and that it would be going on in some households over the Christmas period. Disrupting Christmas was seen widely as 'poor form' – largely because of the intensity of within-family visiting occurring on the street over this time, the premium this is seen to place on standards of home decoration, and because of its anticipated effects on the practice of decorating the exterior and interior of houses with Christmas decorations.[8] For the majority of the households in the study, and particularly Peggy, Christine and Carol, it was imperative that their living rooms would look respectable and 'straight' for Christmas. Now the council – 'true to form' – was adding another level of complication. 'Rather than being over and done with by Christmas, like they said they'd be, here we are with them for Christmas – it makes me PIG SICK, but I'd believe anything of This Council!' says Peggy, a sentiment felt widely on the street.

Having been in the offing for some eighteen months, it is perhaps not surprising that households' responses to the anticipated presence of modernisation were widely divergent. In large part, however, those households which were designated as in the vanguard of the work made their preparations. These were households with tenants with disabilities – identified by the council as priorities – and households at one end of the street, where the work was due to commence. Peggy and Harry were in the first of these categories; Claire and Nathan were in the other. By comparison, other households, including Carol and John and Christine and Malcolm, opted just to carry on with their lives and wait for something to start happening, although modernisation's future presence continued to exert its effects.

When I first met Peggy and Harry in the early summer of 2003, they had already packed up their things in various boxes and placed these in the limited number of storage places available to them – in their greenhouse, in the 'conservatory' (a DIY makeshift structure that abuts their greenhouse) and in the outside 'coal hole'. 'Valuables' (Peggy's collections of china, her 302 thimbles, her china figures and her Ainsley)[9] and 'me sentimental stuff' (mementos of her and Harry's silver wedding anniversary, of her 60th birthday, of holidays and school portrait photographs of all the grandchildren) were all wrapped individually in old newspaper, placed in boxes and locked away. 'If anyone nicks them there'll be hell on', says Peggy. Around the same time Peggy also started making decisions about the contents of her new kitchen. Having chosen her kitchen from the range available, new (peach) tiling and cushioned vinyl flooring, she decided that she 'wanted a change'. She declared that 'all the blue stuff [mainly cooking utensils and jars bought to match the old kitchen units] had to go', and began to replace these with things more appropriate to her colour aesthetic of stainless steel and black. All the rejects were placed in a box in the 'coal hole', for viewing. Peggy told me how her daughter Samantha had already been through the box and 'taken what she wants', and that the current partners of her sons can do the same if they want. 'The rest of it can go to the boot sale'.[10]

Through the same period, Peggy and Harry began to strip the wallpaper off all their rooms, beginning with the bathroom and their bedroom, and then the hallway. They placed all of this matter in black plastic bin bags and then in the wheelie bin, theirs or a neighbour's just up the street if theirs was full. Significantly, they left the living room till last; fed up with the interminable wait, Peggy declared that they were not going to 'rip up' the room where they spend the majority of their time and where they receive most of their visitors until they had a definite start date for the modernisation work. At the same time as they stripped the paper off, Peggy and Harry went shopping for their new wallpaper. Peggy found a pattern that she liked for their bedroom on one trip; on another she found a 'bargain ceiling chandelier' that she liked in Argos.[11] This too is for the bedroom. Another shopping trip saw her return with the wallpaper for the living room. She is less happy with this. The current living room wallpaper has only been up for two years and she likes this a lot, so much so that she went shopping to try to find its replacement. Unfortunately, this doesn't seem to be a possibility, although Peggy looked in every retail outlet stocking decorating supplies that she can think of, taking bus trips to all the regional shopping centres in the process. What she eventually returns with 'will just have to do – maybe it'll grow on me'. The other problem is that she can't find appropriate borders to go with the wallpaper. Dawn – one of her daughters-in-law – tells Peggy that this doesn't matter and that she will make borders out of the new wallpaper instead, a practice that is new to Peggy. As Peggy buys, the new wallpaper

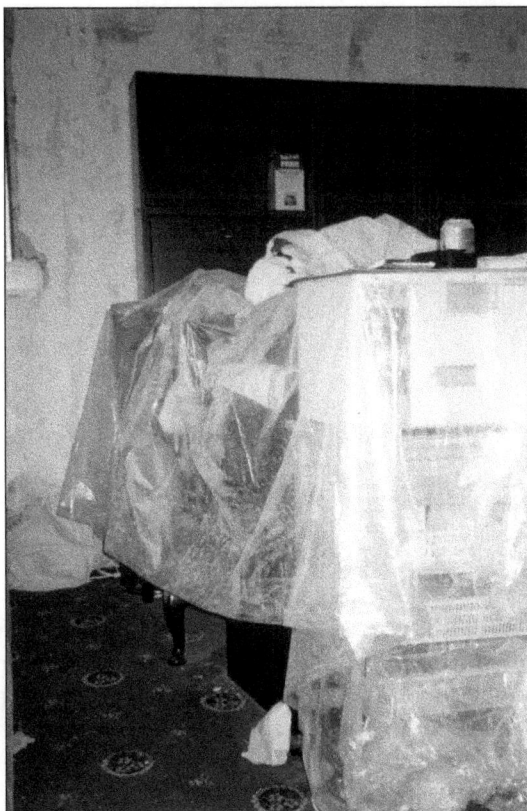

Figure 3.1: Peggy & Harry's 'pyramid'

rolls are stashed away in the cupboards in the display cabinet that stands in the couple's living room.

Finally, some months after I started visiting this couple, but before the modernisation work began, Peggy started talking about the carpets. She tells me that she has decided that the red bedroom carpet can go, and that she has sorted out where to already. Her 14-year-old granddaughter Naomi's boyfriend, Jason (who has been living on the settee in their house for three months, having been thrown out by his mother), has just been allocated a council flat in another village, to the delight of all the adults concerned, because they hope that the relationship will 'fizzle out'. Peggy and Harry's bedroom carpet is now marked out as 'for Jason'. Having started thinking about carpets, however, Peggy is now talking about the living room and hall carpet. She tells me that she hasn't yet made up her mind about this, but she remembers the last modernisation of the street, over 20 years ago, and the mess that generated. This current carpet, like the wallpaper, is only two years old, and Peggy likes it a lot. When I visit the next week, however, Peggy tells me that she has ordered a new carpet from her catalogue for the living room and the hallway, and that Samantha can have the current one: 'It'll do her', she says, 'until she's in a position to get herself a new one – beggars can't be choosers.'

With a week to go before the modernisation is due to enter the bungalow, Peggy and Harry (and me) strip off the wallpaper in their living room, a wall a day. They remove their less bulky furniture – two occasional mahogany tables – to the conservatory and begin to construct a pyramid of their bulkier furniture, three easy chairs in green velour. Finally, they bring out a number of dust sheets and pieces of plastic sheeting which they place over the furniture pyramid and the display cabinet (Figure 3.1). A stack of green plastic garden chairs – 'the new seating' – is brought into the living room and the TV and TV-stand are left *in situ*, uncovered, as things that cannot be removed or covered over because of their centrality to the practices of everyday life – Peggy and Harry usually watch a film in the afternoon each day.

At Claire and Nathan's, the anticipatory preparations were rather different. Although my first meetings with them occurred later in the fieldwork, they talked with me at some length about what they had done, and the effects of their practice were visible throughout the house. Claire and Nathan tell me how one Sunday afternoon they piled up all their furniture, with the exception of a cream leather settee and armchair and their beds, and crammed it all in the back of their Nissan Micra. 'It's amazing what you can get in the back of a Micra', says Nathan. Claire adds: 'It was nearly dark when we took it to the tip'. Like Peggy and Harry, this couple stripped off all the wallpaper in the house, and the walls, particularly in the living room, became doodling spaces for Abigail. Biro and felt-tip pen scrawl adorned most of these walls (Figure 3.2).

Packing-up has been a feature of Claire and Nathan's practice too, but what they pack away is very different to Peggy and Harry. Two bedrooms are full of piles of cardboard boxes, all of them packed to capacity with children's toys. The toys are placed carefully, not chucked-in anyhow, and another storage cupboard houses more of Abigail's things, including her doll's house. Also upstairs, by the boxes, is a large battery-operated kids' car, in pink (Figure 3.3 and cover image).

Somewhat differently from Peggy and Harry, Claire and Nathan have also removed all the carpeting and lino in their house. They are walking around on the untreated wooden floorboards and concrete flooring. The carpet and lino have all been placed outside, in piles in the garden. Nathan tells me how he thought the council would take them away when the work began, but they won't, so now – he thinks – he'll have to burn them. Either that or he'll take them to the tip. But the carpet is soaking wet – it has been in the garden for over a month – and it is too heavy to move far. Besides, this is not the sort of matter that he wants to put in their car.

Like Peggy and Harry, Claire and Nathan are also having their kitchen changed. And, as with Peggy and Harry, a proposed change in colour has precipitated a mass ridding of cooking utensils. Claire says: 'We were blue and yellow but I don't want that any more.' But the ridding goes further than this. All of the appliances, which are fully functional, are being jettisoned. One of these – the cooker – is second-hand, a gift from Claire's mother when they

Figure 3.2: Abigail's doodles

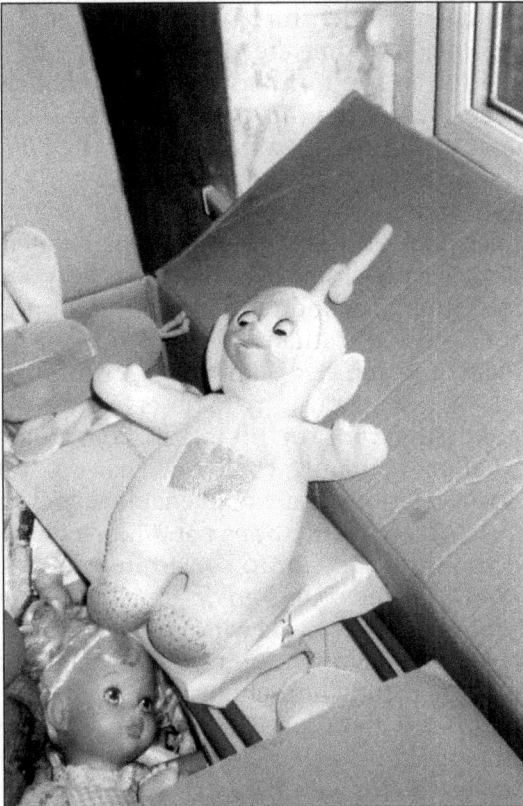

Figure 3.3: Abigail's toys

moved in together. The remainder – the fridge-freezer, washing machine and tumble drier, and the microwave – are to go; Claire wants matching chrome ones instead, and the couple have already started buying their replacements, which are being stored at her mother's. Nathan says, 'We'll just take them to the tip.'

In juxtaposing the anticipatory preparations of Peggy and Harry and Claire and Nathan, it is evident that there are some parallels between the two households' practices. The act of modernisation is deemed by both (particularly Peggy and Claire), to be an opportunity for getting rid of things, in Claire and Nathan's case almost all their things. At the same time, the forthcoming event is clearly read by both households as one from which certain valued things need to be protected in advance. In Peggy and Harry's case, they deploy various layers of packing matter and types of protective matter, including newspaper, plastic and cotton sheeting kept expressly for this purpose, whilst Claire and Nathan rely on boxes. Peggy and Harry also physically move their valued things to secure out-of-house storage zones, whilst Claire and Nathan displace them to rooms that will be largely unaffected by the council work. Stark contrasts between the two households, however, are the temporalities of ridding, their enactment in practice and the trajectories of things. So, whereas Peggy (and it is Peggy who makes these decisions in this household) comes to certain decisions quickly – a reflection of her desire for change in the kitchen – other things take far longer to become open to the possibility of ridding, and some are only reluctantly let go. Furthermore, it takes a long time for all these things to exit the bungalow, over seven months. And indeed, some of the things due to exit – the carpets – are still *in situ* as the council workmen enter the property. By contrast, Claire and Nathan jettison almost all of their discards in one go, leaving themselves with very few things, most of them also earmarked as 'for chucking'. It is, however, in the trajectories of these things that the differences between the two couples are most clearly displayed. Whereas Peggy and Harry for the most part rely on redistribution and re-use, mostly within the family, to get rid of their things, Claire and Nathan opt to abandon most of their things at the tip or – as with the carpets – destroy them through burning. Now, although I did not have the opportunity to observe these things, the state of the matter currently destined for the tip in this household is such that the re-use of some of it, almost certainly, could be imagined. Nathan and Claire, however, lack the social relations that would enable them to redistribute their things: as Claire says, 'All my family want new.' Moreover, unlike Peggy and Harry, they appear to find it difficult to constitute any notion of deserving cases beyond the family. As the couple go on to tell me, they don't mix with anybody living round where they live. I will come back to this point later. For the moment, however, I switch attention to the various events and practices occurring in the two other study households.

Unlike Peggy and Harry and Claire and Nathan, Christine and Malcolm and Carol and John were not having kitchens installed, for they had both purchased and installed their own fitted kitchens relatively recently, both of them bought at B&Q.[12] Christine and Malcolm's is birch with a laminated wood floor – 'it nearly killed us putting it in last Christmas' says Christine.

Carol and John's is pine. Neither do these two households engage in any of the mass packing of valued things enacted by Peggy and Harry and Claire and Nathan. Instead, their anticipatory preparations are largely centred on specific rooms and/or zones. In Christine and Malcolm's case, this is the loft; in Carol and John's, it is the living room.

The modernisation work due to occur in Christine and Malcolm's house was relatively small-scale in comparison with that planned for other dwelling structures, largely because of the work they have done on the interior of the house themselves. This couple are having new windows fitted, including a bay in the living room, a new shower installed and the loft insulated. It is the latter event that precipitated the excavation of their loft, the first time they'd done this in the time they'd lived in the house. They also timed this excavation to coincide with their conversion of their front garden to a paved-over parking area for Malcolm's new car. Needing a skip for the garden makeover, they also used the skip for dealing with some of the detritus from the loft. Christine describes the loft excavation in a long involved narrative featuring apprehension ('what were we going to find up there after all this time?!'), memory (old photos of her and Malcolm as children, their wedding day), filth and excess ('even now it makes me go all scratchy just thinking about it all', 'how much stuff is it possible to have?'). But what she also makes clear is that this excavation was principally about sorting, specifically keeping and discarding things. What stayed? Some predictable forms of material culture: her wedding dress, the bridesmaid's dresses she had worn as a child, Kylie's first baby toys and – intriguingly – her potty. What left? An old fur coat that a pigeon had died in; a pair of pull-on fashion boots; an old rocking horse (given to them when Kylie was small by a family relative, then deemed 'too big', but which couldn't be thrown away because 'it would've been too problematic'); all Kylie's toys; old curtains; a coffee table; old rotten suitcases and piles and piles of boxes from previous appliance purchases. Into the skip, but carefully concealed under piles of earth and grass, go the toys, curtains, suitcases and the coffee table (Figure 3.4).

What remains, including some of the boxes and the old clothes, go in the household's wheelie bin, and then in three other bin bags which are driven round to Christine's dad's house by Malcolm to go in his wheelie bin. Finally, Christine rings the council bulky waste collection service to arrange for the remainder of the packaging and the rocking horse to be collected. In contrast, Carol and John's approach to the forthcoming event of modernisation was to use it as an opportunity to buy a large amount of new furniture (paid for in instalments and timed to fit the council's advertised programme of work) and to rid themselves of most of the furniture in their living room. Carol narrates this in the following way:

Carol: The three-piece – that's two settees and two chairs – they were bought brand new but there's wear and tear in them now so we decided to get a new one, but we decided to wait until modernisation to get that. Hopefully we can get rid of them by asking a couple of people that we know who might take them off our hands – probably

Figure 3.4: Christine and Malcolm's skip

somebody over the road. If the local neighbour doesn't want them there's somebody else in the village who might have them. If they don't want them then there'll be a few phone calls made to see if any charities will take them off our hands.

Nicky: How old are they?

Carol: Four years old about – that's broken in the middle; this one isn't, this one's fine but there's a bit of wear and tear in the arms. Everything else is fine on them

Nicky: You wouldn't get them re-covered?

Carol: It's not worth it because we priced it and it was going to cost nearly £1,200. And that one's broken so really it was pointless. So hubbie said, 'Right, we'll have a new three piece' [...] These two (a bookcase and corner unit) – I got those, I bought those off my friend in the village. I've had them about two or three year, so they're going because they're a bit worn and battered and I think it's time I got some new furniture – new, not passed on and passed down. All the

Figure 3.5: Carol and John's 'old' dresser

furniture I've had has been passed down apart from the three-piece.
So that's going. And I will try to find a home for that (dresser/display
cabinet, Figure 3.5) locally, if anybody'll have it, and the (TV) unit.

At the same time she recounts how her dining room table and chairs are
also going to go to a friend.

Unlike Christine, however, Carol does not begin to relocate these things
until the week before the work is due to start in their house. One Monday
evening a small van is parked outside her house; the table and chairs are on
their way to her friend's house. The next evening the display cabinet was
shifted over the road to a neighbour's bungalow by John and the neighbour,
along with the TV unit and the bookcase. The same neighbour – a man who
lives on his own and who has no immediate family that is known of – has
also said that he will take one of the settees off Carol's hands but not the
other, but since the household's new three-piece suite is not due to arrive yet
the settee cannot yet cross the road; it's needed for Christmas. In the same
week the new pine units arrive and go straight in the living room. This is the
source of much anxiety and frustration. As Carol says:

The only reason I didn't want the furniture in the house was because we were getting modernised. And I wanted it out of the way, of all the mess and all the rubbish. But because THEY'VE delayed for SO LONG, because we were supposed to be getting started in [month], technically it'd have been done and been finished with, if they'd have stuck to their routine and their time schedules like they said they were going to, and that would've been ample time to get my furniture in and it wouldn't have been damaged. Yet the situation now is that I've got my old furniture and the new furniture coming in, and it's going to get made a mess.

Modernisation here is anticipated as simultaneously threat and opportunity: whilst it has allowed, even compelled, Carol and John to invest in the new, the time scale of its enactment has brought new and old things together in advance of any work happening, with the potential risks to the new being already imagined and heartfelt.

Although the acts of ridding that Carol and John engage in resonate in some ways with Claire and Nathan's jettisoning of their unwanted things, the trajectories of this furniture have greater affinities with what happened to some of Peggy and Harry's things. Ridding here is largely about redistribution and re-use. But, unlike Peggy and Harry, whose large family provides the conduits for many of their things, it is the relations of friendship and the neighbourhood that Carol relies on to enact their ridding. Without the family conduits open to Peggy and Harry, Carol has to negotiate the rather more delicate social dynamics of inviting known, but not closely known, people in to her house for the specific purpose of viewing, and possibly rejecting, particular (largely second-hand) pieces of furniture.

By contrast, Christine's actions have considerable parallels with the wholesale ridding of Claire and Nathan. Although Christine and Malcolm do not take their things to the tip – I suspect because Malcolm's new car is 'his pride and joy' (Christine) – they nonetheless ensure that this stuff is carried away, through the medium of the skip and several wheelie bins. Understanding such actions has taken a not inconsiderable period of time. Initially, when the skip and loft clearance events happened, I thought that this was simply a matter of convenience and value creation; that hiring the skip for the drive construction provided sufficient motivation to do the loft and ensured getting value out of the skip hire. The fact that Christine had taken the trouble to bury the loft matter under the other contents of the skip, however, did nag away; I sensed that concealment did actually matter to her, but from whom and why? Somehow, asking Christine directly about why she had done this seemed way too nosey. Instead, and after a while, I asked Peggy about why she thought Christine might have done this. The response was immediate: 'Christine didn't want any of THAT LOT getting hold of her stuff'. One reason to accept this interpretation is that Peggy routinely talks to Christine in a way that ascertains everybody's business. So, I have few doubts that Christine did indeed say something like this or its equivalent to Peggy. Another is Claire and Nathan's near-dark tip journey, in which the

importance of concealment from others' eyes is also suggested. But what
lends further credence to this interpretation is its resonance with remarks
that Claire made in another unrelated conversation with a mother living on
Alternative Terrace about getting rid of some of Abigail's baby things. Here,
in a conversation with Sandra whom we will meet in Chapter 4, she recounts
why she and Nathan burnt Abigail's cot and took a whole load of her baby
things to the tip:

> *Claire:* I wouldn't like give it to just anybody that I didn't like.
>
> *Sandra:* Would you not advertise it?
>
> *Claire:* No.
>
> *Sandra:* You wouldn't give it away?
>
> *Claire:* No – there's some people in the village who would probably
> use it but I wouldn't give it to them cos I think they should just go
> and get a job themselves. I'd rather just burn it or take it to the tip.

For households such as Claire and Nathan's and Christine and Malcolm's,
getting rid of their things is most definitely an act that is partly about pre-
venting certain others – the 'smackheads, thieves and rogues' (Chapter 1)
– who live in the immediate vicinity from getting hold of them. Like Claire's
family, Christine and Malcolm's families also invest heavily in the new.
Moreover, they too do not mix with many unrelated others on the street
– only Carol and Peggy. Correspondingly, it is perhaps not surprising that
these households devote considerable amounts of care to ensuring that their
unwanted things either go the waste route (Christine's skip) or are removed
from the local neighbourhood in a way that marks them out as rubbish matter (Claire and Nathan's tip journeys and burnings). What these two households are doing here is to mark their social alienation by what they do with
their unwanted things. The ridding that anticipates modernisation emerges
here not just as a means of making family (Peggy and Harry) but of fabricating the other and of constituting Wear Road through othering. Whilst Claire
and Nathan and Christine and Malcolm manufacture the other by refusing
the passage of their things to these others, Peggy and Harry's and Carol and
John's actions have much the same effect, through the distinctions they draw
in selecting who gets to know about, look through, scrutinise and appropriate their unwanted things – family, friends and deserving cases only.

Being modernised

With the entry of the workmen into their houses and bungalows, the majority of the tenants on Wear Road found themselves living in the midst of
overlapping waves of 'improvement' activity that lasted for over five months.
First, a team of six window fitters ripped out all their windows and exterior
doors and made a start on the installation of the replacements; at the same
time a team of three electricians started pulling up the carpets (if these hadn't
already been rolled up or removed by tenants) and taking up the floorboards.

Following on behind – usually some weeks behind – were the plasterer and kitchen/bathroom fitting teams. Finally, many weeks behind them, a plumber made his way up the street.

As might be inferred from this, for many tenants 'being modernised' constituted something akin to an invasion of their homes by a council army. The first morning was all too much for Peggy and Harry, who pronounced that they just couldn't stand it and left for the shops. When they returned, they retreated to sit out (with me) in the conservatory, covered in layers of coats, surrounded by their boxes and keeping warm from Peggy's constant smoking. It was a similar story elsewhere, as Malcolm's mother retreated to Christine's and Malcolm's house on a daily basis, as Claire took refuge in her mother's, and as Claire and Nathan's elderly neighbour moved in with her daughter. For Carol, however, and for a few others, camping out with the relatives was not an option, as there were no relatives around. Moreover, unlike Peggy and Harry, Carol did not have anywhere to get away from the workmen during the day, because she had to look after Zuki, whom the workmen were continually threatening to let out. Instead, she had to attempt to carry on with daily life with all this going on around her.

It is hard to convey what living in such circumstances is like. The photographs taken at Peggy and Harry's at the time convey something of the story (Figure 3.6), as too does this extract from my field notes describing the scene at Carol and John's:

> It is hard to convey the sheer enormity of the mess in this house.
> Upstairs the floor is simply joists, with the beds balanced on these.
> The bairns only have the beds to sit on. Going to the toilet is a
> balancing act and there is no bath or shower. Downstairs the kitchen
> is in a total state of devastation – wiring is hanging from the ceiling,
> dust and rubble are all over every surface and chopped-off electrical
> wiring litters the floor. All the appliances are pulled away from the
> walls and are also covered in rubble and dust. It is here that Carol
> is having to try to cook John and the bairns' tea, and where she has
> to try to get them ready for school in the morning, with the men
> already in the house. (January 2004)

As the workmen said to many a tenant, 'Nobody should be having to live in this mess; you should have been relocated.' Instead, the tenants received a £12/week 'inconvenience payment', something that was widely regarded as both joke and insult. Nonetheless, most got on with the business of trying to cook, eat, wash up, bathe, do the laundry, look after children and sleep in their homes – although as Carol says, 'I've given up, we're just going to have to have sandwiches – again!' Like many others though, she has her down times, and is almost in tears one afternoon when she finds the workmen have sat on the kids' beds to eat their dinners: 'Look at this', she says, showing me the filth on the duvet covers from their overalls, 'now I'm going to have to try and get these washed and dried before I go to get them from school.' For

Figure 3.6: Peggy and Harry's kitchen during modernisation

Peggy the stress is too much: she has another mild transitory stroke, from which she makes a full recovery.

If this is what's going on with the people, what's happening to their things? As the council teams rip out windows, frames, doors, kitchen units, baths, washbasins and toilets and chuck these, literally anyhow, on the tenants' front garden areas, their paths and the pavement, other tenants come out and complain about the mess, alleging that the men are 'ruining my grass' or 'ruining my drive'. At the end of each working day, however, a council pick-up truck is driven up the street to collect and carry away the ripped-out matter. 'They take it straight to one of their tips', says Harry, 'I asked them.' However, the tenants' own furniture, appliances and personal belongings – or what remains of them in Claire and Nathan's case –is all *in situ*, in their houses.

Like Peggy and Harry, Carol eventually covers up all her living room furniture with plastic sheeting, blankets and dust covers, some of them borrowed from Peggy (Figure 3.7).

The couple, however, do not roll the living room carpet up until the men have been in their house for a fortnight. 'I knew we should've done something about this,' says Carol, 'look at it, it's cack full of dust and grit.' At the same time, however, one weekend immediately after Christmas, this couple set about stripping off all the wallpaper decoration from every room in the

Figure 3.7: Carol and John's kitchen during modernisation

house, clearing out the two younger children's bedrooms and demolishing the interior wall between their kitchen and utility room. That Sunday afternoon, John took a car load of nine bin bags of kids' toys to the tip, but there are still nine bin bags full of kids' toys out in the back garden waiting for another tip journey. 'They were pretty good about it.', says Carol, 'We asked them what they wanted to keep and what they wanted to go. But there's just so much of it that I just haven't got the time or the energy to take them all to the charity shop – it's just too much stuff.' Also piled up outside in the back garden are the bricks from the interior wall – 'I've been lobbing the occasional one or two in the wheelie bin,' laughs Carol, 'but the men have said to shift it round the front and they'll take it away in the truck.' Meanwhile, the kitchen area is coming in for discussion. Knocking down the interior wall may have created a 'dining room space', but Carol and John are now acutely aware that the kitchen they bought and installed only a couple of years back doesn't look quite right: designed to fit into one particular spatial configuration, the units now end abruptly where once there was a wall.

Over at Peggy and Harry's there is one early casualty of modernisation work, the TV-stand. Later the next week Peggy goes Christmas shopping with one of her sons and buys a replacement, assumed to be identical, self-assembly TV table from Argos, which she places in the pile of bulky furniture in the middle of their living room. Meanwhile, the damaged stand remains, and stays in the house for another three weeks, until the electricians and plasterers have been and gone and Dawn has redecorated the living room. At this juncture the TV-stand has to be got rid of, somehow. Harry – who would have repaired it, but whose role it is to get rid of Peggy's discards – asks a neighbour whether he wants it. He does and the TV-stand goes the same way as all Carol's unwanted furniture. Harry also tells me that this same neighbour

– the man who lives on his own – has also had their previous three-piece suite, their bed headboards and that he will be getting their mattresses when the new ones arrive. 'Saves me from having to ring the council and pay for things to be collected', he says. One of Peggy and Harry's sons assembles the new TV-table. It looks much the same as the old one, but it has a space in it to accommodate a DVD player as well as a video recorder. A few weeks later, one of Peggy and Harry's Christmas presents is a DVD player and they also receive a few DVDs. Peggy and Harry are now buying one DVD a week and watch DVDs in the afternoons as well as the film on one of the terrestrial TV channels. Peggy has also bought a new DVD storage rack to go in the hall, which she has worked out will last them till October at their (more accurately, her) current rate of acquisition.

The other casualties of modernisation at Peggy and Harry's are some of the mementos. During the hot summer months Peggy had noticed a pool of water on the floor of the conservatory but had thought no more about it. When the couple came to unpack their boxes of mementos the water-ice decorations from Peggy's 60th-birthday cake were no longer there – 'They'd melted. But that was my own stupid fault. It's 100 degrees in that conservatory in July!', says Peggy. Also missing are the photographs of the same birthday: 'I've hauled everything out and I can't find them anywhere', says Peggy. She is very upset about this loss, particularly because these are the last photographs of certain family members who have recently died. I say that they must be somewhere and that she wouldn't have thrown them out. But Peggy says, 'I must have. I'd believe anything with all this concoction of drugs I'm taking; I must have just thrown them out by mistake when we were packing up.'

As I draft this chapter, of the four study households on Wear Road, none are yet finished with modernisation and only Peggy and Harry have begun to reclaim their homes through redecoration. Carol and John and Christine and Malcolm still have the workmen in, and a three-piece suite is due to arrive in Carol's next week. Carol wants to shift the old settee over the road, but the windows team is due to start on that side of the street shortly, so she's not sure that the neighbour will want the furniture any more. Meanwhile, at Claire and Nathan's all work is at an impasse because the gas supply has still not been connected, and the gas company claim that nobody has requested this connection. The plumber has connected their new washing machine, but the washing machine refuses to empty. Peggy and Harry's kitchen is still not finished – twelve weeks after work began in their bungalow. The electricity board have not been to move the meter that used to be on their outside wall, but which is now inside the house where a kitchen unit should be. Furthermore, the outer wall of their new kitchen that used to be their pantry is already showing signs of damp. 'Modernised – we'll still be being modernised next year!', exclaims Peggy. All these tenants, however, are looking forward with anticipation to the impending commencement of work in the bungalow next to Peggy and Harry's and opposite Carol and John's. As the council foreman came out of this property he said: 'Boy, it's posh in there! It's All Cream!!' He is told by Carol and Peggy how the woman who lives there – who mixes with nobody else on the street – vacuums daily and insists on her husband's shoes coming off before he goes indoors. 'She'll be running round after them with a broom and insisting they take their boots off.', says Peggy, 'Mark my words. But we'll all be laughing ourselves silly watching.'

＊

There are three general observations that I want to make from this unfolding sequence of events. First, as with the anticipatory preparations, the practice of being modernised is one through which social distinctions are made on Wear Road. As we can see from the above, schemes of decoration – notably the use of cream – and the related practice of cleaning the house are of critical importance to the constitution of 'posh', as compared to respectable. Merely seeing that everything is cream is enough for the council foreman to declare the house and the woman living in it to be posh, whereas for many of the women on the street, the daily cleaning of the cream is understood to be indicative of such social pretensions. Having cream things and keeping the house immaculate are not just about respectability, then, but about constituting the self as better than the neighbours, as cleaner than the neighbours, whose decorative choices are known by both parties to enable them to get away with slightly less intensive cleaning practices whilst retaining respectability. Having experienced and lived with the mess and detritus of modernisation, known its contaminating effects on things and the impossibilities of keeping things clean in its presence, the juxtaposition of modernisation with an aesthetic in cream is widely anticipated by these neighbours, particularly the women. They are gleefully looking forward to watching this tenant attempt to maintain 'posh' amidst the mess of modernisation. Indeed, the seats for watching had already been reserved in Carol's bay window when the fieldwork came to an end.

A second point concerns the practice of protection. As we see with Peggy and Harry's mementos, protecting things is no guarantee of their enduring through modernisation. Instead, wrapping up things and displacing them has been the means to the loss of certain valued things: so, whereas the various china collections survived intact, the water-ice decorations and the photographs did not. Seemingly, the act of merely displacing valued things has the potential for their loss. Nonetheless, the utilisation of protective matter in relation to other things has worked to protect their value. Most of Peggy and Harry's furniture and Carol and John's new furniture survived unscathed. But other things – the uncovered things in use in everyday life through modernisation – have not, and bear the trace of modernisation in their current form. Peggy and Harry's TV-stand is discarded precisely because it bears too much of this trace and because Peggy cannot bear to have anything but pristine things in her house, because of their incompatibility with respectability. Their living room carpet – now *in situ* in Samantha's and moved by her brother – has gone there with the loan of a carpet cleaner: 'She'll have to clean it for a week, but it won't come up right – the cack will still be in it' (Peggy). And Carol's carpet, appliances and kitchen units all still bear the trace of the rubble, dust and electrician's wire cuttings in their surfaces. Although some may be able to live with these things, on a street where respectability and 'posh' will have to be re-forged in things, it is more than likely that others will not and that the trace of modernisation's presence in their fabric will be sufficient reason to cast them out.

Finally, it is impossible to overlook the sheer volume of waste-making involved in being modernised. The work itself – and the parallel practices of tenants living through it and trying to accommodate to it – generates huge piles of discarded matter. For example, from Carol and John's: eighteen bin bags of stuff from the kids' bedrooms, a huge pile of bricks, eight windows and their frames, two exterior doors and a bathroom suite, as well as a three-piece suite, living room furniture and a dining table and six chairs. And this pattern is repeated through approximately twenty other houses and bunga-lows. That all concerned find this accumulation of things, and their ridding, a weighty, troublesome matter is clear. Comments such as, 'There's just too much stuff' abound, and even in households such as Carol and John's, where ridding practices normally involve and prioritise redistribution and re-use to known and unknown others, it is the tip that becomes the primary conduit for ridding; as it does for the council workmen too. Indeed, what emerges very strongly here is the connection between the tip and disposing of large accumulations of cast-out and ripped-out matter. The tip is the quick-fix, easy, convenient solution to displacing these accumulations from the spaces of habitation. As the place to which this matter can be carried away, it is the place that permits the practice of modernisation to be visually closed off from spaces of inhabitation. Indeed, without the tip's capacities to absorb unwant-ed matter, the ripped-out matter would remain *in situ*; in the front and back gardens of these dwelling structures, a constant reminder of modernisation's effects on matter, and their consequences.

Conclusions

Although the nature of the work being enacted through modernisation has distinct resonances with that occurring in Ginny and Lesley's house in the previous chapter – in that it is improvement related, with the express intend-ed effect of increasing the comfort, convenience and safety of tenants' lives – the relations and temporalities of its enactment are very different. Being modernised as a council tenant, then, emerges here as something that is felt to be done to tenants, by councils, rather than something over which tenants can exercise any degree of control. Furthermore, and unlike in Lesley and Ginny's case, the timing of modernisation work is exclusively of the council's making. Indeed, its very enactment is entwined in the politics of local gov-ernment finance and council housing budgets, themselves shaped annually by central government. Moreover, as we see clearly in the previous sections, even the actual timing of modernisation's presence in particular dwelling structures is driven entirely by the council and its agents, the various teams they employ. When things are done, even precisely what is done when dur-ing each day, are events which tenants have very little capacity to shape. Furthermore, rather than frame this work through sequentially orchestrated projects spread out across years – as owner-occupiers are able to do – the improvement work that is modernisation is temporally compressed, with significant consequences for carrying on the practices of everyday life, notably cooking, washing, bathing and even just sitting. The accommodations here, then, are all one way, of tenants and 'their' dwelling structures to the council through the medium of its modernisation programme. Modernisation, then, is a moment when councils re-appropriate housing from their tenants, in so doing simultaneously wrecking homes and everyday life and re-affirming the alienation of life as a council tenant.

A further difference between the two versions of improvement work highlighted thus far is located in what precisely is being corrected through modernisation. In the previous chapter we saw how in moving in, both the material fabric of dwelling structures and the technical systems installed in houses can be the site for othering previous occupants; how improvement work can be construed as a correcting presence; and how ridding and replacing such things is critical to the process of accommodating the other. By contrast in this modernisation programme the script of correcting is one where the local authority – through its designers, planners and their agents of implementation, the foremen and workmen – gets to re-author previous local authority acts of modernisation, something which is well understood on a street on which generations of the same families have lived for decades. When the work of demolition, ripping out and replacement occurs here, then, it is the presence and trace of previous local authority work, working practices and materials that are being stripped-out.

The effects of all this seem considerable. For one, it means that modernisation does not quite have the aura around it that the local authority rhetoric of up-to-date, modern homes suggests. Instead, modernisation is undermined by the trace in dwelling structures of previous modernisation programmes; it is constituted as part of an ongoing history of street and housing modernisation, rather than as a one-off act of making modern homes of contemporary living standards. Secondly, though, whilst the enactment of specific modernisation programmes certainly testifies to the alienation of living as a council tenant, the existence of multiple modernisation programmes in the fabric of these dwelling structures rather complicates the appropriation story (Miller 1988). For what this suggests is that councils, as well as tenants, have to do the work of appropriation. Indeed, I would argue that in enacting modernisation schemes such as the one on Wear Road, councils are attempting to reclaim their housing structures from the legacy of previous modernisations, through ripping out, wasting and replacing the fabric of these dwelling structures. Modernisation here, then, is about attempting to re-author the state as a caring council through changing the material fabric of these dwelling structures. And the materials used to enact this re-authoring certainly do matter to selling the representation, hence the importance of the use of uPVC, rather than an appeal to wood and to authenticity. In re-authoring the state through fabricating more modern dwelling structures, then, the council is attempting to use these 'modern' products to come to a new accommodation with its tenants. Whether tenants see this accommodation in quite the same way, however, is more open to question. Indeed, as I emphasised previously, for some at least the aspiration is to dispense with the council's presence in their homes by exercising their right to buy.[12]

Rather than end on this note, however, I want to conclude this chapter with the older take on 'appropriating the state on a council estate' and its connections to the constitution of particular, largely class-based, femininities (Skeggs 1997). As both of the previous sections have shown, modernisation has been the impetus for a huge volume of ridding and jettisoning on Wear Road, the vast majority of it instigated by women. It would be all too easy to take some of these acts at face value, and read them as indicative of a pure and expressive consumerism. Peggy's declarations that she fancied a change, Claire's statement that she didn't want a blue and yellow kitchen any more and that she wanted chrome appliances, Carol and John's purchasing of a new three-piece suite and new living room furniture could all be interpreted in this way, and undoubtedly will be by some readers. Whilst acknowledging that such acquisitions do indeed display high investments in the new and in fashion, and that they are, in turn, responsible for massive amounts of waste-making, at the same time I would argue that they are fundamental to the work of appropriating the state. Stripping off all the wallpaper and ridding interior decorations, furniture and furnishings in these houses is not just about making preparations for modernisation but an act which prefigures tenants' re-appropriation of dwelling structures as homes. They are the means through which tenants can reclaim dwelling structures back from the council, by making them accommodating homes again. To appropriate the state on this council estate and to do so respectably, then, is something that cannot be done without wholesale ridding and rampant acquisition. In this sense, the extent of the ridding and wasting that accompanied the modernisation of dwelling structures on Wear Road is both an effect of modernisation and an accommodation to it. Having worked to trash the home aesthetic, interiors and surface appearances valorised within particular femininities, and turned their ideal homes to dust and rubble, modernisation is itself accommodated by these women through an intense period of ridding, wasting and acquisition, which simultaneously reconstitutes their ideal homes, through decoration, furniture and furnishings, and reclaims them back from 'the council'.

I cannot close this chapter, however, without commenting finally on another facet of the gendering of being modernised and the ridding that accompanies it. Much of this chapter illuminates the continued perspicacity of Bev Skegg's respectability thesis with regard to the constitution of working class femininities. What it also shows though is men's accommodation to the making of these femininities and respectabilities, through the enactment of ridding. The chapter provides ample evidence of this within households, from Peggy's instruction to Harry to get rid of the damaged TV-stand, to John's and Nathan's repeated trips to the tip, to Christine's dad's provision of his wheelie bin for some of their loft matter, to one of Peggy's sons removal of their living room carpets and transportation of it to his sister's house. But what the chapter also demonstrates is how certain men living on Wear Road – men living alone and with no known-of family living locally – are constituted by many of these women as deserving cases for the receipt of their discards. The deliberately un-named neighbour of three of the study households is a case in point; an individual whose one-bedroom bungalow emerged during modernisation as the metaphorical 'black hole' and as the increasingly unlikely site for an immense accumulation of unwanted matter. So much so that what the flow of matter into this bungalow through modernisation started to suggest was the impossibilities of its containment. Indeed, from being constituted as the deserving other, this neighbour's social positioning on the street started to be recast, as the tenants began to speculate on what he could possibly be doing with all their old stuff.[59] I can think of few better testimonies than this to modernisation's continued forging of social relations through the trajectories of things and specifically through the conduits of ridding.

NOTES

1 In the UK, council tenants rent dwelling structures directly from local authorities, living in what is referred to in other countries as 'public housing'. Throughout the chapter I use the terms 'local authority' and 'council' interchangeably. It will become evident however, that those living in council housing on Wear Road refer to 'the council' as a homogenous presence, usually in terms which indicate its constitution as a defining, constraining presence in their lives. Overcoming this sense of alienation is a consistent motif of living as a council tenant, and exerts critical effects on what many tenants do with the interiors of their rented homes (Miller 1988).

2 One of a small number of Tenants Choice Modernisation Schemes, affecting some 250 properties per annum in County Durham, these programmes are represented by the council as the most extensive form of improvement work enacted. They are targeted at dwelling structures identified as needing modernising 'to bring up to modern day living standards' (http://www.durhamcity.gov.uk/html/residents/keyservices/housing/repair/repair8_2.html: accessed 16 January 2004).

3 This modernisation programme worked to obscure any straightforward correspondence between external aesthetic and housing tenure, as many of the tenants were acutely aware. Indeed, for the 16-year-old teenage daughter of one of the study households, the transformations wrought by a bay window and uPVC front door have meant that she is no longer ashamed to let her friends see the outside of the house where she lives. They now drop her off outside her house, rather than at the top of Wear Road. It is against this background that the popularity of bay windows and patio doors within Wear Road's modernisation programme is probably best seen, for what their installation conjoins is aspiration with distinction. Not only are both features deemed by the tenants selecting them to mark out their houses as appearing to be what they are not – those of owner occupiers – but they mark out their houses as different from those of other tenants too. What effect such changes may or may not have on the external aesthetic of those houses already in owner-occupation on Wear Road remains to be seen, although the gradual appearance of wrought-iron railings along with paved-over front gardens (for off-street private car parking) is certainly suggestive.

4 The calculation made by those tenants aiming to buy their homes post modernisation is that the council will have paid for the work of modernisation, leaving them to find the mortgage repayments only. The difficulty for many, however, is that – on being modernised – council valuations of particular properties have increased, in some cases beyond the capacity for some to be able to afford to buy.

5 An interesting aside here is that throughout the ethnographic fieldwork Peggy made repeated value judgements which worked to differentiate her and her respectable neighbours from others whom she radically othered (Chapter 1). Included within this category of others were the current generation of teenage mothers, which – as we can see – Peggy herself once was.

6 Moving from the owner occupied sector to being a council tenant is relatively unusual as a housing trajectory in the UK, in which both the aspiration and the trend have been the reverse. That Peggy and Harry did this is about the conjuncture of two points; Peggy's wish to move to a bungalow for their older age, and Harry's desire to remain living in South Hightown,

and specifically on Wear Road. Since the only bungalows on Wear Road at this time were in council ownership and since the sale of the couple's own house (bought during the first wave of 'Right to Buy' in the early 1980s) did not realise enough capital for them to move to a bungalow in another part of South Hightown, to satisfy their housing choices Peggy and Harry had no choice but to revert to being council tenants.

7 Swapping houses between council tenants is not uncommon on the Rivers estate, and is organised through the medium of the local post office. It is however a marker of Wear Road's standing within the Rivers estate that during the fieldwork I encountered two younger couples with children who refused the offer of tenancies on this street precisely because they were on this street.

8 The connections to dwelling are both obvious and profound. Unlike the previous chapter, in which dwelling is fabricated through estate agency, here dwelling is forged through an attachment to place, and to place within place. Living, as the state of being at home, for the inhabitants of Wear Road, is achieved through living in a very particular place, and not just in a house. Throughout the fieldwork I came across numerous pointers to this form of dwelling. One such is 'the return'. Typically involving individuals who had either been studying away or working away, the return entailed the purchase of a property in South Hightown, itself narrated as the fulfilment of 'a dream'. Another pointer came from the comments of local police officers regarding what they saw as the highly constrained spatial horizons of local 'youth', for whom 'Durham City is a world away'. Indeed, at one point during the fieldwork, and in near frustration, these officers volunteered to take these 16-year-old boys out of the village, 'just to broaden their horizons a bit'. To their astonishment, their well-meaning attempts at community liaison were turned down; they suspected because of the departure this offered from routine and consequent threat to emotional security it posed. It could, of course, also have been indicative of suspicion on the part of these boys, but the general point still holds.

9 Christmas decorations, internal and external, are taken very seriously on this street. Windows in particular are primary display locations, as are front doors. For those households caught up in modernisation over Christmas, therefore, partially completed windows and doors precluded certain forms of display. They also worked to exclude certain households from the competitive display that infuses doing Christmas on this street.

10 Ainsley is a make of decorative china, manufactured to be collectable (see Chapter 5).

11 Peggy and Harry are keen on going to boot sales in the summer months, and use these as one way of acting on Peggy's frequent declarations of being fed up with certain of her things.

12 Argos' significance as a retailer for a number of the households participating in the ethnography is indicative of its appeal to value, to saving and to the bargain (Clarke 1998). Although these meanings transcend class, there is no doubt that they had greater resonance for those living on the Rivers Estate than for those living elsewhere in South Hightown.

13 B&Q is a mass market DIY-supermarket with stores all over the UK. Its product lines appeal primarily to value and the bargain. In installing their own kitchens, both Carol and John and Christine and Malcolm exemplify the continued importance of the kitchen in appropriating the state on a council estate (Miller 1988).

14 Although, of course, the legacy of having been a council dwelling structure will live on in the valuation of the property and in its location on a street that discloses its housing history in the very fabric of its design and planning.

15 When I returned to Wear Road in the summer of 2004, Peggy told me how she and Harry and Carol and John had, at different times, gone to peer through the windows of this bungalow, at a time when they knew the tenant was out. Neither couple could see any trace of their gifted furniture, but neither has any idea of the manner of its exiting. As Peggy said, 'He must be getting rid of it at dead of night, because none of us has seen the going of it. But what he's doing with it, well it's a mystery.' – a comment which conveys deliciously this tenant's transition from 'deserving case' to 'shady figure'.

Chapter 4

Accommodating sleep

In this and the following three chapters the emphasis shifts from the temporal registers of moving in and out of dwelling structures, and from the major dislocations in the accommodating capacities of dwelling structures, to the everyday. The everyday is punctuated by the rhythms of the mundane, by routine, familiar and taken-for-granted practices and by temporalities which emphasise the repetitive and habitual nature of doings, rather than the exceptional or unusual event, such as moving house or modernisation. These are the doings of lives that are just going on. Washing, bathing, showering, shaving, laundering, ironing, making beds, cooking, cleaning, washing-up, vacuuming, shopping, playing with children, watching TV, listening to recorded music. All these, and more, are facets of everyday life within dwelling structures, and all involve us in doing something with, through and to things that we have to hand around us. But the mundane practice I want to highlight in this chapter is one which appears at first sight to be rather more passive than these. This is sleeping.

Sleeping is a profoundly cultural practice. Where we sleep and how – in what sorts of beds (king-size, double, single, twin, bunk beds, cot); in what sorts of arrangements within rooms; whom we sleep with, or not – matters. There are, for example, various regulatory norms shaping sleep's provision in the UK inscribed in the allocation of council housing to families with children of different genders, whilst sleep's exclusion from certain spaces – lay-bys, park benches, streets, areas of airport terminals – also points to its cultural significance. Within the dwelling structure, however, it is the capacity to sleep amidst co-present others which matters most. This is not just an issue of physical sleep and its potential for disturbance and dislocation in cohabitation, through babies crying, children's illnesses or the tossing and turning of trying to sleep alongside another body that is ill or in pain. Rather, the domestic environments in which we live are constituted through a normative that accommodates the sleeping body within a particular material culture of sleeping. This comprises not only a bed (itself defined through the normative) and particular styles of bedding – think how duvets have supplanted blankets and sheets in recent decades in the UK – but encompasses also a designated room for sleeping, which also accommodates our clothing and which, at least for cohabiting adults, is increasingly likely to be attached to an en-suite bathroom. Or think of how children's bedrooms are seen to require the space to accommodate not just sleep, but also studying, playing with friends and the sleep-over. Sleep, however, is profoundly important to an understanding of dwelling.

Sleep's significance within and to the conceptualisation of dwelling and the dwelling structure is well established through Heidegger's emphasis on the child's bed (Chapter 1) and is founded on its connections with being at home in the world. To sleep (well) is indeed a manifestation of a particular state of being (at home and at peace) in the world. Moreover, being able to sleep is vital to our capacity to inhabit and fully be in the world. In accommodating sleep (well), then, the dwelling structure moves from being merely an accommodation to becoming accommodating. As I show in this chapter, achieving this accommodation involves both a thoroughly corporeal body and the material culture of sleep. The chapter focuses on three instances of dislocation in the accommodation of sleep and its re-accommodation. As with the previous two chapters, rupture points such as these are always illuminating. And in sleep it is the body's corporeality that is the key agency. Bodily capacities – to grow, to age, to become sick, to snore (all of which we see here) – have profound effects on the capacity of a body to sleep. The body therefore has the capacity to disrupt the sleeping accommodations within any dwelling structure. Given sleep's imperative, however, new accommodations have to be forged. One such option, particularly for growing families, is to move house, to a larger accommodation. But moving house is not always an option, and in this chapter I focus on the possibilities afforded for re-accommodation by the material culture of sleep. The first two sections focus on households comprising older couples and those with new and growing children, respectively. I emphasise firstly the unravelling of sleeping together; in order to accommodate the changed sleep patterns of aging, these cohabiting couples move from sharing the same bed in the same room to sleeping apart, forging new accommodations in their dwelling structures. I then consider a set of sleep re-accommodations centred on growing children, focusing on the move to a cot and from a cot to a bed. Indicative of cultural norms of accommodating children within English dwelling structures, notably the move from parents' rooms to a room of their own, these transitions are also important for their constitution of the child in things and for what they disclose about mothers' accommodations to normative discourses of parenting. The final section of the chapter addresses a rather different sleep accommodation, that of the staying-over visitor. Although only a temporary accommodation, this is shown to have profound effects on things beyond the bedroom, specifically through the identification of the visitor with the normative. Together, these three instances of sleep's re-accommodation disclose that re-accommodating sleep involves both appropriation and divestment; that ridding the material culture of sleep frequently extends well beyond beds and bed-related matter to include clothing; and that the ridding of beds and bed-related matter is fundamentally a corporeal matter, in which the absent presence of the body looms large and has critical effects on the routes and enactment of ridding.

Accommodating aging in sleep

One of the core cultural conventions of sleeping in English dwelling structures, unlike in parts of continental Europe, is that cohabiting partners share both bed and bedroom. For two of the older couples participating in the ethnography, however, these conventions had become increasingly problematic, to the point that radical changes were made to their sleeping arrangements during the fieldwork. To begin to open this up, let us take the case of Ted and June.

Ted and June

Ted and June are in their mid and early 70s, respectively. Like Harry and Peggy in the previous chapter, they have been together for decades, in their case for over 40 years. Ted and June have two adult children, one of whom is Janet, and they live in what they describe as a 'three-bedroom box' on a suburban estate on the edge of the Newcastle conurbation. They moved there from Southampton some fifteen years ago when Ted retired, to be nearer – but not too near – their adult children. Unlike the majority of participants in the ethnography, I have known this couple for some years, as the parents of a close friend. Ted used to work in the insurance industry, whilst June – who did not work in paid employment when her children were at school – describes herself as 'a late developer'. She did an Open University degree in her 50s whilst working full-time as a PA. Since moving to the North-east, Harry has been active as a local conservation volunteer whilst June has recently joined the University of the Third Age, taking part in regular poetry reading and reading groups.

One day, when I was visiting them, June started telling me that the couple had just re-arranged their sleeping arrangements. At her instigation, she had decided to take over the spare bedroom, leaving Ted (and their cat) the double bedroom at night. June's telling of this story emphasises that, having lain awake listening to Ted's snoring for years, she had come to the sudden realisation that 'actually I don't have to put up with this any more'. Moreover, she has found that sleeping in her own bed in her own bedroom has other advantages: unable to sleep through the night any more, she is able to sit up and read or listen to the radio or CDs in the early hours, without feeling that she is going to disturb Ted.

Ted and June's sleeping re-arrangement, however, extended well beyond utilising all the bedrooms and beds in the house. Indeed, their re-arrangement of sleeping was accompanied by the movement of various items of clothing, in, out and through the bedrooms. A large mirror-fronted wardrobe, running the full width of one of the walls, stands in the couple's formerly shared bedroom. One side of this used to be taken up with June's clothing, the other with Ted's. On moving into the spare room to sleep, June took out all the clothing on her side of the wardrobe to move it into the other bedroom – 'otherwise we were constantly crossing over one another on the landing' she says. But, as she did so, she found herself subjecting it all to a ruthless degree of detached scrutiny. In the following extract of recorded conversation with June, we see why certain things did not get relocated in the wardrobe in her new bedroom:

Nicky (reading diary as prompt): ... one black polo shirt – 'bad buy' [quoting from diary] – laughter – three pairs of jodhpurs – 'ridiculous' – cackles of laughter – one printed Indian skirt – 'not me' – one pale blue fine ply jumper – 'never worn for more than 10 minutes' – one pair of van Dahl court shoes – 'down at heel, no longer me' – one pair of ankle-strapped buckle sandals – 'not worn for many a summer' – one viscose skirt – 'not long enough to cover the imperfections nor wide enough to disguise the girth' – laughter – one pair of flowery patterned socks – 'too tight around the ankles – enough to cause thrombosis' ...

June: The black polo shirt was bought with this viscose skirt – it didn't do anything for me – it ended up looking you know [she does a cockerel impression]. The three pairs of jodhpur-style trousers, well I looked like – it's not Charlie Chaplin, there's another famous comedian, Max Wall was it? He wore those tight trousers – dark tight trousers so his legs looked spindly ... they went up here [demonstrates – *Nicky*: Up to your boobs] – yes [laughter] – if I'd tried hard enough they'd have covered my eyes [hysterical laughter]. Oh dear, oh dear – hmmm terrible!! The pleated Indian skirt – well the elastic was so tough it sort of creased you, if you ate anything it stopped it going down any further. So I thought, 'Oh no, this has got to go!' And this jumper – I'd put it on and take it off again and think, 'This is no good.' The sleeves were too long but if you wore it without a blouse it didn't look right, and if you wore it with one it didn't feel right ... the van Dahl shoes, well they looked, the heels had gone down, so they wore like this.

Nicky: But they went in the charrie shop? It says here.

June: Yes, but I was in two minds about them, I think they should have gone in the bin.

What we see here is a lot of negative talk about this clothing, cloaked in ironic distancing humour. The clothing is described in terms such as 'bad buy', 'ridiculous', 'not me' and 'doesn't do anything for me'. Talking about things in this way marks them out as mistake acquisitions and/or as items that disrupt the coherent narration of self and identity through things. But what this talk also shows vividly is the centrality of wearing and embodiment to these not-me declarations. The clothes June releases are ones that she regards as too long for her (short) embodiment and/or as displaying body parts and bits that she regards as best covered up. Indicative of June's repeated efforts to shop for her body on the UK high street, these acquisitions could all too easily be read as purchases that are her mistake, and indeed

June represents these purchases as such in the conversation above, at which, importantly, Ted was present. But another conversation with her on her own suggests a rather different story. June, like many women of her age, cannot drive a car. Consequently, when she goes shopping she tends to do so with Ted, who does drive. Going shopping with Ted is an act that she feels has to result in acquisitions being made; if not, Ted – she says – will feel that the trip has been a waste of time. So, June frequently finds herself in the position where she buys things she knows to be not really suitable, just to accommodate to the practice of clothes shopping with Ted and to bring their shopping trips to a close. Notwithstanding her own personal frustrations with the lack of provision of clothing for women of her age and shape on the UK high street, June buys many items of clothing merely to keep Ted happy. The periodic ridding of her wardrobe using the medium of charities' neighbourhood bag-drops and the local charity shops is her primary way of managing this particular shopping accommodation.

Although the majority of these clothing discards are rejected for these reasons, a secondary thread is also evident in June's talk: failings in clothing design and manufacture. We hear here about skirt elastic that is so tight that it doesn't expand and about socks that would cause a thrombosis if they were to be worn. And then there's the jumper that for some reason doesn't look right worn either with or without a blouse, so it stays on for only ten minutes. All of these items of clothing are seen to be examples of clothes whose materiality refuses a corporeal body; clothes that in the materials of their construction constrict upon the presence of a living body in their wearing. Seemingly, this too is sufficient a reason to precipitate their ridding.

At the same time, Ted clearly felt encouraged, prompted and/or impelled by June's actions to subject his clothing to the same degree of scrutiny. This is how the couple begin to relate this act:

Nicky (again reading from diary as prompt): So we have one pair of Indian-type sandals.

June: Hand stitched in real leather, of course. These were mock Ecco. They weren't Ecco with the Velcro. They were an M&S version, thick soles, you know. Straps which fixed over with Velcro.

Nicky: 'Uncomfortable.'

Ted: I never wore them, only wore them once indoors.

Nicky: Why didn't you take them back?

Ted: Couldn't be bothered.

June: They were in a sale – not only that, he would put them on with his socks [laughter], so they were never going to look right.

Ted: They were weird really.

Nicky: Well why did you buy them then?

Ted: Well I needed something to wear indoors. Because I'd thrown a pair of slippers out – June said that I was shuffling around the house.

June: He says that they were uncomfortable, well I don't know whether they were uncomfortable but they were unsuccessful, put it that way ... And then of course we had these polo shirts.

Nicky: 'Bored with the colours.'

Ted: June said they didn't do anything for me – I wore them several times in the garden, odd job shirts. They just looked sissy really.

Nicky: Why did you buy them?

Ted: They were cheap.

Nicky: 'Four business shirts – no further use.' Suit shirts?

Ted: Work shirts.

Nicky: 'Slippers – dustbin.'

Ted: Well they were terrible Nicky – dreadful – they looked as though the mice had got into them. All the padded stuff was out of them and they stunk, and I'd worn them in the garden and all the backing was off of them, so when you walked it was squelch, squelch, squelch!

Ted's clothing discards appear at first sight to display similar characteristics to June's. There's the same reference to 'bad buys' (in his case clothes that had been in a sale and which were therefore cheap), to the no longer worn because of no further use (business shirts and ties) and to items that are seen – mainly by June – to do nothing for his embodiment. But what is also present here, which isn't in June's clothing discards, is the utterly worn-out, notably slippers that have fallen apart (and also a shirt with a ripped back). The other point of distinction is that June appeared to play a key role in pushing certain items of clothing out, declaring these to 'accentuate the negative'. Looking at clothing in an aesthetic sense and in ways that highlight embodiment, and not just in a way that looks for evidence of wear, is something I sense Ted finds neither easy nor comfortable. Instead, and suggestively, he prefers to rely on the visual judgements of his wife to jettison such clothing.

Having sorted through their clothes, what then happened to these things? The following extract, which directly follows the above discussion, conveys something of the complexities of their trajectories and the value judgements that shape these, as well as the household's conflicts over how to manage the ridding of various clothing items.

Nicky: So the slippers couldn't go to the charrie shop?

Ted: No way! You could never have walked in there again – they'd have pushed you out the door [laughter].

Nicky: They went in the bin then, but June's fashion shoes, as you called them, the van Dahl's which she reckoned were worn out .

June: They had to have a second chance [laughs].

Ted: Well if you compared the two there was no question.

June: [laughs heavily] There might have been ten minutes more wear left in mine but it's not that, it's the question of putting one's feet in them and discovering the imprint of this other person's foot is permanently there ...

Nicky: 'Three pairs of boxer shorts'?!

June: To the charrie shop??! [hysterical laughter]

Nicky: They don't take underwear usually.

June: Well they didn't know they'd got it!

Nicky: You mean you gave them the black bin bag full of it?

Ted: Obviously. I'd only worn one pair and they'd been washed. And the rest had never been worn

June: Oh dear, oh dear, oh dear!

Ted: They were snow white – you'd only have to smell them [raucous laughter].

Nicky: You wouldn't get near – 'Out with the tongs!!'

June: Well they should have gone in the jumble. Really!!

As is evident from the above, respectability figures centrally to the constitution of June's clothing discards' trajectories. Clothing matter that is not too worn and that which has apparent amounts of wear left in it is clearly designated as for the charity shop, and is usually dropped off at the charity shop nearest the supermarket car park, a matter of acknowledged ease and convenience. By contrast, other items are declared to be either 'jumble' or 'rubbish'. With long experience of making clothing and of helping out at jumble sales, June is an expert at making these sorts of clothing evaluations, and she makes these decisions rapidly. Critically, she also understands precisely how second-hand clothing relates to the absent presence of the body. By contrast, although Ted clearly understands that giving tatty, old things that are falling apart to a charity shop is not an option (the slippers), and that to do so would not just be disrespectful but constitutive of a loss of face to him, he either doesn't appreciate or is contesting the way in which charity shop donations are understood by June to preclude certain sorts of donations in clothing. The discussion of the boxer shorts is particularly revealing here. So, whilst for June (and for me) boxer shorts, and particularly washed ones, are not the sort of things that go to charity shops, for Ted it is 'madness' that they should be excluded from donation. Whereas evidence of washing connotes wearing, and therefore the absent presence of the body for June (and me), washing equates with the body's absence, that is cleanliness, for Ted.

A similar tale of contrasting value judgements emerges from what happens to the van Dahl shoes. Declared to be 'down at heel' and with too much trace of her absent presence present in their soles, June placed these shoes in a location that connotes 'rubbish' in this household, namely with the matter to go out for the weekly black sack refuse collection. Ted, however, on seeing them declared them to be 'fashion shoes' and rescued them for the charity-shop bag – to June's clear embarrassment. That he is able to do this is not just about his understanding of shoe aesthetics, but is in large part indicative of the way in which rubbish is managed in this household, and the way it is collected by the local authority. Here, as with Peggy and Harry in the previous chapter, dealing with rubbish declarations and placing them outside for collection is understood as a taken-for-granted facet of men's work in the day-to-day running of the household. So, in this household, rather than contest what she describes as the 'bin monitor's' practice, June once more accommodates, in this case to his value judgements as to what is and is not rubbish. That she does so, however, has much to do with the sorting and collection of various types of household rubbish that goes on in this part of the North-east. Indeed, it is precisely because Ted, in compliance with local authority requests, does the work of sorting out and grading the household's various categories of rubbish that he is able to rescue the van Dahl shoes.[1] It is tempting to speculate that had Ted and June been living in South Hightown the same van Dahl shoes would have been instantly jettisoned into the wheelie bin by June, where they might well have been unseen by Ted and routed into the waste stream rather than rescued for charity.

Ted and June's changed sleeping arrangements clearly had profound consequences for the future of certain things in their house, and were the precipitating events for a considerable amount of clothing ridding. As we see now with Peggy and Harry from the previous chapter, the same act of sleeping – or not – is as charged in the homes of other older couples in the ethnography.

As we have seen, Peggy and Harry live in a one-bedroom council bungalow on Wear Road in South Hightown. After visiting this couple for some while Peggy tells me that sleeping is something which she finds increasingly difficult. In part this is about inhabiting her increasingly arthritic body; to lie comfortably for her is a rare event. But sleep's absence is something which she also connects to her body's framing by drug regimes. Peggy takes what she describes as 'a daily cocktail' of drugs, which amounts to nearly twenty pills a day. One effect of this is that she finds herself dozing off at what she sees as odd times of the day, such as late morning and early afternoon. Sleeping through the night though is, for Peggy as it is for June, an impossibility. She frequently finds herself getting up in the middle of the night to doze in her chair in the living room. She does this, she says, when the snoring and choking noises from Harry get too bad to sleep. This is clearly an issue for Peggy as much as it is for June. Indeed, Peggy asks me for the loan of the tape recorder, just so that she can record her husband in full flow, so he can hear himself.[2] A few months on, just before modernisation work is to begin in their bungalow, Peggy tells me that she has taken matters into her own hands, insisting that they replace their current double bed, mattress and headboard with two single beds, single mattresses and headboards. She says that they are both tossing and turning so often in the night that it's impossible for either of them to get any sleep. Harry – like June's Ted – is not happy about this development, in itself an indication of its subversion of cultural norms. But Peggy has already ordered the new beds, mattresses and headboards from her catalogue and instructed Harry to sort out getting rid of the old ones. He has done so by activating his usual conduit – the man who lives on his own in the one-bedroom bungalow – if he wants them, to which the answer is 'yes'. Although yet to exit the bungalow when the fieldwork finished, the double bed, mattress and headboard will do so when the new mattresses arrive.

When I returned to Wear Road in the summer of 2004, Peggy proudly showed off their new single beds, mattresses, headboards and covers, whilst confirming that the old bed, mattress and headboard had indeed gone to their neighbour's – though quite where it might have gone from there she could only laugh and speculate on (see Chapter 3, note 14). More important, however, are the parallels and differences between Ted and June's and Harry and Peggy's sleep stories. Both stories centre on the corporealities of sleep and the potential for re-accommodating these corporealities within particular dwelling structures. For both Peggy and June, the impossibility of sleeping through the night is about their own bodies' changing sleep requirements in older age. But it is also about the impossibility of accommodating these changes within a cultural convention that frames sleeping in cohabitation in terms of sleeping in a shared bed. That both Ted and Harry snore in sleep makes their sleeping co-presence a huge issue for both women, but what is particularly interesting is both women's eventual insistence on and effecting of different sleep accommodations. How they do this is simultaneously a subversion of and accommodation to the normative: at the same time as resisting cultural convention completely, both Peggy and June mobilise the discourse of care to articulate the new arrangements, presenting this as enabling their partners' sleep to be undisturbed by their wakefulness. Ted and June's and Peggy and Harry's homes, however, offer entirely different possibilities for sleep's re-accommodation. So, whereas June can appropriate the spare bedroom in their house as her bedroom, Peggy's only option is to reconfigure the beds within their one bedroom. Although she can now get herself lying comfortably without disturbing Harry, she still has to lie awake listening to the snoring. As a consequence, Peggy has recently tried to sleep during the day, resorting to time rather than space to try to accommodate her need for sleep. She still finds herself having to retreat to the living room in the middle of the night, though. Whilst June can mobilise the space within the dwelling structure to re-accommodate sleep and make this particular dwelling structure accommodating again, Peggy's re-accommodation can only be partial, and is up against the limits of accommodation in this particular dwelling structure.

As we can see from the two stories, however, the effects of the dwelling structure are not just felt in physical sleep, but extend to the material culture of sleep itself. In reconfiguring their sleeping arrangements, both Ted and June and Harry and Peggy set in motion the things that surround and frame sleeping. In Harry and Peggy's case, this is literally the beds and bed-related matter – the double bed, mattress and headboard are got rid of and replaced, by single ones. In Ted and June's case, though, the beds and bed-related matter stay *in situ* whilst other things, including the people, move. Here it is the connections forged in dress between the sleeping and waking body that seems to precipitate the circulation, and related shake-out, of clothing. Seemingly for June, the waking body is regarded as needing clothing to be co-present in the room of sleeping, not to be stored in another bedroom. To re-accommodate physical sleep, then, is about the re-accommodation of sleep's material culture within the accommodation of the dwelling structure. As I show now, the same tendencies emerge in relation to accommodating children in sleep.

Accommodating children in sleep

As with cohabiting adults, there are clear cultural norms shaping the accommodation of children's sleep within English homes. When they are very young, children may sleep in their parent or parents' bedroom, but by the time they are sleeping for longer periods at one stretch their sleep is accommodated typically in a room of their own, at first in a cot and then in a bed. Whilst once commonplace in England – both Peggy and June, for example, recall sharing bedrooms and even beds with their sisters when young – sharing between siblings, even between siblings of the same gender, is now seen to be inappropriate. Instead, a room of their own is normative, enabling both the psychological development of the child and the accommodation of the child in things. As we see in this section, these cultural conventions require parents to accommodate their growing families in particular ways, but they also precipitate much in the way of circulating beds and bed-related matter. To address this I draw on two of the households in the ethnography with young children.

Ellie and Steve and Sandra and Rob

Ellie and Steve are in their very late 20s and early 30s, respectively, with two children, one six-years old and one eighteen-months. She, Steve and their children live in the old core of South Hightown, in a semi-detached cottage not dissimilar to, but larger than, those on Alternative Terrace. Ellie has a degree in social studies and works part time as a child protection social worker. Steve works in computing. At the start of the fieldwork, Ellie had recently got rid of the couple's cot, as Chloe, their youngest child, had moved on to sleeping in a bed. She did this by passing this cot and its mattress on to one of her friends who was expecting her first child; a path similar to that followed by this cot when it entered Ellie's house. It is a similar story in Sandra and Rob's house. Like Ellie and Steve, Sandra and Rob are in their early 30s and have two children; one is five, the other is a baby of coming up to a year. They both have degrees in health-care studies. Rob is a drug-addiction nurse. Sandra has her own business and the couple live in one of the terraced cottages on Alternative Terrace in South Hightown, in a house that used to be Rob's father's house until he bought it off him.[3] Sandra and Rob's first cot was second-hand when they got it from a friend of Sandra's. Having had Josh, Sandra had apparently declared that she wasn't going to go through 'all that again'. So, once Josh was clambering out of the cot and 'obviously needed a bed', she tried to get in touch with the friend to return the cot. This proved impossible, so the cot went over to her mother's house elsewhere in the region. Here it stayed, in the loft, for around four years, until Sandra was able to pass it on. This she did during the fieldwork, via 'a friend of a friend', meaning a friend of the mother of one of Josh's school friends. When she became pregnant with their second child, which she had during the fieldwork, Sandra was offered a smaller cot by her cousin – a cot that her cousin in turn had had second-hand and which she had used for all of her three children. This Sandra accepted – because this cot was clearly going to be a better option in the smallest bedroom in their house. It was this event which precipitated the ridding of the first cot, although this did not happen until late 2003, and Sandra kept that cot's mattress. When she acquired the new cot Sandra jettisoned its mattress in the wheelie bin, for reasons to do with its visual appearance – 'it was a bit bashed and had a rip in it, and anyway it had been in their garage for a few years', she says. Instead, she placed Josh's old cot mattress in it. Alice, however, has yet to sleep in her cot – she sleeps instead with her mother. Rob works nights. In early 2004, however, further government advice was issued to parents regarding 'sudden cot death syndrome', advising that all babies should sleep on newly purchased cot mattresses. Sandra is highly sceptical of such instructions, but nonetheless she has purchased a new cot mattress from Mothercare.[4] She says, 'However much you question it you don't want to risk your child.' At the moment Josh's old cot mattress lies underneath the cot on the carpet in Alice's room. Hating waste, Sandra somehow can't quite bring herself to throw it in the wheelie bin.

Around the same time that Sandra was dealing with buying a new cot mattress for Alice, she was offered a single bed with drawer space underneath it by a neighbouring mother who is also a grandmother. This (cabin) bed used to be the neighbour's daughter's when she lived with them. Sandra accepted this offer since it provided a better bed for Josh (it has built-in storage), and what she describes as 'Josh's little bed' has gone over to Rob's dad's council bungalow elsewhere in South Hightown, to be held over in store for Alice. Josh is now sleeping on this new bed, complete with the mattress, about which Sandra says, 'Well it was Ruth's (the neighbour's daughter) so I knew where it had come from, so all I did was give it a bit of a hoover-over!'

Given its intimate association with the body, getting rid of beds and particularly the related mattress-matter is an act that has strong resonances with the ridding of clothing. Like closely worn garments, mattresses – particularly those used without protective covers – have the capacity to absorb a variety of body traces, notably fluids, hair and skin. Moreover, as the debate over cot mattresses has highlighted, they are regarded as providing a suitable habitat for various bacteria as well as for parasites. Beds, and specifically mattresses, then are some of the most personalised of consumer objects. But, as we can see from the above, children's beds – including their mattresses – certainly do circulate between households. This is worthy of some comment.

The circulating cots and children's beds emerged here as yet another facet of the workings of the moral economies of mothers (Clarke 2000). Along with circulating maternity wear, baby clothes, baby toys and a whole host of baby-development aids such as walkers and high chairs, cots and children's beds are passed around between families with young children, and constitute clear evidence for the ways in which mothers, and particularly middle-class mothers, make new mothers (and generations) through the passage of baby-related and children's things.[5] But what the movement of the cots also seems to mark is the end of a particular phase of parenting. The passage-out of the cot then marks the closure of a particular period of family formation, and is also a sign of pregnancy's end for particular women – whereupon the cot is usually released into a newly forming family, and often one with a close social tie to the ridding family, be this through kinship, friendship and/or locality. Of note too, however, is the effect of regulatory discourse on the practice of cot circulation. This is considerable. So, whereas both Ellie's outgoing cot and the various incoming cots to Sandra and Rob's came and went with their mattresses, Sandra now feels compelled to hold back Josh's mattress from the cot she gets rid of. Conjoining, as it does, risk and maternal responsibility with parenting knowledge, passing on a cot mattress to another mother to potentially put at risk another baby is something that Sandra would not do. Indeed, to do so would be to risk becoming the ultimate Bad Mother, the woman whose (unthinking) actions brought about the Death of the Child.

Beyond the cots, the passing around and holding-over of children's beds disclosed in Sandra and Rob's household is also significant for the ways in which it shows accommodating children's sleep to be about children's changing corporealities. Josh's 'little bed', which will in turn become 'Alice's little bed', is a configuration regarded as appropriate for the body of a pre-school age child. The larger cabin-style bed, however, with increased storage capacity, is seen by all this family as a more appropriate bed for Josh now. For Josh too it works to differentiate him from his baby sister: he proudly tells me that he has 'a big bed – she's got a cot!' For Sandra and Rob it provides more space to accommodate his things. Both Sandra and Rob fear though that this bed may be no more than a temporary sleeping place for Josh. Mindful of the current fashions in children's beds in places like IKEA, where bunk-style beds have been adapted to incorporate a work/study/PC station area below an elevated sleeping area, they are all too well aware of what Josh is still blissfully ignorant of, that his new bed is the previous generation's answer to accommodating the sleeping child and their things in one small room.

Accommodating children's sleep, however, is not just about the provision of appropriately configured children's beds. It is also about creating appropriate rooms for children, through things. As the only couple to have had a new baby during the ethnography, and the only couple who reconfigured a child's room in things during the fieldwork, it is once again Sandra and Rob who are highlighted here, this time in relation to their creation of a nursery for Alice.[6] Unlike their practice with their first child, which saw them putting together a nursery before his birth, projecting and imagining their future family in the domestic, Alice's arrival saw the gradual creation of her room after her birth, in time snatched when Josh was at pre-school and when she was asleep. In itself this is indicative of the complexities of accommodating a second child into domestic space and into the routines and rhythms of a household's everyday life. It is also an elaboration of an already established family identity rather than the projection of a future family. However, creating Alice's room was a complicated act of doing things with things, in which Alice's presence worked to displace and get rid of other things. Formerly Alice's room was Rob and Sandra's 'junk room'. It was where Rob stored his clay-pigeon shooting guns and his various fishing rods, and an old TV of Sandra's also used to live here, along with an old hi-fi system and speakers given to her as an eighteenth birthday present. The guns and fishing rods had been in what the couple described as 'a makeshift cupboard'. On deciding that this had to become Alice's room, Rob set about the cupboard with a sledgehammer – 'he likes doing things like that', says Sandra. This matter – old chipboard – went in the wheelie bin, as not good enough even to burn on the couple's fire. Sandra then set about stripping off layers and layers of wallpaper: 'It took me absolutely ages – there were layers down to when Rob was little; stuff with soldiers on it.' This too went in the wheelie bin, slowly – bag by bag over a month. Sandra then re-wallpapered the room in pink, with a paper with a pink-princess motif. Unusually for them, since they tend to be the recipients of the things that other people known to them want rid of, the couple also bought a pink carpet, and a small wardrobe, a chest of bedside drawers and a bookcase from Argos (Figure 4.1).

The guns have been moved to a new storage place in the kitchen, and the fishing tackle has gone down the garden into the shed which Rob built as a home gym, where he has his punch ball. The TV is over in Sandra's mother's loft and the hi-fi system went to the tip, 'it was too old to be any good to anybody – a shame, but there you are' (Sandra).

In creating Alice's room from a former storeroom, Sandra and Rob engage in acts of destructive ridding and displacement, but in so doing they are also struggling to accommodate their growing family within the accommodation that is their home, which emerges here as a dwelling structure that is shifting from being accommodating to an accommodation. As Sandra said on one occasion, 'When it was just me and Rob, or even me, Rob and Josh, it was OK, but now we're bursting at the seams in here.' Feeling like this has precipitated a number of discussions about moving house, but for various reasons this is on hold: Rob wants to retrain as a paramedic nurse, which will mean a large pay cut to begin with; and the house has deep emotional ties for him, for this is the house he has lived in all his life. Indeed, Alice's room used to be his bedroom. At the back of their minds, too, is whether to emigrate: Rob's brother lives in Australia and the couple are 'sick of this country – it's a better life over there' (Rob). But Rob does not want to leave his elderly father behind. So, for the moment, the family are staying put, and solving some of their storage problems by using the storage space in the houses of both their parents. However, Sandra and Rob's struggles to accommodate are not just about an additional child, but this child in things. Already Alice's room is full of her things: mobiles hang from the ceiling, so too does a clothes holder; the bookcase is stuffed full of soft toys, and a few first baby books, and the cot too has toys in it and on its rails. These are the things that people bought to mark

Figure 4.1: Alice's room   Figure 4.2: Alice's stuff

her birth and for her first Christmas. As Sandra says, 'If people didn't keep buying her all of this stuff we wouldn't have this problem!' (Figure 4.2).

It is the connection between things as possessions – 'Alice's stuff', in Sandra's words – and her sleeping place that connects what is going on in this household with Ted and June's re-accommodations of sleep. As we see from both instances, sleeping in any one room is not just about beds and bed-related matter, but spills over to include other things too; notably the clothes that we put on (or not) or which someone else puts on us when we are very small, and some of our most personal possessions, including jewellery and family photographs, or – when we are children – our toys. Seemingly then, when we live in a dwelling structure, it is not enough simply to have a place to sleep but we need to surround ourselves with at least some of our things as we do, just to make it accommodating of us and to us. So, when we fabricate a bedroom for a new person, as is going on when Sandra and Rob make a nursery for Alice, it is of critical importance that the act of making is simultaneously an act of filling it with things, things that come to be seen as possessions. It is for the same reason that when June moved out of the bedroom she shared previously with Ted, things moved with her. Moreover, as was clear from this enactment, the things that moved with her actually had to be seen to be her, to define her. So much so that that which was no longer her (if indeed some of it had ever been) was got rid of. Re-accommodating sleep emerges here as a microcosm of the acts of moving out and moving in; an act which provides the space for a re-evaluation of the self in things through the mobilities in things that are set in chain by the movement of the person.

Accommodating visitors

As with cohabitation and accommodating children in sleep, having visitors to stay in English homes is suffused with cultural conventions. At minimum, such visitors are regarded as needing a place to lie and something to sleep on. This could be a sofa bed in a living room, or a futon, or it could be the settee – as with Jason in Chapter 3 – but for the majority of participants in the ethnography, the expectation and taken-for-granted assumption was that staying-over visitors should ideally be accommodated in a bed in a spare bedroom. For some households participating in the ethnography, this was not a problem; for others, as we will see, such cultural norms worked to effect considerable upheavals in both inhabitation and things. Having visitors to stay had quite dramatic effects on the accommodation of sleep and of things.

Geoff and Hilary

Geoff and Hilary are in their 50s and live in a large nineteenth-century stone-built detached house with a walled garden in the old core of South Hightown. They have lived here for some four years, moving here from another of the Durham villages in a relocation which they describe as partly inspired by the need to find more space for their things and partly an investment move. Like Geoff, Hilary has a first degree, but she also has a higher degree. Hilary works full time at a senior level in local government; Geoff, who was born in the North-east, recently took early retirement from the engineering industry. He now busies himself with running the house and local conservation volunteering. Hilary's family is from the West Midlands. The couple do not have children.

Geoff and Hilary have an active social life and a considerable social network. They are both amateur musicians and Hilary sings in a local choir, as well as playing tennis regularly. With a large house of three storeys, Geoff and Hilary have two guest bedrooms – one double and one single – and they also have a guest bathroom. Both bedrooms are kept prepared for staying-over guests, so it is no difficulty for this couple to accommodate friends at short notice, as they do regularly. Their house is an accommodation that can also readily accommodate visitors in ways that are accommodating. For other households, though, their homes posed greater problems in visitor accommodation. On the one hand there are those like Peggy and Harry, Sandra and Rob and Ellie and Steve, who are already up against the limits of accommodation in their dwelling structures.[7] On the other, there are those who live alone and who have the room to accommodate staying-over guests but for whom such accommodations are in various ways more problematic and anxiety-laden than they appear to be for Geoff and Hilary. To open this up, I draw on two further study households, both of them comprising middle-aged, married and formerly married women living alone.

Judy

Judy is in her late 50s and is university educated. Born in Essex, she and her family moved around a lot in her early years, as her father was a teacher in the armed forces. When she was young they lived in Libya and Singapore, before returning to the UK for her secondary school education. Judy has been divorced for approximately sixteen years. She has two adult sons, one of whom works in the film industry in London, whilst the other lives relatively nearby with his partner and is employed in club/bar management. Judy lives in a three-bedroom semi-detached suburban-style house with a garden, on the same estate as Ted and June on the outskirts of the Newcastle conurbation. She has lived here since her divorce and it is in this house that she brought up her two children, as a single parent. Prior to this, Judy and her ex husband lived in four other houses in Newcastle, and also abroad, in the Middle East. Judy's elderly mother also lives nearby, in sheltered accommodation, and although Judy works full time (in university administration), she spends a great deal of her time caring for her. Judy takes her to numerous and various hospital appointments; visits most evenings on her way home from work to make sure that she is alright and to talk with her; and she does her weekly shopping for her every weekend. Judy also has a dog, which she walks daily in the mornings before work, and three cats.

Pauline

Pauline is also in her 50s, though she is a good few years younger than Judy, and at first sight she is everything that Judy is not: confident, out-going and with an enormous friendship network. Pauline lives in one of the terraced cottages on Alternative Terrace in South Hightown. Like Judy she has a dog. Pauline tells me that she has been here for about twelve years, since she separated from her husband. Unlike Judy, however, Keith and Pauline's separation is one that has been about trying to 'live together apart', as Pauline describes it. So, the couple have their own houses but visit one another at set times during the week. Keith comes to Pauline's on Thursday evenings and nights, whilst she goes over to his house in another village in County Durham at the weekends. Ellie is Pauline's adult daughter; her son lives in the same village as Keith.[8] Pauline originally hails from Liverpool and moved to the North-east when she met Keith, who was then active in local housing politics. The couple lived initially in Newcastle, before moving to South Hightown. Pauline works part time as a therapist, combining this with her own semi-professional singing career. Like Judy though, Pauline seldom has staying-over visitors to her house, other than Keith and the grand children.

✳

One late afternoon in the first month of the fieldwork I am round at Judy's. My field diary recounts the scene:

Judy says, 'You must come and see my bathroom.' This she describes with pride, and she tells me all that she's done. She has put up a

new blind (pale blue, from B&Q), a rail and shower curtain at the
back of the bath and another rail and curtain at the front side of
the bath. Both curtains are cream and plain. She describes this
process as one that 'nearly killed me'. Apparently she kept doing an
hour and then going and sitting down in front of the TV. All these
things were bought from B&Q. The old curtain – there for 16 years
– which was blue with flowers on it – had got covered with black
mould and slime. Judy proclaims, 'I threw it out – I actually threw
something out!!!' It went out in the black sack refuse collection. She's
also cleaned all the tiles – pale blue – with a Dettox anti-bath-mould
cleaner, which she confesses is only the second time she's done this
since she's lived in the house. And she's also bought a new bath mat
from Fenwick's.[9] The old bath mat went the same way as the old
shower curtain. (February 2003)

When I ask Judy about these various enactments, she tells me that they
were prompted initially by a problem that was having structural effects on
the house. Somehow, water from the shower was getting behind the back of
the bath and trickling down the wall into the kitchen below, where it had
begun to cause a large amount of plaster above the sink to lift. The installation of the curtain rail at the back of the bath was an attempt to rectify this
problem, but as I draft this chapter – almost a year later – the problem has
yet to be solved and the plaster is still coming off the kitchen wall. Possibly
as important for the trajectory of things though is another revelation: Judy's
elder son and his then new girlfriend were coming up to stay the following
weekend. Looking at the changes enacted by Judy, particularly their emphasis on cleaning up (the tiles) and the ridding of old and, by her admission,
'filthy' things (the shower curtain and bath mat), my sense is that what is
actually going on in this partial makeover of the bathroom in things has a
very great deal to do with the impending visit of a potentially significant but
as yet unknown other. What Judy appears to be doing with her bathroom
is to look at this room in things through the eyes of the visiting other, and
to see herself as others, particularly female others, might see her. Perceived
to be unclean and grime-laden tiling, mould-covered curtains and old bath
mats have – through the dirt present and visible in their material surfaces
– the capacity to suggest a set of risky social meanings: un-cleanliness, uncar-
ing, not respectable (see also Chapter 3). Furthermore, whilst Judy might be
prepared for well-known others to make such inferences about her through
the state things are in, should they choose to, to risk the new and unknown
girlfriend making them is – I would suggest – an altogether more risky social
practice. Indeed, not only would such things constitute a potential source
of shame for her elder son, but they also have the capacity to comment on
Judy's investments (or lack of them) in particular versions of femininity. My
interpretation of these events, then, would be to see them as a partial accommodation to the normative. In ridding and wasting what she perceived to
be old and dirt-encrusted things, and replacing them with the new, and in
setting about the tiles with anti-mould cleaner, Judy is acknowledging in her

practice the power of the normative; cleaning up, throwing out and buying the new to accommodate to a set of social identities (mother, woman) that are judged through a normative located in the surface appearance of things (Chapter 3).

All this has considerable resonance with a set of enactments at Pauline's in the early summer of 2003. Like Judy, Pauline rarely throws anything out. However, one day when I am over at Janet's house Pauline comes down the street to tell me that she is literally in the throes of throwing four mugs in her wheelie bin. Pauline goes on to tell me how she is in the midst of tidying-up 'me minging house' in preparation for having staying-over visitors. My notes at the time recount Pauline's turn of phrase: 'These are going to have to go.', she says, 'They're like drinking out of plant pots! I can't think why I bought them!' She goes on to add: 'This [said whilst lobbing them in the wheelie bin] is most unlike me, but I really can't think of anyone who'd want them or who'd thank me for them.' Later that same day, when I went round to Pauline's, she showed me the four new replacement china mugs which she had been out and bought.

Having drunk several cups of tea in Pauline's kitchen from the jettisoned mugs, I can indeed vouch for her judgement that they were like drinking out of plant pots. They were shaped like clay flower pots and were large and manufactured from a thick pottery. Furthermore, their shape made holding them by the handle difficult and allowed the tea to cool very quickly. What is interesting about these mugs though is Pauline's additional comment. Not only does she clearly regard these mugs as a mistake-category purchase, but she sees this mistake as a major disruption to her narrative of her own sense of self. On another occasion, Pauline represents herself to me in terms which emphasise her own investments in the alternative style of the bricoleur, and her immense pride in this. So, having bought these things and having them in the house is certainly a problem for her self-narration. But what is also problematic is their ridding. As Pauline says, throwing things away in the wheelie bin is 'not her'. Instead, she usually effects ridding – of her things, many of her daughter's things and things other people give her to get rid of – through her vast social network, mapping things with people who she thinks will appreciate them. But, as she says here, Pauline cannot imagine anyone thanking her for these mugs; they are not the sort of matter that she can rid through the gift, precisely because their form and their aesthetic are seen to be discordant with her sense of self. The wheelie bin is the only place Pauline can think of in which to place these things.

There seems little doubt that, like Judy, Pauline uses the imminent event of being visited to see her house in things through the eyes of the other. Indeed, she tells me how she has made a huge effort to clear the house up prior to the friends' arrival, placing fresh cut flowers from the garden (not the supermarket) in the spare bedroom, and buying the new china mugs. Furthermore, and again like Judy, she uses the event of the visiting to destroy certain problematic consumer objects, things whose physical presence poses problems for the narration of identity. Indeed, whilst Pauline's jettisoned mugs were clean and un-chipped – things which, unlike Judy's shower curtain and bath mat, did not pronounce their history in consumption in their material surface – the known experience of drinking tea from them was sufficient to get rid of them. Although primarily about the narration of identity through things and the ability of certain things to disrupt this, the trajectory of the mugs certainly testifies to the power of the staying-over visitor to effect the ridding and wasting of things.[7]

But to return to the events of visitor anticipation, it is perhaps not entirely a point of coincidence that both these events occurred in the households of two women living alone who rarely have others visiting them and staying-over. Both Judy and Pauline, through their actions in advance of being visited, demonstrate that they are well aware of the power of the normative as this effects women, its relation to the appearance in things of their homes and particularly to the apparent cleanliness of things in their homes. Furthermore, in enacting intense bouts of thorough cleaning in preparation for the accommodation of the visitor, they acknowledge in their practice how their social relations of inhabitation allow them to resist (or ignore) this normative in their routine everyday (non-cleaning) practices. The presence of the visitor, however, is clearly understood by both Pauline and Judy to constitute the entry of the normative into their homes.[10] Normally excluded, and in Pauline's case rejected by her subversion of conventional cultural norms of living together in cohabitation, the entry of the normative through the figure of the visitor has an intense power to trigger an evaluation of the self in things. It is this, I suspect, which lies behind the ridding and wasting of certain – considered problematic, troublesome and/or inappropriate – things to the wheelie bin, rather than their temporary displacement elsewhere in the house.

Finally, however, I want to highlight a key distinction between Pauline and Judy's accommodation of their visitors. As Judy told me on another visit, to accommodate her elder son and his girlfriend did not end with the bathroom makeover. Rather, and unlike Pauline, Judy gave over her bedroom and her (double) bed to this couple, transplanting herself to the spare bedroom and its single bed. In the process she disclosed herself to be what she described to me as 'the thoroughly modern mother!' Moreover, in this way she hoped to differentiate herself from her own parents' attitudes to accommodating adult children in sleep – 'strictly separate beds!' But what this accommodation also entailed was a further set of preparatory works. Like Pauline, Judy regards her bedroom as 'a tip'; it's the place in which things which have no apparent home can be dumped and where piles of clothes in varying stages of laundering accumulate. In short, it is the ultimate back-stage zone. To accommodate her son and his girlfriend within this room, however, required that Judy devoted time and energy to sorting out her bedroom in things, by imposing a degree of visual order on what others might potentially judge to be disorder. In so doing, and in a series of manoeuvres which resonate with June's sleep re-accommodation, Judy found herself casting out some of her not inconsiderable accumulation in clothing, including clothes given to her by others but which had never made it into the wardrobes and others which were piled up in front of it. These she removed to the spare room before placing them out in a charity donation collection drop. In re-accommodating her own sleep to accommodate the sleep of others, albeit only temporarily,

Judy's actions show that to disturb the spatialities of sleep in homes is to set in motion a trail of other things. As with June, it is clothing which is got rid of in this re-accommodation, precisely I suggest because of the way in which clothing – specifically the taking on and off of our clothes – connects the states of the sleeping and the waking body.

Conclusions

In this chapter we see how ridding is central to routine, mundane every-day life: at the same time as being integral to key, but relatively infrequent, moments in which our inhabitations of dwelling structures are either rup-tured or disturbed, such as moving in or modernisation, ridding also just goes on, as part of mundane ordinary life in inhabitation. Sleeping (and its accommodation) is just one instance of this. As all three sections disclose though, the ridding that is integral to sleep's re-accommodation often goes well beyond beds and bed-related matter. It spills over to include clothing, previous rooms in decoration, things formerly held in storage, and even – as with Pauline's and Judy's visitors – the contents of bathrooms and kitchens. Indicative primarily of a material culture of sleep which frames the sleeping body not just through particular sorts of beds but as a waking body, and which positions this body in proximity to the storage of its clothing, it is inevitable that when sleep gets displaced so too do our clothes. And disturb-ing things always contains the potential for things to be got rid of. But, as we also see, ridding frequently occurs in close temporal juxtaposition with acquisition. Pauline's mugs, Judy's bathroom accessories, and Sandra and Rob's cot are all examples of things that are got rid of because more appro-priate things are either acquired or projected in to their place. Not only does this testify to the coincidence of and close relation between appropriation and divestment, but it suggests that certain of the things to hand around us are provisional accommodations. Open to comparison with other potentially more suitable things that are either readily available through retail outlets or which are offered up through social networks, such things are continually open to being rid from dwelling structures.

Getting rid of the material culture of sleep, however, is done in two dis-tinctly different ways. One the one hand, we see through this chapter how households go to considerable lengths to avoid ridding through wasting, by passing things on, handing them on through social networks and using rid-ding things to make these socialities. This is particularly the case with chil-dren's beds and clothing, and I will have more to say about this in the next chapter. On the other hand, we see how in other instances ridding things is intrinsically connected to their wasting and destruction. Pauline's plant-pot mugs and Judy's bathroom accessories are both instances of this, but June's comments about various items of clothing also make clear how she regarded their only appropriate ridding trajectory to be wasting. In all these instances the destruction of these particular things was of critical importance to their divestment. This requires elaboration.

In all these instances, destruction relates to the perceived impossibility (rather than possibility) of gifting. Pauline's 'no one would thank me for them' comment in relation to the plant-pot mugs is critical here. To get rid by passing on, or as Carol expressed it in relation to her second-hand three-piece suite (Chapter 3) 'by getting someone else to take them off my hands', is fundamentally about being able to imagine certain things being handled by others in new social lives. It requires the divestor to project these things into another social context (either known or imagined) and – as a consequence – to project themselves into this context. This is readily achievable in relation to certain things, notably the material culture of childhood, which allows mothers to imagine themselves as part of a wider sociality of mothers. But clearly, certain other sorts of things are far more difficult to project with. So, and in order to forestall the unimaginable and unwanted projection, the only safe course is wasting, destruction.

Intriguingly, however, and in contrast to normative practices of mothers, the material culture of children's sleep is becoming increasingly difficult to project with. Framed through regulatory discourses of risk, once grown out of by one child, the mattresses that go with any one cot are increasingly likely to be jettisoned, as Sandra did, via the wheelie bin; made waste because they are too socially and culturally risky to hand on. It was a similar story with many of the other discarded mattresses in the ethnography. Posture sprung, bulky and impossible to accommodate in cars – other than on the roof racks of estate cars or MPVs – these were the things which those living in South Hightown resorted to ringing the council to carry away, via the bulky waste collection service. Either that, or – like Claire and Nathan – they burnt them in their gardens. Such wasting in ridding is indicative of the potency of the absent presence of the body and the bodily. Mattresses are akin to the garments worn closest-in; they are things which have the capacity to absorb into their materiality the corporeal absent presence, and to be haunted by its proximity. So, whilst some might disregard such cultural prohibitions – like Sandra, because they know the body it has come from; or like Peggy because of the certitude that surrounds her practices of mattress care – for others to waste these things in their ridding is the appropriate, indeed the only, thing to do. Wasting, here, works to dissipate the corporeal absent presence, by making waste the configuration that holds the haunting.

I want to close this chapter, however, by returning once more to the connections between sleeping and dwelling. As all the instances discussed above disclose, a dwelling structure's capacity to hold sleeping bodies appropriately and to allow them to sleep well (physically and culturally) is critical to its continued status as an accommodating home. If sleep is disturbed, and can not be re-accommodated through working with the material culture of sleep, the dwelling structure shifts to becoming merely an accommodation. At a premium in relation to households with growing families, for whom this transition has long been recognised as a trigger to moving house, we see in this chapter how this does not go away in older age. Indeed, it is precisely because they have not downsized that Ted and June are able to continue to sleep well in their house, which remains, as a result, an accommodating accommodation for them. In contrast, for Peggy, their bungalow is strictly an accommodation; somewhere she lives in but does not dwell. This, I would argue, has more than a little to do with the fact that she can barely sleep there.

NOTES

1 The work of sorting and grading the rubbish in this household is enacted in the garage. The garage is also where Ted does his wood-carving and where he does many of his DIY jobs.

2 Interestingly, even when hearing the recording of his snoring in sleep, Harry continued to deny that this was actually him, protesting that this sound could have been the neighbour through the wall. Harry, of course, has a point: he has no means of knowing that this sound is him since he was only present in sleep. For Peggy, this response only worked to further her exasperation with Harry, whose capacity to dispute obvious 'proof' is portrayed to others by her as further 'proof' of his intransigence.

3 Like many of those who live on Wear Road, Rob is 'born-and-bred' in South Hightown, and is another example of the persistence of this form of dwelling in the village (see also, Chapters 1 and 3). Sandra, however, is from the West Midlands, and the couple met at university.

4 Mothercare is a UK retailer primarily stocking baby-care products, prams and buggies, young children's clothing, and a small range of maternity wear and nursing bras. It has a presence on most UK high streets and appeals to mass-market value.

5 The social significance of Claire and Nathan's burning of Abigail's cot (Chapter 3) is brought into relief here. It is indicative of Claire's refusal to make connections between herself and other proximate mothers and between Abigail and their children. The burning of the cot is an example of how destruction can make distinction.

6 Carol and John and Claire and Nathan also engaged in this practice post modernisation, but since these makeovers occurred after the end of the fieldwork, they are not included here. Although their room redecorations resonate strongly with Sandra and Rob's creation of a nursery, there is one key difference – both couples painted and carpeted the children's new bedrooms in a colour chosen by their daughters, pink.

7 For some of these households, notably the residents of Wear Road, accommodating visitors was not part of everyday life. With their families living either close by or on the same street and with few relatives living at a distance, their lives carry on without needing to make such accommodations. Visiting here is of the daily and/or weekly popping-in variety. For those like Sandra and Rob and Ellie and Steve, with friends and family spread rather more widely, accommodating visitors was more of an issue. However, whilst their ideal was Geoff and Hilary's accommodation, the practice in their homes was a sofa bed in the living room at best. It is also worth highlighting that June's reclamation of the spare room in their house for her sleep itself poses other problems for sleep accommodation. To accommodate staying-over guests, June would either have to revert to sleeping with Ted or the guests would have to sleep on the sofas.

8 Once again, we see in Pauline and Keith's children some of the same intense attachment to place disclosed in relation to Wear Road (Chapter 3). As with Rob, and as with those who have 'returned', this attachment is distinctly middle class, and contrasts markedly with its expression on Wear Road, where extended families live out their entire lives on the same street. However, such attachment to place stands in contrast to the mobilities displayed by Pauline and Judy or, for that matter, Ted and June and Geoff and Hilary. It is a clear marker of how contemporary dwelling can be achieved through place attachment, and of how such attachment transcends any straightforward identification with social class.

9 Fenwick's is a large department store with branches in many Northern cities in the UK.

10 As a postscript to this, though, I should add that Pauline's visitors were the perfect guests, in that they brought with them a gift, in this case a decorative table lamp in a Victorian style. This now sits in a corner of Pauline's kitchen, as a permanent reminder of them and their stay. As well as effecting the ridding of things, the visitor and the act of visiting are frequently the medium for the entry of new things into the house; things which Pauline's actions suggest require them to be displayed, rather than hidden away or relocated.

11 As others have commented, visitors – real and imagined – exert powerful effects on what is done to rooms and on the stability of rooms in things (Clarke 2002). This was certainly a recurrent thread in the ethnography. Participants talked about clearing up for visitors; about

how they used to clear up prior to my initial visits, but about how they didn't bother any longer; about how certain rooms were suitable for visitors to see but not others; and apologised for 'the mess' in their kitchens and bathrooms when they hadn't washed up or when there were piles of unlaundered clothes on the floor. These acts of clearing up were usually all ones involving the tidying up and putting away of things; of re-ordering the displacement tendencies of consumption in everyday life within households. All, however, are indicative of the visitor's identification with the normative.

Chapter 5

Collections, clothing and toys: the accommodations of everyday life

In this chapter I turn to consider some rather more familiar consumer objects than beds, mattresses and the material culture of sleep, focusing specifically on collections, children's clothing and toys. As will become clear, there are reasons for focusing on these particular objects, notably that they are central to the ways in which we inhabit our homes through things. Furthermore, the practices that frame the objects' lives in domestic space illuminate the primary temporal registers of everyday life, and of the social life of objects in the home. These registers encompass the enduring and the transient. Enduringness and transience, however, are shown here to connect fundamentally to the mobility and immobility of things as constituted by practices of inhabitation in dwelling structures.

The chapter begins by examining how collections are accommodated within the households participating in the ethnography. Comprising some of the most enduring of objects in the study households, these collections are for the most part prominently displayed. Placed in display cabinets and locations out of the way of the ebb and flow of people moving around and through the dwelling structure, collections comprise some of our most intensely cared for accommodations within the domestic. Used to narrate a life being lived and to memorialise lives lived, they were the things that invariably were not got rid of during the fieldwork, as well as the things which participants were most anxious to constitute social futures for. In contrast to collections, both children's clothing and toys move around and through the rooms of the dwelling structure. However, whilst both sets of things do pass through dwelling structures, the accommodation of children's clothing is shown to be more transient than many toys. The transience of children's clothing is demonstrated to be intimately bound up in practices of laundering. In contrast, whilst toys certainly do move around the house, as they are played with and tidied up, they endure in homes in ways which children's clothing frequently does not. The chapter reflects on the similarities and dissimilarities between accommodating collections, children's clothing and toys in dwelling structures; highlights the correspondence between holding and enduring and mobility and transience, and emphasises that, whilst the vast majority of these transient things are rid in ways which connect to their re-use and redistribution, others are deliberately and intentionally wasted. As the chapter makes clear, the relations of love are present in both acts of redistribution and acts of wasting. As with the previous chapter, I close by highlighting the importance of mundane practices of inhabitation to constituting accommodating homes and to understanding contemporary dwelling.

Accommodating collections

Collecting is a practice which manifested itself in various ways across almost all the households participating in the ethnography and, more than any other, it disclosed the class distinctions between them. In a certain sense all the households in the ethnography could be regarded as having collections, through their use of storage systems to display, as well as hold and order, consumer objects such as CDs, DVDs and videos. In this section, though, my interest is in things that were represented to me by participants as 'collections', that is assemblages of related objects acquired for their relatedness and whose meaning is located in this relation, but also in relation to their authoring subjects. Of primary concern here, though, is the manner in which collections are accommodated within domestic space. As things whose enduringness is critical in the narration of the self, accommodating these collections safely and securely mattered. Yet, to accommodate in this way is double-edged: the enduringness that is a product of their protection and safe display brings with it a weightiness which I show to be felt most acutely by those whose accommodations in collections span the temporal registers of generations.

On Wear Road, to have a collection or collections in things was something that three of the four adult female household members took for granted.[1] As we saw in Chapter 3, Peggy has various collections, all of them comprising things that are constituted by their manufacturers and retailers as 'collectables'. There are three collections, all of them in china, and all are displayed in the living room of the bungalow: 302 thimbles with place names on them, Ainsley china and a set of pastoral female figures. The 302 thimbles are housed in various identical display cabinets, bought specifically for their safe keeping from a collectors' shop in Scarborough. The various china pieces are located on the mantelpiece over the gas fire, on the window ledge and on and in the couple's display cabinet (Figures 5.1 and 5.2).

In Carol and John's house, the collections are a set of ceramic pigs, whose faces Carol finds appealing, and a set of cottage-style houses manufactured by Lilliput Lane, a mass-market manufacturer of 'collectables'. The pigs and the cottages stand on the household's display cabinet and in the hearth. Christine's collection is almost identical to Peggy's; it's a set of china figures of women in pastoral dress. These live on the window ledge and mantelpiece in the household's living room, and on the display cabinet.

Another couple, Sharon and Barry, live elsewhere on the Rivers estate. They are in their early 40s and have a Rottweiler dog, Zak. They live in a one-bedroom bungalow of a similar size and design to Peggy and Harry's,

Figure 5.1: Peggy's thimbles

Figure 5.2: Peggy's Ainsley, china and memorabilia

but unlike Peggy and Harry they are owner-occupiers, having bought the bungalow, which they had rented for some years, a year ago. Barry and Sharon both work shifts at a hotel in Durham, in the kitchens and as a chambermaid, respectively. The bungalow though is Barry's primary project. He spends almost all his free time working on it, has recently installed his own loft conversion and is currently working on installing a new fitted kitchen. The irony of the loft conversion, however – which is not lost on Barry – is that this has yet to provide the couple with any extra space for themselves. Instead, it is the primary storage zone for the major part of Sharon's large collection of porcelain dolls. Amounting currently to some 150, these dolls are also in the couple's bedroom, and on the top of the display cabinet in their living room. As Barry jokes to his friends: 'I built a loft conversion to house a load of fucking dolls!!'

Early on in the ethnography I attempted to get these four women to reflect on why the collection was important to them, and why they collected what they did. To my surprise, at least initially, they seemed to find this difficult to answer and difficult to narrate a story around. Responses such as, 'I don't really know – perhaps it was something to do with seeing them at a collectors' fair one day at the hotel that got me started' (Sharon), or 'perhaps it was me mother that got me started, I don't know' (Peggy), were typical, as well as indicative of the futility of pursuing this line of enquiry any further. Instead, and what emerges much more forcefully when we consider the extent of this practice in this area of South Hightown, is the normativity of collecting as a practice amongst women, and its connections to the making of social respectability.

Looking across the various collections of individual women, what seems to matter here is not just the similarity in their content, but their display and their visibility in display to real and imagined others. In part this connects to normative practices of furnishing houses and bungalows on this estate. Along with a fashionable three-piece suite, all these households included in their living rooms a display cabinet comprising a lower cupboard and, above this, glass-fronted cupboards, with shelves inside. Having such an item appeared to be normative in this area of South Hightown; throughout the ethnography I did not encounter one household on the Rivers estate without one. But, merely having this piece of furniture is not enough. Instead, having seems to require that the furniture's capacity to store and display valued things be satisfied, in much the same way that Peggy and Harry's new TV table's obvious gap seemed to require that this be filled with a DVD player (Chapter 3). So, having the furniture suggests the necessity of having a collection. But, it doesn't solve the problem – and I think it is a problem for these women – of what to collect. Their solution, I think, is to look around them, using the socialities of their everyday lives – including their mothers, sisters and friends as well as their routine shopping trips to the high street – for suggestions as to what things might be both appropriate and acceptable as collections. It is, I suggest, this safety in the known and assumed practices of others which accounts for the prevalence of the manufactured and retailed 'collectable' on this particular estate.[2] But what this manufactured collection also confers is respectability through social conformity. Thinking back to a previous project (Gregson and Crewe 2003), in which collections of things like snow domes, 1950s Pyrex dishes and Fuzzy-Felts loomed large, and in which collecting was practised through the appropriation of everyday consumer objects from previous decades, almost all of them sourced through a variety of second-hand outlets, the differences between these and the objects and practices of collecting discussed above are considerable. To collect in ways that encompass the kinds of self-determination, knowingness, and the mobilisation of irony and nostalgia disclosed in that project, and to display such things in this part of South Hightown would be unthinkable. Instead, in this area what matters acutely is to fit in with and/or out-do the neighbours' valuations in things, not subvert or contest them.

As we will see shortly, elsewhere in South Hightown a very different form of collecting practice is in evidence. For the moment, however, and as a bridge to this, it is worth looking at a different version of the manufactured collection in another household. Linda and Paul are in their 50s. They have been married for nearly 30 years and have two adult children, who no longer live with them. They and their two cats live in what they describe to me as a 'semi-detached box' on the same large estate as Ted and June and Judy. Linda works in healthcare administration. Paul used to be employed in the offshore construction industry, but now works as a customer adviser in a large DIY superstore. For some years now Linda and Paul have been collecting antiques. They have several ongoing collections in their living room. Most of these are Wedgwood and include nineteenth-century cups and saucers and a few eighteenth-century pieces, as well as some more contemporary Wedgwood collections. There is also another collection of Crown Derby coffee cups and saucers and a number of single items, including an eighteenth-century mantelshelf clock and a Viennese cuckoo clock carved in wood. The china collections are displayed in purpose-bought antique display cabinets and on the fire plinth. Linda and Paul take great pleasure in their collections. Searching out antique shops when they visit places and going to antique fairs are mutual interests, and Paul in particular likes the bargaining that goes with acquisition in these arenas. The couple worry vaguely about how much of an obsession their hobby might seem to others, but acknowledge how central collecting has become to their identity as a couple: 'Look at it', says Paul, 'wherever we go, we go to antique shops, whenever we're on holiday we're in antique shops, it's us, it's what we do. It's all we do.' Paul also appreciates looking at these things in the couple's living room. For him these things are markers of how far he has come socially, from his roots in a Northumberland coal-mining village. He says, 'I think it's because I come from a position of having nothing – you want these sorts of things.' In contrast, for Linda – whose background is more identifiably middle class – the collections are things she takes pleasure in viewing. Whilst Linda's relationship to these things foregrounds aesthetic appreciation and reverence, Paul's is about the narration of social advancement and a distancing from his familial past in things, a past which is not dissimilar to, and indeed has many resonances with, those living on Wear Road.

Unlike the research subjects discussed thus far in this chapter, Linda and Paul have stories which they narrate about why they collect the things that they do, and which are located in their own biographies and identities. But what connects their objects of collection to those of the previous study households is their safety as a collection of objects. Albeit that these things are 'antique' and therefore of much greater financial value than the Ainsley, the thimbles, the dolls and the pigs on the Rivers estate in South Hightown, they are nonetheless things that were manufactured and retailed as to be collected (McKendrick 1959/60; McKendrick, Brewer and Plumb 1983) and to be displayed. Although definitely not collecting through mass-market collecta-bles, and confident in their own capacities both to know the authentic and to create the appropriate transaction in exchange, Paul and Linda's objects of collection testify to the anxieties that surround collected objects, and the potency of the safe, manufactured collection in such circumstances.

Back in South Hightown, Geoff and Hilary have a very different sense of the practice of collecting. As we saw in the previous chapter, Geoff and Hilary are keen amateur musicians, and have contacts that take them to play in various locations across the UK and in continental Europe. As part of this interest they have amassed what they describe as a large collection of musical instruments – many of them stored in their capacious loft – and a room of sheet music, which Geoff has catalogued (Figure 5.3).

At the same time, the couple have another collection, with sub-collec-tions, books. The books, double-stacked on the shelves, fill two attic rooms, and the expansion in this collection is one of the main reasons why Geoff and Hilary moved house (Figure 5.4).

Geoff and Hilary's stories about all these collections are ones that high-light the strength of their emotional attachments to these things and their importance to their abilities to narrate their identities. Here, just as one instance, is how they talk about their collection of musical instruments:

Nicky: So, as the interests have progressed have you accumulated more and more of these?

Geoff: Yes!!

Hilary: We've got a huge number. Whereas say a violinist would have say one or two, we've got quite a lot of recorders because recorders come in different sizes, and we have copies … so we have got a lot

Geoff: There's a phrase – it's what they call The Magic Toyshop, where you had to have every instrument that's ever been known, and we're rediscovering all these old instruments … you see someone who plays something nicely and you think, 'Gosh I must try it myself.' The trouble is you get at least 50% of these things that you quietly forget about [laughs].

Nicky: So there's this lingering accumulation.

Geoff: Yes! And we're too proud to get rid of them … the recorders I would be sad to lose any of those. I wouldn't want to replace them; I'd like to keep them. But a lot of the other – the lutes for example – I wouldn't mind the lutes disappearing or the sackbuts or the cornets. If I was replacing them I wouldn't have any sentimental attachment to them. But saying that there is an attachment thing because if I let them go that's saying 'I'm never ever going to play that instrument again' – that's why I hang on to them.

There are three key differences between Geoff and Hilary's collections and those of the other households discussed in this section. First, these are

Figure 5.3: Geoff and Hilary's sheet music

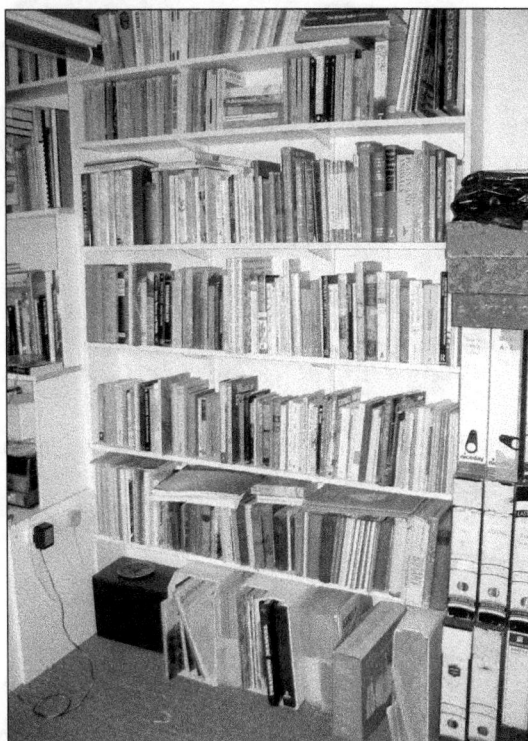

Figure 5.4: Geoff and Hilary's books

self-authored collections, constituted through things whose manufacture and retail is not about the production of the collectable but about the trans-mission of the word and sound. Secondly, these are 'open' collections, ones which are being continually added to and accumulated, not finite. Moreover, the continued accumulation of these collections was in part the precipitate for their moving house, with the collections occupying many of the upper level rooms in this large(r) house. Thirdly, their location in the upper-level rooms means that these collections are largely invisible to others, and cer-tainly absent from the two reception rooms in this house, although one of these rooms is used for playing music. As we see now, though, the nature of Geoff and Hilary's collections exert important effects on Geoff and Hilary's ability to contain them as collections.

In one instance of recorded conversation, Geoff and Hilary described to me how their music playing requires them to take along not only the musical instruments but sheet music to weekend events and/or social visits involv-ing music making. The sheet music contains various parts; some pieces are for two or three parts, others for up to eight. As Geoff explains, losing any of these parts would render the whole value-less, and has posed them with a dilemma of how to counter the potential for loss at such meetings:

> *Geoff:* 'It's awful actually, we've actually got a stamp with our names on it! Because when you go to these weekends people have the same bits of music so you don't know whether – and also they subscribe (to an early music publisher) – so you've got to make damn sure that it's going to come back to you.
>
> *Hilary:* Say if the Tenor One part didn't come back – then it's no good to play on other occasions if one of the parts is missing
>
> *Geoff:* It's not a possessive thing in that sense; it's a securing against shall we say wandering!

A similar worry is raised over the book collections. Hilary likes to loan out her books for friends to read, as a marker of sociality, but the couple are acutely aware that running a library through social networks risks loss too:

> *Hilary:* … I like lending books … Often when you're talking to somebody something will come up and I'll say, 'Oh I can lend you that.' Perhaps more than Geoff does. Because I want other people to enjoy books because I enjoy them, and then there is the issue of can I get them back. And Geoff has actually become quite good at keeping a record of what we've lent out.
>
> *Nicky:* It's a bit embarrassing to ask for things back – or have you done that?
>
> *Hilary:* Yes actually, I have – there was one person – that was a bit of an issue. We lent this person a cheap paperback that we'd bought in America and a year later he hadn't returned it. I chased him up

and his view was that paperbacks are something that you read once and then bin ... I thought that was wrong, that books are worth something and should never be discarded. That's why I chased it up, but you [said to Geoff] you thought I was being a bit. Did you feel I perhaps shouldn't have lent it?

Geoff: Well I felt you ought to be aware of the fact that if you lend something you may not get it back. Because people have this viewpoint. I remember, years ago X [name] he said that he was on an ocean liner – that must have been a long time ago – and there was a guy next to him reading a book and he said, 'Gee, that was great' and threw it over the rails!

As we see here, managing loss is socially awkward, at various levels. Whilst Geoff thinks Hilary should be more aware of the loss potential in loaning and able to let things go through loaning, as an inevitable risk of the practice, Hilary continues to try to negotiate the difficult turf of asking for the return of the loan and therefore of her possessions.

Leaving aside the intricacies of the differences between Geoff and Hilary over what to do about lending, both the collections of books and sheet music establish that mobility and movement are critical states for the collection. As we see so clearly with Geoff and Hilary's books and sheet music, in going journeying – to music events or through loaning – these collections become open to another social life. They have the capacity to be appropriated (consciously or entirely inadvertently) by others, to be lost or even discarded, which is why Geoff and Hilary stamp the mark of ownership on them. My contention here, though, is that it is for precisely such reasons that the other collections discussed in this section are accommodated differently, in display cases, or in specific locations in living rooms, such as mantelpieces and hearths. Although designed and manufactured to be displayed, keeping collections shut behind glass doors or in one place is a way of keeping them safe and secure. Accommodating them thus retains the collection as a collection, simultaneously restricting their movement and ensuring their enduringness. Indeed, in fixing collections in domestic space, immobilising them even, these households not only preserve the integrity of objects but ensure that their collections endure, to the point where their social lives exceed their own. Although acknowledged by all the households with collections, it is once again Geoff and Hilary whose collections bear most heavily upon them in this sense, though the collections that are most potent in this respect are different to the ones they have amassed together.

Hilary's maternal and paternal families disclose very different class histories to the other participants in the ethnography. Moreover, the trace of this history lives on in some of the things in Geoff and Hilary's reception rooms. Above the fireplace, for example, hangs an early twentieth-century watercolour painting of Hilary's mother and her two siblings as young children, all of them on a pony. Adjacent to this is the photograph from which this was painted, which also includes the figure of the children's governess. Elsewhere in the house there is a large wooden trunk dating back to the medieval period, on which figures of the apostles are carved. And it is through these families too that Hilary has inherited a collection of eighteenth- and nineteenth-century china, housed like all the other china collections in the ethnography in a display cabinet, but this time of solid oak. With no children to pass these things on to, however, the future passage of these inherited collections is now exercising Hilary's mind. They will, she says, have to pass them to her sister's children, but the trouble with this is that her sister has sons rather than daughters, and these are collections which historically have been passed through the female line. Hilary is at one level matter of fact about this: she explains her current difficulties with these things as indicative of her mother, grandmother and great grandmother's incapacity to conceive of a future in which women did not have children and in which each generation would not produce daughters. Yet Hilary also acknowledges that the eventual passage of these things to her sister's sons will break the family in things: 'It's sad because really it is the breaking of the chain', she says.

Whilst managing the passing on of their own accumulating collections is a concern for Geoff and Hilary, the difficulties posed by these other things far exceeds them. Hilary's inherited things – amongst them the chest, the painting and the china collections – are classic examples of enclaved objects. Indeed, some of these things have endured within one family of women for over 150 years, and have been used by these women to constitute this maternal family and to delimit it, from others and from a sense of 'the patriarchy'.[3] To hold these things, then, is not just to be their custodian, but to accommodate this matrilineal family in generations. That Hilary and her sister between them cannot pass these things on in accordance with the familial tradition is, then, a considerable burden: it signifies their collective failure to satisfy the conditions for inheritance laid down by previous generations, the cessation of a particular maternal line and their inability to continue to accommodate their extended family in things. Indeed, in having to compromise by passing these things through the male line, Hilary and her sister know that they will be letting loose the ghosts in these things, across two generations. The absence of another generation of daughters to accommodate the absent presences in these things means that these things will be but partial accommodations in their new homes, never quite belonging with those who accommodate them. But for Hilary and her sister, it is in the now that the haunting persists, in the anxieties that are an effect of accommodation's loss.

Accommodating children's clothing

In contrast to collections, clothing's accommodation within households is characterised by flow and mobility (cf. Banim and Guy 2003). It is not just that clothes move in, round and out of the house in their wearing, but the everyday life of clothes in domestic space is one in which clothes move from wearing to laundry zones, through washing machines and sinks, to gardens or tumble driers, over ironing boards and under irons, and thence back into wardrobes and chests of drawers. Unlike collections, theirs is not a fixed accommodation in dwelling structures, but a flow or passage through the rooms of the dwelling structure and some of the things contained within them. I will argue that this has intense implications for clothing's continued presence and potential for enduringness within our homes, but to begin to open this up, let us look more closely at practices of clothing management and care within domestic space.

Thinking back to the fieldwork and to the several households with young children living in them, one of my most pervasive memories is that whenever I was in these homes, the sounds of whirring, spinning and rinsing water were a constant background accompaniment; the washing machine, seemingly, was always going. At the time I merely noted this, thinking that – since visiting obviously coincided with household members being at home – this was purely a scheduling issue. What was highly visible though were the piles of children's clothing in varying states of laundering present in the rooms of these houses. Ellie and Steve's kitchen work surfaces were invariably covered in piles of un-ironed toddler clothes; the radiators in their kitchen and living room always had drying children's clothes on them; a clothes-horse (always loaded) stood behind a settee; and a few piles of ironed clothing were always on the back of the settee or on the household's dining table. Upstairs in the girls' bedrooms, other piles of clothes lay on the top of chests of drawers. It was a similar picture in Sandra and Rob's house, although not in Jo-Anne's, because almost all of this work is done by Jo-Anne's mother in her own home. Elsewhere, on Wear Road, the washing machine is always going in Carol and John's and Christine and Malcolm's, and there are usually a few piles of laundry in Carol's kitchen/utility area waiting to be ironed. However, here laundry never spills over into the living room and is usually ironed immediately by Carol; once again, a marker of the importance of social respectability on Wear Road and its management through the spatial ordering of things. Indeed, in Christine's house washing is ironed and put away as soon as it is dry.

Ellie's elaborations on her childminder's stipulations about clothing provisions for her toddler go part way to accounting for the amount of clothes washing that goes on in this household. Each day at the childminder's requires three sets of clothes, as Chloe does 'wet play', is changed, has her lunch and wipes or spills her food on her clothes, and is changed again, before being picked up at 5 p.m.. Meanwhile, Ellie and Steve's eldest child Rachel participates in various out-of-school activities which generate a continual flow of worn clothing and laundry – Irish dancing classes and competitions, climbing and swim club. In part, then, the constant audibility of washing machine cycles in these households is a marker of the intensely structured social lives in activities of young children in Britain today, and of their requirements in dress. But, as the practices at the childminder's suggest, where there is washing there is always cleanliness and its close parallel, dirt.

One incident that occurred on Alternative Terrace during the school summer holiday period revealed much about these associations and particularly about their potency for mothers with young children. One early evening, on a day when it had rained heavily earlier on, Josh and Mark were out playing in the back lane. It was Sandra's birthday, and she was having a glass of wine with me, whilst Rob fed Alice. Suddenly there was an enormous amount of shouting and excited yelling from the two boys. Sandra immediately rushed out of the house to see what was going on; the boys were jumping as hard as they could in a relatively deep puddle of muddy water in an area where some of the residents of Alternative Terrace park their cars. They were covered in mud splats. Sandra yelled at them to stop immediately, and knocked on Jo-Anne's door to get her attention. Whilst Rob washed the mud off the cars, the two boys were dragged back into their respective houses; their clothes were stripped off immediately; and they were then flung in the bath by their mothers, who scrubbed them and washed their hair at the same time. Once they were dry and dressed again, both washing machines started up, though Jo-Anne threw Mark's vest and pants straight into the wheelie bin, saying, 'These are too cacked to even go in the wash – look at them!'

Not being a mother, these actions at the time struck me as somewhat 'over the top'. Remembering back to the distinct attractions of rolling about in the mud as a child, and – if I'm honest – mud's continued attractions, I could see why these two five-year-old boys were having a great deal of fun in these puddles, particularly after having been cooped-up in their homes all day. More detached observation, though, certainly testifies to how these two mothers feel about dirt's presence in relation to their children: this is something which has to be scrubbed away from their bodies immediately, in a drop-everything way – remember this is Sandra's birthday and she is supposed to be relaxing. Furthermore, the dirt has to be eliminated from their clothing too, hence the immediate activation of the washing machines. In part about good and appropriate mothering, this unfolding sequence of events also highlights the potency of cleanliness and purity in relation to young children in contemporary Britain. Washing away the dirt from them and their clothing, and doing this immediately, is both the means to reclaiming these meanings and indicative of dirt's capacity to undermine them.

Returning to the specifics of the action, what we see here is how removing children's clothes and placing them in a trajectory that connects them to a sequence of laundering practices is no inevitable seamless flow of action. Instead, as Jo-Anne's jettisoning of Mark's underwear into the wheelie bin shows, clothing can be got rid of in its passage through these various laundering practices. There are, of course, several reasons why Jo-Anne may have chosen to jettison this clothing (see Chapter 2), but – rather than speculate on these – I want instead to connect this act to the piles of children's clothing in various states of laundering that are visible all around Ellie and Sandra's houses.

Alice's nursery bedroom almost invariably holds piles of laundered clothes which have not been put away in her small chest of drawers There is also – usually – a black bin bag in or near her cot. My initial assumptions about these piles were that these were excess capacity for the drawers, but on asking Sandra directly about them, it became clear that these items of baby clothing were 'on the way out', waiting for the next charity bag drop in the neighbourhood, or to go in the black bin bag of household clothing discards that Sandra continually accumulates and takes routinely, every three or four months, to a charity shop. It is a similar story in Ellie's. Some of the piles of laundered clothes, particularly the toddler clothes, are for taking to work or for charity collections. For both these mothers, then, laundering provides

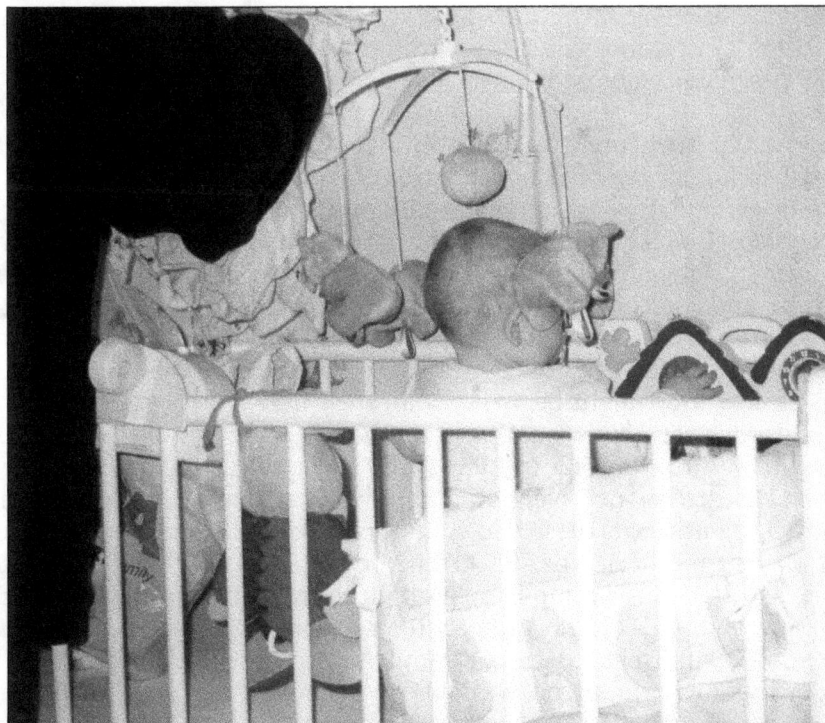

Figure 5.5: Sandra manages the baby clothing

the space for evaluating the continued presence of particular items of children's clothing in their homes. How much longer can this be worn? Has she outgrown this? Is it too small? These questions are constantly asked of these clothes. Correspondingly, very young children's clothing is frequently and routinely got rid of, and it is laundering that provides the space for the scrutinising that precedes this (Figure 5.5).

It is a similar story, albeit with a slight twist, at Carol and John's. With two slightly older younger children, both of them girls in primary school, Carol finds that managing clothes is no longer simply a matter of her own evaluations of 'fit' between clothing and children's bodies. Instead, she has to accommodate her evaluations in clothing to her daughters' emergent identities in clothing, which are evident even in relation to the five year old in Year 1 of education. Carol's response to this problem is ingenious, and one which mobilises the constant work of the washing machine in this household. So, although Carol continues to routinely release items of younger children's clothing, as she always has done, through dropping them off at a charity shop, she answers the younger children's queries of 'Mum, where's my X?' by saying, 'Oh I don't know, they must be lost somewhere in the wash.' Given the volume of household clothing that passes through this wash, and the constant work of the washing machine, the household's washing machine's capacity to absorb this loss in clothing is currently greater than the girls' capacity to remember some of their clothes. Moreover, forgetting these things is enabled by Carol's practice of juxtaposing these losses with the acquisition of new-to-them clothes from other mothers, which she disguises as new purchases by using retailers' bags which she keeps specifically for this purpose.

Inevitably, such pretexts will only have a limited purchase as ways to manage children's clothing's release from this household; as Carol says, the girls will eventually work out that all is not quite what it seems, and the household will make the transition to a rather different practice in clothing management, already in evidence with Carol's teenage daughter, Zoe. Like Christine and Malcolm's daughter Kylie, Zoe routinely gets rid of clothes. Both Kylie and Zoe continually scrutinise their clothes, looking at their wardrobes not just in terms of how they look to themselves in their clothes, but in terms of how they might be seen within their peer group. Correspondingly, both girls routinely throw out things that they see as potential causes of trouble in this respect. Indeed, in Kylie's case so acute is this that she jettisons clothes that she has not even worn and which still have the label in them. Nonetheless, although these two teenagers make their rejections independently of their mothers, what to do with the rejected clothing remains their mother's work. Both Zoe and Kylie prohibit their mothers from going in their bedrooms, and both mothers respect their daughters' desire for independent space. So, having rejected certain clothes, these two teenagers place their laundered or unworn but still wearable rejects out on the landings of the two houses, whereupon they become re-appropriated within the two mothers' value systems around clothing. Carol takes this clothing to a charity shop whilst Christine uses a work acquaintance of her mother's (living elsewhere in the region) as the conduit for getting rid of Kylie's clothing discards. In both instances we see how the mothers appropriate these clothes within the moral economies of circulation and redistribution that they have enacted since becoming mothers, and which are also clearly displayed by Sandra and Ellie.

Kylie and Zoe's practices of scrutinising their wardrobes of clothing resonate strongly with June and Ted's clothing rejections in the previous chapter. Indeed, we see again here how, once the wardrobe doors are open, clothing becomes open to potential release. No longer contained or shut away, clothing's passage out of the wardrobe as well as through laundering regimes positions it within a normative which is not just about the narrative of the self through clothing or even appropriate mothering through clothing, but which increasingly sees clothing's ridding, and not just its holding, as normative. Sandra's held-over charity donation piles, Ellie's accumulations to take to work and Carol and Christine's charity shop drop-offs or gifts to work friends of their teenage daughters' cast-outs are all illustrative of the routine nature of this ridding, and indicative of the way in which the proliferation in second-hand clothing exchange is present in within-household clothes care regimes. But what they point to as well, is the transience of clothing's accommodation within our homes. Whilst some clothing endures in our homes – notably things of sentimental or symbolic value, such as Christine's wedding dress and her bridesmaid dresses (Chapter 3) – other items of clothing, and particularly children's clothing, pass through our homes, worn for a few months only, as with many baby clothes, or never worn at all, as with Kylie's fashion rejects. That they do so is more than a little to do with the manner of their accommodation within them.

Accommodating toys

Like clothing, the accommodation of toys within households, and particularly households with young children, is about their circulation around and within homes, but, as we see in this section, these accommodations differ in their temporalities and exert key effects on toys' open-ness to ridding.

At first sight, toys' presence in the homes of the households with young children looks much like children's clothing. On going into Ellie and Steve's living room, toys are strewn across the floor; some are to be found on kitchen work surfaces, dropped by Chloe in exchange for a spoon with which to eat yoghurt. Others are located on the dining table. Most of these toys are described as 'educational' by Ellie, and are bought from the Early Learning Centre. There's a farmyard with animals, various spatial cognition development aids, first jigsaws, Lego, a few soft toys, and numerous defunct telephone and mobile phone handsets now serve as multi-purpose toys, enabling 'phoning mummy' games, 'playing offices' and learning numbers. Upstairs, in their bedrooms, the girls' rooms are full of various toys including favourite soft toys and, in Rachel's room, a legion of Barbie dolls.

Similar accumulations festoon Sandra and Rob's living room, although most of these toys are selected via the Argos Catalogue, rather than from the Early Learning Centre. During the daytime the living room in this house is a play-room-come-baby-room. Alice's 'walker', a play mat and some of her soft toys are always on the main floor of the living room in front of the fire, whilst beside the settee by the garden door is a large pile of Josh's things, including Micro Machines, jigsaws, cardboard box 'pretend boats', a train set, a candyfloss maker, a trampoline, a Spiderman outfit… (Figure 5.6).

This is only some of Josh's things. There are others upstairs in his bedroom, but these are out of bounds for playing with during the daytime, as Rob is asleep in bed for much of the morning and early afternoon. Elsewhere in the living room are other indications of Josh's presence. Squeezed between the TV and the fire, with a tiny chair in front of it, is a three-year-old PC, given to the household by me in August 2003 when I upgraded my home computer. This is the platform for Josh's computer games, and it has various games stored beside it. In the kitchen is a Spiderman bike, bought at Easter 2003 for Josh as a special present around the time of Alice's arrival.

As Sandra talks about these things, she makes it clear that two temporalities order toys placement in their house, a daily rhythm and a longer term one. Each evening, she says, once she has got the two children to bed and asleep, she tidies up the living room, moving Josh's things from where he has left them into piles behind the settee or to the main pile by the door, and moving Alice's stuff to one side. She does this, she says, not just to tidy-up in itself, but as a means to 'get my room back – I need that'. Sandra's tidying-up of Josh and Alice's things, then, is not just a way of reimposing order on the displacement tendencies inherent in children's play, but is also

Figure 5.6: Sandra and Rob's living room

a means of reclaiming psychological space for herself, by removing from her immediate field of vision the things that most define her as the mother of young children. So, when she finally sits down – usually exhausted – at the end of each day, she wants to view the TV not across a floor strewn with the things of a five year old and a baby, but across open space.[4] Rather than look at the TV through 'Mother', she wants to watch late-evening TV programmes through an adult field of vision.[5] The second rhythm of toys' movement in this household is between the two floors of the house. As we saw previously, what is in the living room is only some of Josh's things; the rest are in his bedroom. Every few months or so, Sandra decrees that they can 'have a change around'. Some of the toys that are downstairs go back upstairs and vice versa. The decision as to what moves where is entirely Josh's. However, the negotiated agreement that this particular mother and son have come to is that the size of the pile in the living room cannot increase.

What we see going on in this second rhythm in toys in Sandra and Rob's house, is a way of teaching Josh to accommodate to the others around him through the relation between his things' location and those of others. But what we also see through the two rhythms is how the practices of tidying-up and moving the toys around are about holding things over, rather than ridding. Together with the gift economy in toys (at Christmas, Easter and birthdays), holding is why the toys accumulate in this house. Indeed, in the entire fieldwork, there were only three instances in which mothers used tidying-up their children's toys as a means to get rid of these toys. Two of these happened in Ellie's house; one in Carol and John's.

As a child protection social worker with a social studies degree, Ellie has academic knowledge of the psychological development of the feminine subject, but whilst abstract knowledge is one thing, enacting it with her eldest daughter, currently nearly seven, is another. Occasionally, Ellie's constant fears and worries about what she sees as Rachel's precocious development in things – and that of her peer group – spills over and erupts. This fear is always directed, explicitly, at some of the things Rachel has. Early on in the ethnography, Ellie recounted to me how she had 'lost it' during Christmas 2002, grabbing a plastic bag, filling it with piles of Rachel's make-up for parties, and jettisoning the lot in the wheelie bin. Similarly, and around the same time, the Barbies got to her. She counted them up: there were twenty-seven in the house, literally all over the house. Ellie said to Rachel that she could keep six, later negotiated up to seven. The rest she bagged up, ostensibly for redistribution via work. But, such were her feelings about these Barbies that Ellie actually dumped them in the wheelie bin; an act which she regarded at the time as an entirely cathartic release, but which she now admits to feeling a tiny degree of guilt about, hence the gradual accumulation of new Barbies in the house.

At Carol and John's, the acts of ridding children's toys in tidying-up were exclusively about preparing for modernisation (Chapter 3). Amongst the eighteen bin bags that went to the tip were nine containing nothing but Natalie and Amie's toys. Although I did not witness these events, it was clear from Carol's general unwillingness to talk about them at length, that the whole process had been fraught. Whilst Carol and John had asked the two girls what they wanted to keep and what they could let go, letting go was not something that either of these two girls (aged 7 and 5) wanted to do at all.

As is vividly testified by these three instances, and their rarity, getting rid of children's toys once these children have reached a certain developmental stage is a difficult experience, for parents and children alike, precisely because these children know that these are their things and that they mark their presence in the home, because they know that the things help to define their emergent identities and because of the way these toys figure in their imaginary play worlds. By contrast, getting rid of baby things is altogether easier work for mothers. Indeed, this was something that all the mothers in the ethnography related, recounting this as an act primarily about ridding, but also as one encompassing the process of memorialising their child(ren) as a baby/babies through keeping a favourite soft toy and, usually, a couple of garments. Again, all these things – even on this occasion Claire and Nathan's – were got rid of by releasing them into trajectories that enabled their revaluation, by placing them in charity shops. But children's toys tend to hang around in homes. Their expulsion is a rare event, and instead these things accumulate and accumulate, bringing about not inconsiderable problems in their accommodation. Indeed, notwithstanding parents' acquisition of a whole host of configurations aimed at easing their storage – for example, shelving, container boxes, plastic stacking systems and beds with built-in storage systems – these things continually spilled-out of their children's rooms and play rooms, eventually filling up other zones of in-house storage too, such as lofts and garages.

It is against this background that I want to turn to a table-top sale held in South Hightown during the spring of 2003. Although not well attended, there were some twelve tables (many of them doubles or trebles), of which six were dedicated exclusively to the sale of children's things (clothing as well as toys). One of these stalls was that of a woman from the Rivers estate with a five-year-old daughter, who sat playing amongst her things as her mother attempted to sell them. The mother told me how her daughter did not want to part with any of them, but that she herself was absolutely sick of the stuff littered all over her house. In another corner were a couple from the older area of suburban-estate style housing within South Hightown. I was told that their two sons, aged 17 and 15, wanted absolutely nothing to do with any of this stuff from their childhood, which had been stashed away in the couple's garage for up to fifteen years. The sons were working at Tesco and doing competitive sport whilst their parents attempted to sell 'their stuff'. The pile of toys was nearly as high as the parents, and extended well beyond the confines of their tables, but at the end of the morning barely a dent had been made in it. A few older women had bought a couple of jigsaws, but that was it. Elsewhere in the hall, the ten-year-old son of the event's organiser – again from one of the areas of suburban-estate style housing – was attempting to sell several things he no longer wanted. He was using this as a means to raise funds for a *Blue Peter* appeal, but was also satisfying his mother by doing this and using it as an opportunity to get rid of certain things.[6] Included on this table were a number of Action Man toys, which he described to me as 'way too babyish' for him now, some Action Man accessories and a large number of early PlayStation games which he had 'done' and had no wish to play again, as he was far more interested in the PS2 games coming his way via a school friend's much older brother. In another corner of the hall, entirely distinct in their things, were his much younger sister (getting rid of nothing and buying as much as her mother would let her), his mother and his grandmother.

I think what we see in these three instances of attempted sale of children's things in South Hightown is a microcosm of the lives of children's toys in households in contemporary Britain. As one of the primary ways through which parental love for children is expressed, if not the main way if we think back to the boxes and boxes of Abigail's things that defined Claire and Nathan's house in its modernisation (Chapter 3), toys accumulate in households with children precisely because parental love has to be continually reaffirmed through child-centred purchases and acquisitions. This though poses problems, for both parents and children.

For parents, particularly those without the dedicated playrooms available to some, the presence of such accumulations and their trail through the house almost invariably becomes too much sometimes. Indeed, the act of the first mother at the table-top sale is similar in sentiment, if not volume, to Ellie's jettisoning of the Barbies and to a story that Sandra tells of rescuing what was to become Josh's trampoline from a woman at the tip.[7] Whilst some parents might be able to manage their ambivalence towards the things that they (or others) might have bought for their children, for those without the capacity in their homes to accommodate these things within dedicated playrooms, negative emotions exert their effects and children's things are cast out via the wheelie bin, abandoned at the tip, tossed by the road side, or – as we see at the table-top sale – placed in locations that seem to allow for their revaluation.

However, one of the most striking things about this table-top sale is that, whilst young children's clothing certainly did exchange hands and in quantity, the toys did not sell. The following extract of recorded conversation between Sandra and Claire contains several pointers as to why:

Sandra: … he's pointing out to you constantly on the television, 'Can I have that? Can I have that?'

Nicky: Is it like that?

Sandra: Yes

Nicky: All the time?

Sandra: Yes – but then I haven't got a clue what's in for girls at the minute. Apart from Barbie stuff, cos all girls want Barbie stuff. [… to Claire] Have you got Sky? [Claire: No] It bombards you with toy adverts, it's on all the time, every 15 minutes you've got loads of toy adverts, especially on the kids' channels – there's about 10 kids' channels. It's just adverts all the time.

Nicky: So how do you navigate your way through the constant 'I want, I want, I want'?

Sandra: You narrow it down to things he's going on about when the adverts aren't on. So when he goes on and on about something for weeks and weeks we get it, and the other stuff can't matter that much.

Nicky: Is that the same with Abigail?

Claire: She just gets hold of the Argos book and goes 'I really want that' sort of thing, so then it's the one she talks about the most.

Sandra: And you say, 'Well if you had to choose which one would you get?', 'I like this one, which one do you want?' You work it like that when you're looking through the *Argos Catalogue*. And whenever you're looking through, whichever bit of the *Argos Catalogue* you're looking at he'll come and pinch it off you.

Claire: Uhuh – straight to the toys bit. But I would never take her to a toy shop, would you?

Sandra: Oh no!

Claire: We once took her to Toys"Я"Us, and it was awful!

Nicky: What was it like?

Claire: She just wanted the whole shop, and she had this pram that she already had, and she had it like full – she just picked this pram and she filled it up with toys and we like had to peel her away! Never again!!

Nicky: When was it you took her there then?

Claire: For her third birthday to pick her own presents – it was awful, I've never felt so embarrassed. I was stupid. I'd never let her do it ever again. She always goes 'Oh there's Toys"Я"Us' when we go past, and I go 'Yeah, yeah'. I would never let her in the place again!

Given the pervasive presence and potency of Sky and the *Argos Catalogue* within these two children's consumer culture, as well as the forbidden city of Toys"Я"Us, it is perhaps not surprising that the only purchasing of children's toys going on at this sale was by grandmothers buying gifts of Barbies for their granddaughters. Yet another version of love's enactment across the generations through the acquisition and gifting of consumer goods, one can perhaps hazard a guess that these unknowing acquisitions might not have been the most appreciated of gifts, for either parents or the receiving child.

For children, toys' accumulations pose other problems. Hinted at in the instance of the ten-year-old seller, toys are things which are used in part to constitute and to manage children's identities, as well as to play with and fantasise through. Whilst toys help define identities, their potential to do this is increasingly locked in particular ages and phases, a tendency exacerbated by toy manufacturers and retailers through their increasing differentiation of children as consumers. We can see this most starkly around the Action Men and the old PlayStation games. Action Men appear here as things which this ten-year-old boy regards as his past, and which he at least has no desire to memorialise through keeping. The PlayStation games are similar, yet different too. These games are no longer challenging enough for him; they are games that he says he has the skills to master easily. But in addition, these things are neither the latest games nor state of the art in their graphics and effects. Managing his identity within his peer group requires that this ten year old attempts to play the latest games, compares his performance with others in his peer group and is able to talk about their effects and graphics. As well as leaving little apparent room for PlayStation 1's trace in things in his bedroom, I would suggest that it is for precisely the same reason that Action Man and his accessories have been sent in the same trajectory. Identity for this particular child is in the temporalities of the now, not about memorialising and conserving a past in things.[8]

Again though, and a salutary lesson from this sale, nobody bought these PlayStation games. Neither did they buy what were then four-year-old Action Men. Although opened up to potential revaluation, these things – at least in the context of South Hightown – appeared to possess little capacity to be revalued as toys or games; they appear here as the ultimate consumer goods located in a consumer culture of the now. Although children's toys emerged in the ethnography as some of the most difficult things to get rid of – precisely because of the strength of their connection to children's emergent identities and to parental love – when they are released they appear to have limited potential for re-appropriation. With a mixture of vehemence and exasperation in her voice, the mother of the two teenage boys at the table-top sale explained to me how she would just resort to driving the whole lot to the tip at the end of the sale and abandoning it all there in one ceremonial act of trashing and purging. My sense on listening to her ire was that she had reason to be angry: markers in their acquisition of the degree of her and their parental love, held over and accommodated in storage in their garage for well over a decade so that they could be released easily and indicative of the degree of their sensitivity as parents and their knowledge of child development, these things had suddenly become imperative to expel from their home as waste; hated, I suggest, precisely for their capacity to turn love into rubbish value.

Conclusions

The accommodations of collections, clothing and toys disclosed in this chapter establish the core temporal registers of everyday life in our homes and their constitution through mundane practices. At one extreme are collections. Framed by collecting practices that simultaneously hold and protect, these practices ensure that collections endure, demanding through their presence and importance in our lives that we establish their future social lives before our deaths. At the other end of the temporal register is clothing, and particularly children's clothing, which emerges here as amongst our most transient of accommodations. And then there are the toys, things which for all parents' ambivalence about them, are held over, accommodated for love in back-zone storage spaces like garages and lofts, until they can safely be got rid of, when we are sure that their presence is no longer required to narrate a self or a life. Enduringness, transience and holding are, however, themselves accommodations of temporalities through spatialities. When we examine these temporalities we can see just how critical domestic space is to their constitution. For collections to endure requires them to be contained, safely; protected, in specially designed, bounded configurations like lockable display cabinets or in rooms from which children and animals are prohibited. In contrast, that so much clothing passes through the house is indicative of clothing's handling within our homes, and specifically the continual flow in cloth through the dwelling structure; from zones of storage like wardrobes, to proximity with our bodies, through the technologies of washing, drying and ironing, our routine everyday clothing is seldom still. Toys disclose several similarities with clothing, flowing round and through the house, notwithstanding parents' continual attempts to 'tidy-up'. But in their holding they also disclose at least some similarities with collections; albeit that their containment is neither as secure nor as visible, for the purpose of their holding is to enable their eventual release and loss to families.

At the same time, the chapter shows – much as the previous one – that it is the mobility of things in the practices of inhabiting dwelling structures which is key to their transience in our homes and to their ridding. Moving things displaces things; it threatens order even though it may also be part of the ordering of accommodating certain things, particularly clothing and toys. Movement, however, always contains the potential for things to be got rid of. Yet, what we see here, as in Chapter 4, is how so much of this ridding is about the redistribution and potential revaluation of things. Whether it be the young children's clothing, Kylie and Zoe's clothing, or the no longer wanted toys of a childhood past, these are things which people continually attempt to pass on and to hand around, even if they don't always succeed in this, as with the toys. Indicative – as with the circulating cots and children's beds of Chapter 4 – of the extent of the second-hand economy and its presence in household practices, the proliferation in this economy seems to suggest the increasing normativity of transience in our accommodation of at least certain of our things. But what it also brings with it is attempts to avoid wasting some of these things by projecting them into imagined social futures.

Finally, and as with the previous chapter, we see here how the practices of the mundane connect to dwelling. Not only does the dwelling structure emerge through these practices as constitutive of enduringness and transience, but it holds both temporalities simultaneously. The two temporalities are critical to both accommodation and accommodating. Indeed, it is in the play between things' enduringness and transience, between what stays, what is seen to define us and what endures beyond our deaths, and what is discarded, cast-out and got rid of, that we make our homes accommodating places to live in, and achieve the state of being at home. Dwelling is manifested through such ordinary practices of inhabitation, that in turn weave the defining temporalities of a life being lived, through what we do with and to the things to hand around us.

NOTES

1 The exception here was Claire, but this house is currently in such a provisional state in things that it would be premature to see this difference as significant.

2 We might note too that the success of retail outlets selling manufactured collectables such as these on the UK high street – of whom Collectables is the obvious example – is strongly related to this particular consumption practice and to the anxieties that surround it.

3 To cite the patriarchy here is not mere ethnographic license. Hilary's maternal family included first generation feminists and the patterns of inheritance they devised for particular valued things included explicit challenges to the social norms of the time.

4 As an aside here, and in connection to a father's comments on a similar theme, I was driving on a day in late January 2004 listening to BBC Radio 4, when the broadcaster, introducing a story on Lego, commented on how he had recently developed an obsession with other people's flooring: 'Whereas some people have carpet and others polished wood floors,' he said, 'courtesy of our two young sons we have wall-to-wall Lego.'

5 It should be noted that Sandra watches BBC 2's Newsnight programme nightly. Tidying-up the toys in this household, then, is a means to reclaiming, however transiently, Sandra's adult

identity and a capacity to engage with television as part of an adult audience, as a woman who is a mother, not as a woman who is defined exclusively as a mother.

6 Blue Peter is a long-standing BBC TV children's television programme. Each year is marked by collecting for a particular, often aid-related, cause. Many of these collections involve household things, rather than money directly, and the collections are turned into money through the medium of the markets in recyclables.

7 One day when they were dropping something else off, a woman pulled in behind them with a car full of children's stuff, including the trampoline. As Sandra asked if she could have it, the woman declared herself to be 'sick of the sight of it all'.

8 That other children may not release their things as easily as this ten year old is clear from the goings-on elsewhere at the same table-top sale, as it is within some of the study households. Josh, for example, has been taught by Sandra and Rob to care for things to such a degree that he now tries to stop his mother from placing anything in the wheelie bin at all. To do this they have to wait until he is either asleep or at school. To release any of his toys is also an impossibility; one reinforced by the couple's intention to hold a lot of these things over for Alice to play with.

Chapter 6

Accommodating appliances

As others have emphasised, kitchen appliances foreground invisible consumption (Shove 2003). They constitute environments within our homes and do actions for us, using energy and resources – electricity, gas and water – to do this. They consume as we consume through them. But it is their dependency on energy which accounts for the manner of their accommodation within dwelling structures. Power sockets, gas pipes, water rising mains, and outlets to drains are built-in to the fabric of dwelling structures. Although additions may be made to the number of sockets in a house and alterations made to electrical circuits, although gas can be installed and changes made – at considerable expense and inconvenience – to the water supply and drains (see Chapter 3), access to energy in any one dwelling structure is constrained, built in to matter and confined to particular outlets. This exerts considerable limits on the location of certain consumer objects in our homes, with kitchen appliances being an exemplar case. Consequently, on moving in to a property, kitchen appliances tend to be positioned in what is usually an obvious location, connected up and then left *in situ*, until something happens to necessitate their disturbance. We may move house (Chapter 2); our homes may be modernised (Chapter 3); we might become fed-up with their look – as Claire did with hers (Chapter 3) – or with the noise they make as they work, or we might want to change kitchen designs. Much more common though, at least through the fieldwork, was that the appliance itself either failed to work or started to malfunction. This is what happened with eight kitchen appliances in this study, and it is these instances of appliance failure or malfunction that the chapter concentrates on.[1]

As with the previous chapters, the emphasis here is on households' accommodations of these things. Appliances are disclosed to be things accommodated primarily for their capacities: specifically, to manufacture environments in our homes and to enable everyday life to be enacted in particular ways. They allow us to cook food in certain ways, to hold food in storage, to wash and care for clothes in particular ways. In short, their capacities are critical to accommodating our daily lives. So, when they go wrong – or are unplugged, as in the modernisation work of Chapter 3 – our lives are completely disrupted; as we saw for instance with Carol's declarations that her family would just have to eat sandwiches for their evening meal, again. But these capacities also create particular accommodations in our homes. They work to make life more convenient, easier even. Washing machines, and particularly washing machines located in warm homes, take away the hard, painful work of washing clothes in cold winters, which both Peggy and June recall in its effects in chilblains on their hands. Fridge-freezers mean mothers do not have to shop and cook every day. Tumble driers allow children's clothing to be dried quickly, even in wet weather. These things, then, provide particular accommodations for us; they make our dwelling structures accommodating environments to live in. They are part of what makes dwelling structures accommodating; places to feel at home in.

When appliances fail, therefore, our homes lose their capacity to be so accommodating. As we see, how households respond in these circumstances varies. The chapter begins with a tale of two microwaves that failed. Their different trajectories open up the ways in which social relations of (co)habitation, and not simply attitudes to repair, exert critical effects on failed appliances. Following on from this, and focusing explicitly on one household with young children, I examine their year in kitchen appliances. Although the number of kitchen appliance failures occurring during the fieldwork were broadly in line with what would be anticipated from 'product life' statistics, the concentration of failure in one household over the study period is indicative of just how heavy appliance use is in households with children. At the same time, we see in this section just how dependent such households are on the capacities of appliances to do what they were designed and manufactured to do. In contrast, for households living in rather different social relations, the capacity to accommodate appliance failure is somewhat greater. As we will see, however, the majority of appliances failing during the ethnography were rid through routes which connected these things to their wasting. This is in stark contrast to the disclosures of the previous two chapters. I close the chapter by reflecting on this and its connections to the manner of appliance accommodation within our homes.

Ping! A Tale of Two Microwaves

One of the first instances of microwave failure in the fieldwork occurred in Pauline's house on Alternative Terrace. The intricacies of food preparation in this household are complex. As we saw in Chapter 4, Pauline spends her weekends over at her partner's house whilst he comes to hers on Thursday evenings. This affects how the couple eat together: when they eat together, Pauline insists on cooking 'a proper meal', which involves using the oven, not the microwave. Furthermore, she will often bake bread when she is at Keith's house, because this is something which she and the rest of their family associate with the weekend. Indeed, Keith and Pauline's adult son and the grandchildren drop in on Keith's house at the weekend, not just to see Keith and Pauline, but because they know that Pauline will have made home-made bread. However, when Pauline is at home for the rest of the week, it is the microwave which is in routine use. She uses it daily at breakfast to make

her breakfast food of choice (porridge), and usually every other evening, to
reheat left-over food or to cook baked potatoes. This is how Pauline narrates
the story of the microwave's gradual demise, a demise which began shortly
after the fieldwork started:

> Now then – me microwave was on the blink, because me porridge was
> like – which I had off to a fine art – it never quite came out right; it
> had great big lumps in it; it just wasn't done enough. And I decided,
> well I'd had this microwave for – well, I've been here for twelve years,
> erh, twelve, fourteen years anyway – it's had a good service, but
> obviously. You could still defrost things but it took a long time. It was
> still workable but it wasn't a good piece of working thingy…

What we see here is how this appliance's trajectory out of the house is
intimately bound up with the adequacy or not of food preparation. Pauline's
microwave begins to become opened up for ridding precisely because it no
longer has the capacity to prepare her routine breakfast food to her satisfac-
tion. This matters intensely. It is important that Pauline's porridge doesn't
have lumps in it, for this is a texture that she doesn't want to eat. Equally
though, particularly given the routine of her workday mornings and the
need to fit in walking her dog before leaving for work, the convenience
of the microwave is something that Pauline does not want to be without.
Although a proud cook, Pauline doesn't want to be standing over the stove
cooking porridge the slow way each morning. She hasn't got the time to do
this, or – more accurately – to do this would require her to accommodate the
time to do this within her early morning routine. She would need to get up
even earlier, eating into the time for sleep that she finds herself increasingly
needing as she gets older. Although this microwave still works in a fashion,
its inability to continue to conjoin convenience with Pauline's textual preferences in porridge begins to signal its devaluation.

Pauline continues the story of her microwave:

> So, anyway, 'cos it was me birthday the family decided to chip in
> and asked what did I want. So I said I'd prefer a microwave rather
> than bits and babs that I didn't really want. So I said I wanted a
> dead basic two-dialer with times, like me being a technophobe, I just
> wanted one with two bloody dials on it, one with medium, high and
> low, and how many minutes. So – and green – [adopts ironic voice]
> 'tis very important to be colour matched in the kitchen you know.
> Anyway, because I wanted a basic one – I think it was only 45 quid or
> something, so it was really quite cheap, but I was over the moon with
> it. So I got it from Argos – well Ellie got it for me from Argos…

What we see here is that, whilst a new microwave is seen as the means
to reclaiming the capacity of convenience, and also non-lumpy porridge, the
purchase of this replacement and the ridding of the old is deferred. Although
Pauline wanted a new microwave, she was prepared to wait three months

for this to arrive, framing this within the gift economy of birthdays. Rather than just going out and buying a replacement microwave – which she could afford to do – Pauline held the act of replacement over, in so doing allowing the presence of the gifted microwave in her house to legitimate the ridding of the old. Its presence as a gift therefore works to absorb the trace of guilt on her part about the old microwave's release.[2]

Having acquired her new microwave, Pauline found herself facing the problem of what to do with the old one. She resumes the story:

> So, anyway, I needed to get rid of my old one. So I thought, well I needed to take it down the tip because you can't put it in your bin really. And then there was this sort of dialogue of whether Keith was taking it down the tip. And I said, 'Well I think I'll wash it before you do' [Nicky: What was that all about?] I don't know – it must have been intuition as it turned out because – I just thought – well it still works, there might be somebody who'd want it, just on the off chance. And I thought if it went down the tip and it was in a clean condition somebody might be inclined to use it if they were that desperate. But if it was minging they wouldn't touch it would they? Well I wouldn't. No you wouldn't. And I just thought, well just on the off-chance because you know me – and I thought, 'Shall I take the glass dish out the bottom and use it as a spare? What can I salvage out of it?' You know what I mean. So in the end I decided to put the glass dish and the roller and the stand in it and give it a good clean and send it down the tip with Keith. Anyway, Keith phoned me back and he said, 'Pauline, I've got to tell you – you won't believe this,' he said, 'I went down the tip with that microwave of yours and I walked in and the bloke said, "I know where that's going." He said that he'd got a home for it. There was this woman and she'd just left her husband and she had two kids – a one-parent family – she had no white goods at all, like really on the bottom. And she'd been to the tip and she'd said, "If anyone comes with anything I'm just really desperate." And he'd said, "Well I'll keep an eye out for you pet."' And he's said to Keith, 'Is it working?' So he said, 'Well yes, it is working actually – it's not state of your art whatever but it is working.' And he said, 'Well I know where that's going. Shove it on the side.', for this woman like. So he said, 'I thought I'd let you know.' And I was just so made up. I was chuffed to Mint Balls. I really was chuffed. It made my day.

Clearly understood by her to be inappropriate physical matter to place in the wheelie bin, Pauline prepares this microwave for its journey to the tip, by cleaning it thoroughly. Although beyond her capacities to find the conditions for its continued valuation through her social networks, because of the malfunctioning state it was in, Pauline still wants to open this microwave up to potential revaluation in its release. Cleaning it thoroughly, doing consumption work on it herself, is the only way she can think of to begin to suggest the potential for revaluation to an unknown yet imagined to be desperate other. For who would bother to clean something that did not work and which was being jettisoned at a site of rubbish value, the tip? I would suggest that it is precisely this cleanliness in appearance which the tip employee spotted as different about this particular microwave when it entered the tip.

Of course, we will never know if this 'woman on the bottom' exists or not. Indeed, she could quite easily be a fictive presence designed to enable tip employees to appropriate things in the throes, even the throws, of their ridding. More important though is the potency of her image for Pauline: as the imagined beneficiary of her jettisoning, this woman's gift to Pauline – through her (imagined) destitution and deservingness – is to release Pauline from her guilt of ridding a microwave with partial value left in it. Furthermore, her presence in the narration enables Pauline to appropriate her new green microwave without guilt. Her ghost, connected as this is to the presence of the green microwave, allows Pauline both to accommodate this new appliance and narrate the release of the old without guilt.

A second microwave failure occurred in Sandra and Rob's house, also on Alternative Terrace. This happened just before Christmas 2003. Sandra and Rob took the microwave straight back to the retailer (Argos), as they had had the appliance for less than a year and it was still under retailer guarantee. Although Argos took it back, they had no replacement models to give them immediately (because it was Christmas – another indication of how microwave purchasing is embedded in the gift economy). Consequently, Sandra and Rob drove straight to Sandra's mother's caravan – a round trip of some 60 miles – to retrieve the microwave from there, this being unused over the winter months. When the fieldwork came to an end this microwave was still in their kitchen. It will stay there until Argos get round to telling them that the replacement one is available to collect.

The differences between the temporalities of this sequence of events and those in Pauline's household are striking. Whereas replacement and ridding took over three months to enact in Pauline's, Sandra and Rob felt it imperative to plug their loss in microwave capacity immediately. Indeed, they reorganised their entire day around this event. What this testifies to, of course, is the importance of a microwave's capacity to prepare food with push-button convenience. In a household in which meals are being prepared for a baby, for a five year old who has just started school and who comes home for lunch, for two adults and for an elderly father too, this capacity is seen as invaluable, essential even. The microwave's capacity to do Alice's baby foods instantly and to satisfy her hunger cries, to heat up quick meals for three or four lunches, and to do the meals across a two hour lunch period which extends from the start of primary school lunch break to include the demands of Sandra's clients is critical. Its capacities to provide hot baby food instantly allows them, simultaneously, to be good parents providing food for their baby when she desires it, to heat up an already cooked meal for their son at noon, and to be a couple with a business. The failure of the microwave in this household, then, is seen not as the loss of a physical thing but as the loss of a capacity, the importance of which is such that it enables them to enact some of their primary social identities.

Pauline's and Sandra and Rob's microwave stories allow us to see how living with kitchen appliances is about accommodating certain things for their capacity to do certain things for us and to allow us to get on with other things. But what they also highlight is the difficulties appliances pose households in their ridding. In taking their microwave back to Argos, Sandra and Rob are not just ensuring that they are going to get a replacement microwave, eventually. They are passing on the physical object that poses a problem for them; using it to claim another physical presence and simultaneously ridding themselves of its presence in their home, though its displacement. For Pauline, however, whose microwave was 14 years old, such displacement options were unavailable. This appliance was way past its guarantee period. Looking back at her narrative, we see how Pauline resorts to the normative in her dealings with the old microwave. She cannot gift it knowingly; seemingly she also takes it for granted that she cannot displace it via the wheelie bin. Repair – unusually in this instance, for this is someone who re-upholstered two sofas and partially rebuilt her outbuildings during the fieldwork – never even figured as an option. Instead, however reluctantly, Pauline accepts the normativity of having to get rid of its physical presence in her house; tellingly by getting Keith to carry it away for her, to the tip. Regardless of what actually happened (or not) to this microwave there, the key point is that this particular appliance was cast in a trajectory which indicates Pauline's inability to continue to accommodate it, the impossibility of its accommodation within either the homes of known others or within the second-hand economy, and the capacity of the normative to enable such acts of ridding. As we see in the following section, carrying away and throwing away are the primary ways that almost all the households participating in the ethnography accommodated appliance failure.

'We haven't had much luck with these things this year'

During the twelve months of the ethnography, Sandra and Rob had two of their kitchen appliances fail outright on them: their fridge-freezer and the microwave discussed above.[3] They also jettisoned a kettle and a toaster, both of which had ceased to work as they were designed and manufactured to. In discussing the appliance failures present in the ethnography then, it is largely the events that unfolded in this household which are highlighted.[4] In a sense such temporal juxtapositions in failure within one household do make sense: since we frequently buy large kitchen appliances when we move into our first non-furnished property, or when we replace kitchens, the manufactured product life built into these things suggests that some at least will fail around the same time.[5] Most households though – at least on the basis of this research – do not think about their appliances like this. Instead, depending on their experience of living with them, they talk about 'being lucky with' appliances or not, and of particular appliances being of good service or not. Pauline's 14-year-old microwave and the way she talked about this as having been of 'good service' is typical of valued appliance talk. In contrast, the first appliance to fail in Sandra and Rob's house is a clear example of the other type of talk.

Right at the beginning of the fieldwork, just one week after they had agreed to participate, Sandra and Rob's fridge-freezer 'packed-in'. This was frost-free technology, purchased on the recommendation of Sandra's mother, who had lauded the virtues of not having to spend time defrosting a freezer to her daughter. For Sandra, such appeals to labour-saving were attractive. At the time of the appliance's purchase, Josh was going to nursery for a few half-days a week and Sandra was building up the client base for her business. Anything that saved her time was regarded as a boon. So, the couple 'splashed-out' and bought a mid-price Daewoo model from Curry's. Eighteen months later, when it was out of the retailer guarantee period, it failed, at which point Sandra was six months pregnant. Given its cost to them and their general commitment to preserving the life in things and to avoiding wasting, Sandra and Rob contacted the Daewoo service engineers and called them out, anticipating that the appliance would be a straightforward repair job. The response was not what they had expected. Sandra and Rob were told that this fridge-freezer was 'not worth repairing': according to the engineer, frost-free technology was only worth investing in if you could afford to pay top-end prices; cheap to mid-range models were designed to fail and were not worth paying the repair cost to fail again. For Sandra and Rob this was devastating news. They knew that their income would drop off noticeably when Sandra was on maternity leave. At the same time, all spare household income was going towards saving for the new baby.

The loss of fridge-freezer capacity also posed the couple immediate food-storage problems. This household are vegetarians and have strong opinions on animal farming practices and on what they feed themselves and their family. They also have a complete aversion to packaging of almost all kinds. Their freezer then is usually filled not with pizzas and burgers, but with home-prepared food cooked by Sandra and made from largely organic or free-range ingredients. With the fridge-freezer not working, the couple had to find an immediate location for their frozen food. They managed to do this by distributing the freezer contents across neighbours' houses on a temporary basis, before disappearing off to buy a replacement fridge-freezer on in-store credit. With an estate car, the couple were able to collect the appliance the next day from Curry's regional distribution centre, rather than wait for one to be delivered a week later. Sandra duly installed the new Beko fridge-freezer ('an ordinary one') in the kitchen, restocking it with the food retrieved from their neighbours, whilst Rob dragged the old one out into their yard. There it stood for the next ten days, awaiting collection by the local authority bulky waste collection service.

To an observer, it is interesting what happened to the fridge-freezer over those ten days. The arrangement of the houses on Alternative Terrace is such that, as in many locations in the North-east, the yard is the main thorough-fare in and out of the house. So, every time that Sandra and Rob went in or out of their house they had to walk past the fridge-freezer. Moreover, when others walked past and saw them they drew attention to this appliance in their yard and asked the story. Correspondingly, Sandra and Rob found themselves having to retell the failure story on several occasions. According to Sandra, after about a week of this Rob started to wreak acts of sabotage and cannibalism on the appliance. He began to kick it as he went past, and then extracted the various wire baskets and food containers to use in his DIY tools' store. Eventually, to much relief, the Daewoo finally disappeared down the back lane of Alternative Terrace on the back of a council lorry one Friday morning, out of their sight and out of their lives.

The story of the Daewoo will be familiar to many living in the UK, conjoining as it does successive technological innovations' appeals to further labour-saving, the apparent nonsense of repair in circumstances where product failure is built in to particular things, and the imperative to recapture appliance capacity through replacement purchasing. But what is particularly striking about this story is the Daewoo's passage out of Sandra and Rob's house, particularly the visibility of this appliance in its failure and the way in which this seems to connect to negative emotions. What I suggest, is that it was the constantly visible quality of this passage out of the household that intensified negative emotions. Walking past it as they walk in and out of the house, seeing it out of their kitchen window as they wash up, having to retell the narrative as others who walk past comment, this is a looming presence in their lives for ten days, making visible its failed capacity because it cannot be removed from their sight. Is it any wonder then that, having caused them so much trouble, and being continually in their field of vision, this appliance starts to attract Rob's ire? Or that his anger towards it, hatred of it even, is directed in such a way that this will have effects on its future trajectory. With dents in its door that are indicative of boot marks, and minus its internal storage systems, this fridge-freezer is being trashed before being carried away. Rob's actions and their indelibility in the material configuration of this particular appliance seem to ensure that its trajectory is not only out of their lives but a final one, to rubbish value.

The jettisoning of both a kettle and a toaster from Sandra and Rob's household has some similarities with the above, but only some. Neither of these smaller appliances had been working properly at the beginning of the fieldwork; the lever on the toaster needed to be held down to toast bread, and the button on the kettle had to be handled similarly. Sandra and Rob persevered with both until early September 2003, arguing that since the two appliances still worked, albeit with their assistance, they couldn't be thrown away. In September 2003, however, Josh started school, and the early morning routine in this household changed dramatically. Rob gets in from work at 8.30 a.m. each morning, and Josh has to be in school by 8.55 a.m. For Sandra to see to Alice and get Josh ready, dressed and fed usually involves a frantic rush. Indeed, she barely has enough hands to manage this routine without holding down both a toaster lever and a kettle button. Josh's first day at school then was marked by the jettisoning of both appliances into the wheelie bin and the purchase of two new cheap replacements from Argos.

The transition in this household's value system regarding small kitchen appliances consequent upon Josh going to school could not be more dramatic. We see here how the capacity to tolerate partial working, and to accommodate everyday life to this by adding in human bodily capacities to the appliance, is overturned by the increasingly intense time-space scheduling requirements of a household with school-age children and adults in paid

Figure 6.1: Ted and June's dishwasher

employment. Quite simply, these appliances now have to do what they have been designed and manufactured to do: to continue to tolerate partial working would require the household to find more time, already a scarce resource, and would appear to value defective appliance's lives over their time, and by implication their lives too. As Sandra said at the time, with new replacements costing next to nothing, to persist in such circumstances would not just have been unusual but open to being read as 'plain barmy'. Whilst happy to appear 'plain barmy' in the supermarket, where she insists on not putting fruit and vegetables in plastic bags, and on having continual disagreements with the checkout cashiers as a consequence, valuing the worn and defective at her expense is a different matter. It is altogether easier just to throw away and replace, and even more so when this enables the work of being the good parent to be accomplished more smoothly and efficiently.

In all four of these instances – the fridge-freezer, the microwave, the toaster and the kettle – we see very clearly how appliance failure and its connection to immediate replacement is actually about reproducing particular ways of living in contemporary Britain. Everyday life – at least for this household – requires that food be stored yet available to be eaten immediately, at press-button convenience. Moreover, as is illuminated by the various goings-on in Sandra and Rob's house, the complexities of the time-space rhythms within this household mean that appliances have to deliver what is required – toast, boiling water, a meal to be eaten, a choice of meals – all the time and every time. In circumstances such as these, repair is not just economic nonsense, but a nonsense culturally, for repair is about a temporal loss in appliance capacities, albeit a temporary loss. Ridding these things, in ways that set them in trajectories that connect them to rubbish value, and replacing them with substitute things, at least for households with young children like Sandra and Rob, makes a great deal of economic and cultural sense. Ridding and replacement work to reclaim the capacities on which everyday life in such households rely and which are taken-for-granted facets of their lives. As we see now, although the practices disclosed in Sandra and Rob's household are undeniably widespread, certain instances of appliance failure remain unconnected to ridding and instead entail the continued accommodation of these things.

Accommodating love through failed appliances

Ted and June have a dishwasher in their kitchen. After several visits to this household, many of which involved drinking tea and eating snacks, it became apparent that the dishwasher did not appear to be loaded with dirty cups, mugs and plates. Instead, Ted invariably washed all these things up. I wondered whether this was a household like Geoff and Hilary's, where the dishwasher is talked about openly as an object of ambivalence. Geoff and Hilary have strong 'green' orientations and are keenly aware of how much energy their dishwasher uses when in use. They are also acutely aware of the potential this dishwasher has to undermine their green credentials, although they counter this in their talk, to some degree, by revealing that they acquired this dishwasher second-hand via a friend. Nonetheless, Geoff and Hilary only use this dishwasher when they have guests for dinner, at Christmas and on other occasions which are heavy on food preparation, that is, when the situation appears to constitute either mitigating or legitimating circumstances. Towards the end of the fieldwork, around Christmas time, Ted and June invited me – along with Janet – for a meal. Again the dishwasher did not get activated, though it took Ted around 30 minutes to do the washing up – which he did while we all talked. On my next visit, I asked June directly about this dishwasher. June raised her eyebrows and gave a huge sigh, 'Ah, the dishwasher' she says, and proceeds to tell me the story (Figure 6.1).

The dishwasher's arrival in their house dates back to when they first moved in. June had the fitted kitchen altered slightly to accommodate a split double oven and a hob (see also Chapter 2). The space where there had been an oven, next to the washing machine, was plumbed in to accommodate a dishwasher. However, as June makes clear in the telling, the dishwasher was her idea. 'He' – meaning Ted – 'was never keen', she says. For some years the dishwasher was used on odd occasions, just as with Geoff and Hilary, when visitors came for meals and at Christmas, but it was always operated by June. Ted refused point blank to have anything to do with it. The dishwasher failed some five years after it was purchased, and was repaired. A few years later it failed again. The couple called the service engineer, who came out to tell them that the appliance was obsolete – 'That was an expensive £80', says June. However, rather than get rid of the obsolete appliance, the dishwasher remains *in situ*. June laughs hollowly about this, and says, 'If it were left to me I'd get rid of it immediately. I'd use one all the time. But it's not just about me. I suppose you could say it fills a hole!'

There's a lot going on in this history of a dishwasher. First, there's the way in which appliance failure and repair can be accommodated within a household in which the patterns of use is intermittent. Unlike Sandra and Rob's household, it doesn't matter here that the capacity is temporarily unavailable, because the dishwasher itself is only rarely put to work. Secondly, manufactured obsolescence is well to the fore, in this dishwasher's repetitive failure and ultimate 'death' by parts unavailability. Thirdly though, it is vital to note that this instance of failure and obsolescence does not connect with ridding. To understand this it is imperative to look at the domestic division of labour within this household, and at Ted's disposition towards an appliance that performs a particular function. As the primary washer-up in this household for decades – itself an indication of June's positioning as the primary cook – Ted regarded the arrival of this machine in their house as an affront and as an insult: he tells me later that it made him feel redundant. Furthermore, when other family members commented positively on the capacities of the machine to make things like glasses sparkling clean, he felt even more affronted. Ted admitted to me that he was actually quite pleased when the dishwasher failed, and that he was even more pleased when it was declared to be obsolete: he the infallible and reliable washer-up was still here. June admits that at the time of its purchase she had no idea that Ted would feel so threatened by the capacities of a machine, but says that she can now see other examples of similar dispositions towards other things in the house. Actually I'm not so sure that these are the same; to me Ted's aversion to the mobile phone, to the TV remote and to programming the video recorder are different, and not about manufactured threats to the domestic tasks that he routinely does. Regardless, for June the effect of this realisation has been to resist all temptation to argue for another dishwasher: the continued presence of the obsolete, defunct dishwasher in their kitchen, then, is about June's accommodation to Ted's self-designated role as household washer-up and, simultaneously, is an accommodation to Ted's valuation of manual over automated capacities. But it is an accommodation which only works in relation to this particular thing. To remove it and/or replace it would set in chain a different set of people–appliance accommodations, filling June's 'hole' in a very different manner.

Retaining capacities through accommodation

Back in South Hightown, but on the Rivers estate, other instances of appliance failure are accommodated rather differently. These connect with the enactment of much more intricate and convoluted economies of repair, but are at a considerable remove from the economies of repair disclosed in Sandra and Rob's and June and Ted's households. Sharon's mother Betty is a council tenant in her mid 70s. She lives alone and has been a widow for over twenty years. She is dependent entirely on the state pension for her income. Betty finds appliance failures problematic to finance. But appliance failures are a frequent occurrence in her household, for she finds herself caught in a circle of endlessly buying cheap reconditioned second-hand appliances (because these are all she can afford), only for these to last for about six months before they fail again. Fortunately for Betty, her son-in-law Barry is able to turn his hand to appliance repair. This though has significant effects on what these two related households do with their failed appliances. Betty's one-bedroom bungalow has a washing machine and two defunct fridges in storage in what was her coal store. She also has a washing machine and fridge in the kitchen, along with a cooker and a microwave. When, at the beginning of the field-work, her washing machine failed, Betty bought a second-hand one via one of the local village pubs. Barry asked around for her, and somehow a second-hand washing machine materialised a week or so later, paid for initially by Barry and then by her. Barry moved the failed washing machine up the street and over to his and Sharon's bungalow on a wheelbarrow; they do not have a car. This washing machine is now in Sharon and Barry's shed, declared to be 'parts'. Along with the other failed washing machine in Betty's coal store, it is being held over in storage as a resource for keeping Betty's existing 'in use' washing machine going.

The repair economy that binds Betty's household to Sharon and Barry's is one that is reiterated in many low income neighbourhoods in Britain and is usually understood through the notion of 'time rich/income poor' social networks (Pahl 1984). And, as might be anticipated from this frame, Betty does indeed return the favour by investing time in cooking a Sunday lunch for Barry and Sharon each week, of roast beef, roast potatoes and a plate of Yorkshire puddings. Perhaps as important in all this, though, are the way economies of repair work to forestall ridding. As well as having the effect of placing appliances in long-term storage, this seems to signal a profoundly dif-ferent understanding of the appliance to that discussed so far in this chapter. So, rather than being understood as singular objects with a particular set of capacities, as a black box, in these households appliances are understood by Barry through an ontology of depth, that is as assemblages of largely invisible but accessible component parts. These components are substituted for one another and mixed together from different models. They are, then, examples of hybrids, put together from cannibalised drums, brushes, motors and cir-cuit boards and the practical human knowledge that experiments in putting these things together.[6]

Putting these three households – Ted and June's, Betty's and Sharon and Barry's – together, two points emerge. First, in these circumstances appliance failure is not followed by ridding but by the continued accommodation of these things. Indeed, as we see with Ted and June, failure's co-presence in the kitchen in the form of an obsolete dishwasher can be a means to reconstitut-ing the couple in cohabitation. Here failure is accommodated for love. With Betty, Sharon and Barry, failures are understood as partial failures only, of components not of the whole appliance. To rid in such circumstances then, would be to get rid of other components that may potentially be of value in reclaiming appliance capacities in the future. Secondly, both instances high-light that the social relations of habitation are critical to understanding appli-ance trajectories. Just as ridding failed kitchen appliances and replacing them with the new works to reclaim patterns of everyday life for Sandra and Rob, not ridding enables everyday life to carry on in some of these households. What the ethnography suggests, then, is that there is no one way of living with kitchen appliances' capacities to fail. There is no automatic trajectory of ridding that locates failed appliances as matter of rubbish value. Instead, we live with appliances in a relation of continued accommodation, in which the relations of habitation and cohabitation impinge directly on the trajectory of these things, even in their failure, and perhaps most acutely in their failure.

Conclusions

Together, kitchen appliances and the energy they harness produce an intensely manufactured environment in our kitchens; an environment which works to produce convenience, unless there are disruptions to energy supplies, and which is supposedly safe and risk free. But what these appliances also provide is particular normative ways of doing practices that are integral to everyday life itself. So, laundering clothes is something that is rarely performed by hand or by a twin tub; instead it is work done by an automated washer and/ or drier. Boiling water is not produced via a pan on a fire, but from a kettle. Similarly, bread is not held over tongs on a fire to make toast but pings from a toaster. Freezers and microwaves combine to store and prepare ready-made meals, circumventing both the need to shop daily and the work of cooking food. And dishwashers do the work of cleaning and drying the implements, tools and containers we use for cooking, eating, eating off and drinking from. Although frequently understood in the research literature in terms of frames that highlight the connections between social change and technology, the changing understanding of time or actor-network theory, the points I would make about these appliances are two: in the automation of tasks, the tasks themselves have not just become separated from us, they have become invisible to us, as has how these machines actually do the work they do. When a kettle boils we do not normally stand and watch it do so. Instead we do something else, we might help sort out a child's school-bag or glance at the TV. Similarly, most of us do not stand and watch the operation of either the washing machine or the dishwasher. We do something else, precisely because we take it for granted that the machine will get on with the task in hand. Furthermore, the majority of us have very little idea of what is inside these appliances, or of how they do what they do. Most of us are not like Barry. Instead, we are framed, through instruction manuals, as operatives of these things, not as their engineers. Our role is to push the buttons in the right sequence, to call the service engineer if appropriate, and definitely not to open up the inner workings of the machine inside, let alone to do what Barry does, experiment with and cannibalise the things inside to make hybrids.

There seem to be important corollaries of these points, three of which are worth highlighting. First, as these tasks have been pushed into the background of our lives, made into practices that go on whilst we do something else, so the appliances themselves have become largely invisible presences in our routine everyday lives. Audible maybe, accessed and encountered through touch, known through the transformations wrought to other things that are put inside them, but rarely the focus of our spectatorship, kitchen appliances only come into the full focus of our vision as things in themselves when they fail to do what they are supposed to do. We saw this very clearly – and some of its effects – with Sandra and Rob's fridge-freezer. Our positioning with respect to these appliances though is far more tendentious than this might suggest. As we feed these machines in everyday life, with uncooked food, dirty clothes and dirty dishes, and as we press the buttons to activate capacities, we emerge less as the agents of these things, and rather more as slaves to their capacities; we feed them to justify their presence and accommodation in our homes. As co-presences which position us as their slaves, and as things that have lives through their capacities to perform certain actions, or not, kitchen appliances are some of the objects about which we display our greatest ambivalence. We may value them for the manufactured environment of convenience they give us, but they are simultaneously things we frequently fear or hate, for the power their capacities have to disrupt the ways in which we enact our everyday lives. Their potential to fail and/or malfunction, seemingly with total unpredictability, is a constant facet of accommodating them; a capacity of which we are all aware.

Second, I want to return to the spatial fixity of appliance lives in our accommodation. Spatial fixity means that appliances too have 'homes' within our dwelling structures. These things literally live in holes and gaps in kitchen units, and in places on top of work surfaces. This is where they connect up to energy supplies and outlets, and this is where they do their work for us. But these holes, gaps and places are not just sites for placement and energy consumption. Rather they become the medium for the invisibility of these things in everyday life. It is, I argue, precisely because of their immobility within our homes and their confinement in and absorption by domestic space that we come to see these things only in the moments of touch that activate them, open and shut their doors and switch them off at wall sockets at night, if appropriate. Correspondingly, and in what amounts to a critical slippage, these holes, gaps and places in our kitchens become spaces which are identified with and known as the sites where certain activities are done, or not if an appliance fails. The holes, gaps and surfaces become the spaces for doing things in our kitchens. This, I think, has critical effects on understanding the general trajectory of appliances in our homes and through our homes. Ted and June are the exception here: for all the other households, a failed appliance was one that was removed from its position in the kitchen, disconnected and, with the exception of Betty's and Sharon and Barry's households, usually displaced from the house in a way that connected it to a site of rubbish value. To be sure, much of this is about manufactured obsolescence, the high cost of economies of repair and the relative low cost of replacement. But what also goes on when appliances fail is loss, in individual appliance's capacity and a more general loss of kitchen environments to do what they were designed to do, to work as manufactured environments. So, when we buy a replacement appliance, what we are doing is not just recapturing an appliance's capacity through another's presence, but countering the loss in our kitchen environments and in the capacity of a kitchen to manufacture an environment for living in. By contrast, repair involves the temporary loss of an appliance and of capacity, leaving our kitchens with highly visible gaps and with an absent presence. Such lost capacities transform domestic environments from accommodating homes into an accommodation that is lacking.

Third, I would highlight that it is the manner of our accommodations of appliances within our homes which discloses why their ridding connects so closely with their wasting. Most of us are not like Barry in our accommodations of these things. Barry emerges in this research as a man whose identity, more than most, is integrally bound to the fabrication of the domestic. Building a loft conversion, installing a kitchen, rewiring the house, doing the plumbing – these are what Barry does and what he enjoys doing. Rebuilding washing machines is just another facet of his identity and this disposition. For Barry, then, the appliance manuals, manufacturer and retailer guarantees and service engineers which frame many households' accommodations of appliances just do not enter the dwelling structure. Appliance capacities here are built, not declared and dictated by a triumvirate of manufacturers, retailers and service engineers. For Barry, to rid makes no sense. But for others, including the vast majority of households in this ethnography, these things are black boxes, capacities, things in which complex emotions spanning fear and hate are invested, and things which are accommodated in their homes through the normative. It is, then, no surprise that households draw on this same normative to simultaneously rid and replace these things when they go wrong, as they inevitably do. The effect of this, however, is that ridding appliances entails wasting. So, the very same households who go to such lengths to avoid wasting so many other things in their ridding chuck small appliances like kettles and toasters in to their wheelie bins, take microwaves to the tip and ring the council to carry away – as waste – their failed large appliances. Few regarded this positively, with most regarding it as 'a waste'. But for all bar Barry and June, wasting these things was integral to their accommodation, for it is their capacities which in turn make dwelling structures accommodating homes, and places to be at home in.

NOTES

1 The list of appliances which exited the households is as follows: a washing machine, a cooker, two fridge-freezers, a tumble drier, three microwaves, four kettles, two toasters and an iron.

2 Pauline's guilt at wanting to get rid of something that still worked is a sentiment widely felt by several of the participants in this study. That she resorted to the gift to alleviate her guilt is also telling, in that this allows the gift (of related others) to absorb and absolve the guilt.

3 When I returned to visit Sandra and Rob in the summer of 2004, they recounted how their lives had continued in the same vein. Their oven – given to them by Sandra's mother when she had replaced her kitchen – had exploded that spring. They had apparently spent the next six weeks cooking on a Baby Belling, before they could afford to go out and get a replacement.

4 Lest it be thought that what is discussed here is in any way exceptional, I would emphasise that during the same period Ginny and Lesley jettisoned two kettles and an iron in their wheelie bin, Judy dispensed with a toaster in a similar manner, and Andrew and Mel's kettle also went the same way. Indeed, absolutely no one repaired or even attempted to repair a small appliance, reasoning that with replacements available at under £10 in either Argos or Asda, to do so was totally irrational. Furthermore, the questionnaire returns from the Environment Day showed that those who had recently got rid of a fridge-freezer, a tumble drier or a washing machine had done so for similar reasons; to buy new was the cheaper option. All had either made use of the council's bulky waste collection service to get rid of these old things, or they had paid for a retailer to carry it away for them.

5 Jo-Anne's IKEA kitchen discussed in detail in Chapter 2 is an example of tied appliance purchasing. Sandra's mother provides another instance. Sandra tells the story in a way which makes clear her own disapproval of her mother's seduction by a new kitchen, but adds that this

was how they came by their then oven – the one which went on to explode. At the time this was a much better offer than the oven that was in the house when she moved in with Rob.

6 It is important to mention that Barry only does this type of work with large appliances. Like all the other households, small appliances such as toasters and kettles are chucked in the wheelie bin when they fail, and then replaced, in Barry and Sharon's case at Argos.

Chapter 7

Accommodating nature

In the previous chapter, we saw how kitchen appliances work to produce manufactured environments in our homes and just how central these environments are to several mundane practices, and therefore to daily life in households. In this chapter I look at how other non-human things, specifically plant matter and the companion animals that share our domestic space, are accommodated in our homes. My argument here is that in accommodating these non-human things, in making gardens from them and living with them as co-presences in our homes, we continually have to manage their effects. Invariably, this involves both appropriation and divestment, but as with appliances, the ridding that goes on here is intrinsically connected to wasting. As we will see, managing the ridding of animal and plant matter in habitation goes to the heart of current understandings of accommodating a domesticated nature. The chapter begins with an exploration of the various gardening practices disclosed, and considers their relation to the ridding of plant matter. It then moves on to consider the accommodations of living with companion animals and the ridding that occurs in relation to them. I conclude the chapter, firstly, by making some more general observations on accommodating domesticated nature and the emphasis it places on the management of excess, arguing that living with these non-human presences requires an eternal vigilance and, in South Hightown at least, a reworking of domestication through the ordering of excess. Secondly, I highlight the importance of a domesticated nature to contemporary dwelling, emphasising how practices of gardening and living with companion animals are fundamentally about inhabitation and being at home in one's home.

Gardening and growth

In a way that is peculiarly and uniquely English, all sixteen of the dwelling structures in this ethnography had areas attached to them that could be described as gardens. Given the location of these dwelling structures in South Hightown and on the edges of the Newcastle conurbation, this is hardly surprising. Indeed, such is the importance of gardens in English culture that it would require a radically different city centre or inner-city location, with

Figure 7.1: Geoff and Hilary's garden

areas of high-rise and/or apartment living, to produce a research setting without them. However, as will become apparent, the gardening practices disclosed by these households are widely different, and competences and degrees of gardening knowledge highly divergent. As we will see, this has huge effects on how accommodations with plant matter are reached. Indeed, they have considerable implications for how plant growth is managed by households.

Four of the households in the ethnography are extremely keen gardeners, devoting much of their spare time and/or their retirement to working on and in their gardens. The four gardens are of contrasting styles, but all are recognisable examples of English garden traditions. Geoff and Hilary's is a walled 'cottage-style' garden, with a pond (Figure 7.1).

Their garden design, plant selection and gardening practices are all framed in accordance with environmental and biodiversity criteria. In this garden, plants are grown for their capacities and not just for their aesthetic appeal. Plants are grown to attract other species and to inhibit or suppress the growth of others. This is indicative of Hilary's botanical training and interests, and of her professional investments in environmental issues. The effects of this are felt in both the gardening talk and practices in this household. Here plants are referred to by their Latin names, whilst routine growth management – such as hedge pruning – is itself accommodated around the lives of other non-human things, notably nesting birds. In contrast, Ted and June's and Linda and Paul's gardens feature planting styles that centre borders of perennials and mature shrubs, set off by lawns of varying levels. With distinct echoes of the eighteenth-century English landscape tradition, theirs are examples of the 'English-country-house-in-suburbia' garden (Figure 7.2).

Both couples routinely visit National Trust gardens through the summer months, to admire, to learn and to inspire. At the same time, they both go to

Figure 7.2: Ted and June's garden

a wide range of garden centres and plant nurseries across the region, searching out particular plant species and varieties for their gardens.[1] On Wear Road in South Hightown, one household stands out for its garden. This is Peggy and Harry's (Figure 7.3a nd b).

Harry has been a keen gardener all his life and, in his retirement, continues to work as a casual gardener for three other households in South Hightown, none of them living on the Rivers estate. His style of gardening though is very different to the households highlighted thus far, emphasising the cultivation of annuals and hanging baskets, of tomatoes via the greenhouse, and of vegetables and fruit bushes. Onions, potatoes, strawberries and rhubarb are his specialities.[2] Like the other three households, lawn management is another vital part of Harry's gardening practice. He cuts the grass at least twice a week during the growing season, edges and aerates the lawns, and routinely 'feeds and weeds' these areas using tried and tested chemical products.[3]

Regardless of the different plant matters in their gardens, all four of these households invest sizeable amounts of time in their management. Ted and June and Harry and Peggy work daily in their gardens from spring through to autumn, weather permitting. Geoff and Hilary and Linda and Paul spend some summer evenings and parts of their weekends similarly engaged. As a result, their gardens are always immaculate, with plant growth being well managed and under control. In three of these households, lawns are kept close cut; trees and shrubs are invariably appropriately pruned; the flowers of annuals are routinely 'dead-headed' and perennials are 'cut back' in the autumn. Moreover, three of the four households compost all of their garden and vegetable waste, using this each year for renewing their garden beds.[4]

Figure 7.3 a/b: Harry and Peggy's garden

At the other end of the spectrum in terms of garden management, are Claire and Nathan, on Wear Road. Neither Claire nor Nathan know anything about gardening, they tell me. Their three-bedroom council house, however, comes with a large back garden, a legacy of the importance of the tradition of vegetable cultivation at the time of their building. As we have already seen in Chapter 3, the primary use of this garden is as a dump for stuff that is being thrown out of the house; and it is also where they burn such matter. Occasionally, however, Claire and Nathan have tried to 'do something' about their 'grass'. In the summer of 2003 they emptied the entire contents of a box of weed killer on this grass. Nothing happened: it still looked the same, long and greeny yellow. Throughout the fieldwork, Nathan says that he will try to do something about the garden, but for the most part the back door out to it remains firmly locked. Abigail is banned from playing out in it: Nathan says,

'I don't like going out in it so there's no way she's going to go out there.' With so little human attention, it is perhaps not surprising that this garden has been taken over by couch grass, bindweed, nettles, thistles and briars. Indeed, the two wire fences that mark the property off from their neighbours' houses are entangled in bindweed. The only area without plant growth is the burning site, a pile of ashes in the middle of what once was a lawn. In gardening terms, this space would typify the 'gone to waste' label; it is a reversion to its natural state. Nathan and Claire's garden is at the extreme end of gardening practice, a manifestation of their lack of gardening knowledge. However, they are not alone in their practice, at least on Wear Road, where other households routinely park their cars on the grass areas in front of their houses and burn three-piece suites in their overgrown and neglected back gardens. The exceptional gardening practice on this street is definitely Peggy and Harry's. Nathan and Claire's lack of gardening knowledge, however, is replicated across many of the other households in the ethnography.

For some of these other households, the response has been to manage garden space by covering it over, either with paving slabs – as Christine and Malcolm have done – or with various structures that define the garden as a children's playground. Ellie and Steve's garden is the best example of this in the ethnography. Half of this approximately 20 × 30' space is covered over with a patio terrace, on which stands a set of garden furniture, a large table, four chairs and an umbrella. There is also a brick barbecue on this terrace and a very large Wendy House for the girls to play in. Further down, the garden is grassed over, but houses a big and small slide, side by side. One is Rachel's and the other is Chloe's. There are no plants in this garden, only a few pots on the patio terrace. Other households however struggle – with varying degrees of success – to manage their gardens within a planting norm. That is, they keep their gardens within the parameters of acceptability in plant growth, but without investing the time that the first group of households devote to this practice, and without the practical and academic knowledge that set this group of households apart. Judy, Pauline and Andrew and Mel are all like this.[5]

Judy, Pauline and Andrew and Mel all make a degree of investment in various practices of gardening. Judy routinely goes to garden centres with her mother at the weekends in the spring, to buy annuals for planting in pots and for hanging baskets. This has a double function: as well as enabling her to do her garden, it is a way of taking her elderly mother out and of enabling her mother to continue to cultivate plants, something which she takes pleasure in but is unable to do in the care-home in which she lives. Judy herself has some practical knowledge about plants and planting through the year, much of it learnt from her mother, from garden centres and from watching gardening programmes on TV. Although she has not the intense knowledge of, or investments in, the garden and gardening that characterise the households of Geoff and Hilary, Linda and Paul, Ted and June and Peggy and Harry – being prepared to let plants 'take a chance' living (and dying) with her and the animals, rather than nurturing them – she is infinitely more knowledgeable about gardening and plant matter than, say, Pauline. Pauline refuses to have anything to do with visiting garden centres, regarding these as 'glorified supermarkets and a rip off'. Neither does she watch television programmes on gardening. Instead, the plants in her garden were either all *in situ* when she bought the house, or have been accumulated through plant gifting from friends and neighbours. In many senses then, the plant matter in Pauline's garden maps Pauline's social networks, and is a random accumulation selected for her, rather than self-selected via garden centres or nurseries. What this testifies to, though, is Pauline's own lack of investments in and insecurities over gardening practice. In letting others determine the contents of her garden via plant gifts, she enjoys the safety conferred through the practice, for what could be a safer form of gardening than growing what more knowledgeable gardeners than her grow? In contrast to both Judy and Pauline, Andrew and Mel's anxieties in gardening are even more transparent. Having attended to some of the excess tree growth in their garden shortly after they moved in (see Chapter 2), the couple's only planting acts in the twelve months of fieldwork were to plant two fruit trees and a couple of pots. On more than one occasion, and in ways that resonate with Nathan's talk, Andrew remarked to me that he really was not at all sure where to begin 'out here', or what to do. And for the time being, so he says, he has more than enough to occupy his non-working time on the inside of the house (Chapter 2).[6]

As we can see from the foregoing, although these three households have gardens and do gardening in ways that acknowledge the presence of regulatory gardening norms, they neither define themselves through gardening nor identify themselves as gardeners. Indeed, through their practices they display many of the anxieties that are associated with more conventional arenas of consumption and identity, particularly fashion and clothing. What I would highlight about these households' gardening practice, however, is that it is continually being accommodated with other facets of their lives. Gardening is something that all three of these households fit in to everyday life, because they feel that they have to; and because if they did not they would end up with gardens like Claire and Nathan's. But as we will see, fitting gardening in, rather than doing this routinely, even daily, means that they frequently have to cope with excessive amounts of growth in plant matter.

As they tell the story, Andrew and Mel's garden posed them with even greater problems on moving in than did their house. Uninhabited for over twelve months, and previously lived in for some years by an elderly woman, the garden had reverted to nature. The grass had become a two-foot-high meadow; the privet hedge was over six feet tall; a laurel tree had reached around twenty feet; various shrubs had grown to fifteen feet and then there were the trees. Five leylandii – all of them around twenty feet, and two large cherry trees were competing with the laurel. The trees were the first things to attract Andrew's attentions, in the spring of 2003. Andrew could see and hear signs of neighbours tackling their leylandii trees: the sound of chain saws was all around, trailers of leylandii matter went by on the road, and various lay-bys and field gates around and about South Hightown started to fill up with piles of abandoned leylandii matter. Andrew asked about in the pub, and was eventually put in the direction of 'a local tree surgeon'. Two men duly turned up at Andrew and Mel's house one spring afternoon when I was round at Janet's, and started sawing at the trees. They left a huge amount of lopped branches and leylandii growth on the couple's lawn. As Andrew reflected when he got in from work and saw the pile, 'Maybe I should have asked them what they were going to do with it!!' Confronted with all this plant matter, Andrew had to work out what to do with it. Sandra and Rob took some of the wood off his hands, wheel-barrowing this up the street to their wood store. But they would not take the leylandii, telling Andrew that this 'wouldn't burn'. Reluctant to put this matter in their new car, Andrew started to ask around the village informal economy, to see if anyone would carry it away. Eventually, after being passed through several contacts, he got in touch with 'Frank'. Frank makes a living carrying away people's unwanted matter: 'If you want rid of anything, try Frank' is a saying on the Rivers estate.[7] Frank duly turned up, loaded the leylandii onto the back of his pick-up, cash exchanged hands and the leylandii disappeared – 'Who knows where,' says Andrew, 'but my guess is to a lay-by near here!'

Having dealt with the trees, Andrew set about the grass with the help of his dad. Andrew's dad bought his large motorised lawnmower over and – after two days' work and several bin bags later – 'a lawn, or a green carpet – take your pick!' (Andrew) reappeared. 'Don't ever let that get like that again', Andrew's dad implored. Around the same time, the cherry trees that had been pruned by the local tree surgeon started, in Andrew's words, to 'look a bit sick'. He eventually managed to get another tree surgeon – this one known by his dad – to have a look at them. 'Well it turns out that actually those tree surgeons didn't know what they were doing', says Andrew. More lopping and pruning ensued, leaving Andrew with more tree matter to dispose of. Again, some went to Sandra and Rob, but the remainder Andrew burnt slowly, along with other leaf matter in a wheel barrow in the garden; a year on, the privet hedge remains *in situ*.

Andrew and Mel's gardening story is one of reclamation and is indicative of the power of the normative with respect to garden appearances. To live on this street, for Andrew and Mel, seemingly, required that the garden did not remain in the state it was in. Also on Alternative Terrace, Pauline's garden provides further testimony to the workings of this normative. Here too gardening is simultaneously about managing growth and a struggle to accommodate. Pauline loves her garden, rather than gardening: she loves the space and the tranquillity it provides her, and she frequently spends the summer afternoons when she is not working asleep there in a hammock. Pauline's difficulty though is in trying to juggle the upkeep of the garden with the various other facets of her life. Working for two and a half days a week, going to Keith's at the weekend, and being a semi-professional singer leaves her precious little time to fit gardening in. Periodically then, on Wednesday afternoons during the summer, and in a routine that is indelibly marked in my body's remembering, I would help Pauline cut her privet hedges. The rhythm to this would go something like this: Pauline would get in from work and announce her arrival with 'Jesus Christ, look at this fucking hedge; it's growing in front of my eyes!' I would go round. Pauline would place an old decorating sheet under the hedge, bring out the ladder and the shears and start clipping. Once the sheet was full of privet trimmings, these would be bundled into a black plastic bin bag. Pauline would make some tea and I would take her place at the hedge. And so it would go on, over two hedges. Eventually the black plastic bin bags – usually three of them – would be shoved in her wheelie bin. Whereupon we would collapse into the garden furniture, drink more tea and endlessly talk.

Over at Judy's, it is the front garden that is the equivalent to Pauline's privet. When she gets in from work and from seeing to her mother and the animals, Judy says that she is just 'too knackered' to contemplate doing anything about cutting the grass. A consequence is that the grass grows and grows, until she needs a strimmer to cut it. As with Pauline's privet cuttings, Judy bags it all up, as household rubbish, and puts it out in the black sack refuse collection. Judy's back garden poses other difficulties. Although most of this is paved over, the flower beds are seen to need routine weeding and digging over. Again this is something Judy finds to be hard physical work, and hard to accommodate within her schedule. It takes her a whole weekend to do one bed, amongst the other things that she has to do, and there are four flower beds in the garden. So, by the time she's done the fourth bed, it looks like nothing has been done to the first. The routine of garden maintenance in this household is a constant battle to overcome the visibility of the weeds.

Pauline's privet cuttings and Judy's grass strimmings and weeds are all immediately routed into the routine weekly household refuse collection. Without the investments in gardening that make composting a sensible practice, their only other option with what to do with this excess plant matter would be to take it to the tip. However, as we saw with Andrew, taking excess plant matter to the tip seems to pose households with a problem: this is not the sort of matter that many households seem to want to place inside their cars.[8] There are several potential reasons for this. One, as Pauline's privet cuttings demonstrated, is that this matter is difficult to tame, even in black plastic bin bags. It spills out of these bags from the top; it escapes through the sides that are split by twigs; it is often damp; and the bags themselves accumulate garden matter to their surfaces as they are used and moved. Whilst transferring this matter to the wheelie bin, or putting it out with the household rubbish, is one thing; putting it in a car, even a car boot, seems another. I would suggest that it is precisely because cars are amongst our most intensely managed and manufactured environments that transporting excess plant matter in them, as opposed to behind them in a trailer, is such a problem. Not only do privet cuttings, grass, twigs, leaves and branches threaten to contaminate the upholstered interiors of our cars, scratching back seats or leaving detritus in the boot, but they threaten to leave behind them the things that may be living in and on them – insects and larvae.

Managing garden growth through cutting plant matter down and back is one facet of accommodating nature in habitation, and is simultaneously an accommodation both to the regulatory practices of gardening and to the normative in English garden aesthetics. Managing the ridding of this matter, however, constitutes the excess in growth as waste. In placing excess plant growth in conduits that connect it to the waste stream, households simultaneously reproduce the intensely managed, domesticated nature that is the English garden and their inner domestic spaces, their homes and their cars, as environments defined against nature's incursions. Keeping excess out emerges as a key way in which households maintain a sense of their homes as accommodating, places in which to be at home.

Cats and dogs: the co-fabrication of interiors and the management of excess

The various companion animals in this ethnography – the thirteen cats, five dogs and one rabbit[9] – are all further instances of a domesticated nature. Moreover, the practices of their management – their feeding, exercise and the manner of their access to the space outside the house – are all as intensely regulated as the gardens discussed in the previous section. Nonetheless, as living beings and cohabitants in the dwelling structures, these non-human agents posed their accommodating households several dilemmas, specifically: how to manage their cohabitation in the dwelling space, how to manage cohabitation in things and how to manage animal bodies. In this section I discuss all three of these issues of living with co-present non-human beings, using as illustration five of the eight households with pets. As will become clear, cohabitation with animals continually foregrounds excess, in ways which go to the heart of issues of domestication and accommodation.

Whilst most of the households with animals allowed their pets to move freely within the dwelling structure, four did not. Almost all of these were households with dogs. In Sandra and Rob's, the dog and the two cats live in the kitchen. The dog has a duvet bed under the stairs, and there is also an old, scratched chair in the kitchen by the wood-burning stove, which is where the cats sleep. In Pauline's, Carol and John's and Sharon and Barry's houses, the three dogs are usually confined to the kitchen space, invariably when their owners are out. All three of these dogs have their (plastic, manufactured) beds (with duvets) in the kitchens of these houses. In Linda and Paul's, whilst the cats are allowed access to most of the rooms, they are 'banned' from the living room, which is where the antique collections are displayed.

What we see here is the way in which animal co-presences, and particularly dog co-presences, in habitation are accommodated through temporary inclusion and exclusion zones. Indeed, of the five dogs in the study only one – Judy's – was allowed open access to all the rooms in the house during her absence. For most of the dog owners this was a taken-for-granted way of living with dogs: it was an accepted fact that, unless they were provided with a bed in the kitchen and made to use this, a dog would use three-piece suites, armchairs and beds for the same purpose, as indeed Judy's dog does. For most of the research participants, this was unacceptable. There are several possible reasons why. Amongst them are the workings of the clean/unclean binary and its mapping into cats and dogs respectively; the strong cultural associations between working dogs and the kitchen; the general ease of cleaning kitchen floor surfaces, and the intense regulatory frame that constitutes appropriate dog ownership as a matter of discipline, obedience and domination, in which what the dog does and its very movement in and through space is highly controlled, restricted by the lead, the hand and the voice. The effect of this practice of cohabitation, however, is considerable: confining dogs to a designated bed and to one room, in the main, works to minimise their potential effects on other things in the house.

This was certainly the case in the fieldwork, although there were of course some exceptions which highlight the capacity of dogs to do otherwise. Pauline's dog, Tess, arrived in Pauline's house as a stray, just before the beginning of the research.[10] The arrangement of Pauline's house is such that, whilst Tess could be left in the kitchen and excluded from the living room, she still had access to the upstairs, where the bathroom door is hard to shut properly. Consequently, when Pauline left her on work-days a frequent motif on her return would be, 'Oh Tess, you've trashed me house' – a reference to the clothes which Tess routinely dragged down from the dirty laundry pile in the bathroom and then chewed on the kitchen floor.[11] Some of these clothes became Pauline-substitute presences in the dog bed in the kitchen; others though went straight in the bin, as too mauled and chewed even for the charity shop. At Judy's, too, old duvet covers that were too covered in dog hairs to reclaim through washing were similarly discarded and carried away, via the wheelie bin. However, the households in which pet co-presences were most marked in things were those with cats.

At the risk of a slight digression here, having lived with cats for many years and knowing several other households who live in similar social relations, my appreciation of the 'living with cats' stories that feature here is considerable. Living with cats is a matter of accommodating to them, an endless quest to find fabrics, furnishings and surfaces that are either robust enough to tolerate their presence or which they are uninterested in. As many will attest, this is not easy. Like me, then, Judy has come to the gradual realisation over the years that cats and decorating styles involving wallpaper do not go together. At the beginning of the ethnography, Judy had a long expanse of scratched wallpaper beside her front door in the living room, where Amy – one of her three cats – marked her passage in and out of the house. Over the course of the fieldwork, Judy gradually stripped this wallpaper off the walls, replacing it with paint. Although she finds the result to be colder, she argues that the new style of decoration will make redecorating easier when the time comes, but acknowledges too that this decorating has been designed to out-manoeuvre Amy's 'wallpapering tendencies'. Similarly, another of Judy's cats – Pansy – scratches at the leather three-piece suite. Both arm rests are described by Judy as 'decorated with hundreds of tiny perforations'. This leaves Judy in a quandary: she does not want to have to go to the expense of having the settees re-upholstered if this is simply going to happen again. On the other hand, neither can she think of a fabric that will be immune to Pansy's attentions. So, the solution is to wait for Pansy's demise and 'throw throws over the worst of it if anybody important comes' (see Chapter 4). The goings-on in Judy's house, however, do not begin to compare with those in Linda and Paul's.

Linda and Paul have two cats. Between them, over the last eight years, these cats have 'trashed' three stair carpets, several sets of brocade curtains and two three-piece suites. Linda says, 'I used to be house proud, but that was life before these two – we decorate to keep them amused!' Linda and Paul's latest attempts to accommodate both carpets and cats under the same roof involve the intense use of plastic. Rather than put plastic carpet-protection strips under the interior door divides as manufacturers intend, their latest decorative tactic is to extend the plastic protection matter all the way up the staircase. 'It's not pretty,' says Paul, 'but it works! They do anything to avoid it!! We can have carpet, but they won't trash it.' However, as this couple are acutely aware, using a protective material that the cats dislike to avoidance may save the carpet, but the visual effect of this – to non cat-owning households at least – has greater risks for them. Although able to represent themselves as being ingenious in their use of furnishing materials and as good pet owners in accommodating their preferences for comfort to living with claws, they know that others may read things differently, and see this as indicative of lives overdetermined by the capacities of non-human presences. Given the cultural prevalence in the UK of views that elevate the agency and importance of human over non-human life forms, seeking accommodations in the fabrics of furnishing between these life forms can be a difficult terrain to navigate, at least – as here – when this overturns the norms of decorating and furnishing practice. It suggests equivalence, where normative understandings suggest a hierarchy of human and non-human presences.

Taken together, Pauline's, Judy's and Linda and Paul's stories about their pets' transformations of household interiors in things, and particularly in fabrics, furnishings and decoration, disclose much consistency in practice. The mauled, chewed and trashed matter is thrown away, made waste, typically through the wheelie bin. And, if it is furnishing related it is replaced, typically in a configuration which is hoped to be more capable of absorbing pet presence without trace. Like living with gardens, then, accommodating pets is a practice which is in turn accommodated, through a form of ridding which connects with wasting. Moreover, it is through wasting and replacement that these households manage to locate themselves within a normative that constitutes dwelling structures as spaces for human habitation, and not for human and non-human cohabitation. In wasting their pets' transgressions in matter, however, these pet owners not only disclose the power of this normative to shape their lives with non-human beings, but disclose the extent of their love for these presences, through what they do with things.

Managing the capacities of dogs and cats to co-fabricate and re-fabricate household furniture and furnishings was a routine facet of everyday life for the pet-owning households in the ethnography. Another constant presence in living with them, however, was their bodily capacities. As with humans, companion animals have permeable bodily boundaries. Like us, they shed hair and skin, urinate and defecate, vomit and bleed. Given widespread neutering practices in the UK, few pets give birth in our houses, but our pets have odours; many of them, particularly dogs, issue noise; and, like humans, they have the capacity to die in our homes. Regulating the bodily capacities of their pets was a matter of intense concern for all these pet-owning households – all of whom, for example, dealt with any in-house 'accidents' immediately. One instance of this occurred on my first visit to Carol and John's on Wear Road. Zuki (the Yorkshire Terrier) was shut in the kitchen while we sat in the living room, talking and drinking tea. Eventually the barking got too much for Carol, who got up from the settee and let Zuki through, after checking that this was alright by me. Zuki came through and got so excited that she urinated all over the settee – at which point Carol exclaimed 'Oh Zuki!!', and rushed for the kitchen paper to mop it all up, before adding that they were getting a new three-piece anyway. We see here how Carol – not then aware of my positive orientations toward pets – continually mobilises the normative in her attempt to accommodate my presence (as a visitor) with Zuki's presence. Letting Zuki into the living room is the only way through which Carol can appear to be an appropriate dog owner, by controlling Zuki's barking; but letting Zuki into the living room is itself socially risky. Indeed, Zuki's 'weeing' on the sofa can only be negotiated socially by mopping, cleaning and telling me that this sofa is going to be replaced anyway.

For the dog owners in the study, though, managing the bodily presence of their pets was not just a day-to-day routine of in-house living. Instead, it spilled out of the house to encompass the once or twice daily activity of walking the dog. Walking the dog in the UK has recently become an intensely regulated practice. In the North-east, as elsewhere, street lamps have anti-dog-fouling notices stamped on them, together with notices of fines if caught in the act. Moreover, dog owners are implored to carry their 'Poop Scoop' (a plastic bag and paper tissues) with them whenever and wherever they take their dog out, and to take any 'Poop' back home with them to place in their wheelie bin.[12] In some neighbourhoods, as in South Hightown, local authorities have introduced neighbourhood Poop Bins, for dog walkers to put their packages in on their way round their walk. Fuelled by associations with dangers to child health, dog defecation in public space, as opposed to the private space of individuals' gardens, has become an intense matter of public debate, with both the imposition of fines and the reporting of offenders on the increase. Although the dog owning households in the ethnography did not let their dogs foul the pavement, regarding this practice as unacceptable, most of those who walked their dogs did not agree with poop scoops. For the majority of these households, dog defecation on fields and on open grass (but not playgrounds) was a natural act involving biodegradable matter, as well as being something that had gone on since dogs and humans first cohabited. Why, they reasoned, start surrounding this matter with plastic – a non-bio-degradable material – and place it in a bin? Why send to landfill matter that is already biodegrading?

More broadly, the debate over dog defecation in public space suggests that the turf of animal accommodation has been critically extended. No longer is accommodating pets just about their incorporation within dwelling spaces, but it is also about eliminating and concealing from public view the evidence of their passage out of these dwelling spaces. Moreover, in attempting to make dog owners rid not only pavements, but fields, grass and all open spaces, of any visible trace of their pets' passage, and appropriate this matter as their household waste, the spaces of domestication are being extended far beyond the house itself to include all the environs of habitation, those we live in and those we move through. At the same time, as well as attempting to purify these environs by concealing and eliminating from view any animal bodily waste, in trying to enforce the placement of this matter back in the households in which pets live, this regulatory frame ratchets up to new levels the practices of accommodating animal life within the home, by focusing on households' accommodations of their pets' excess.

Conclusions

As both the previous sections show, ridding as wasting is a constant facet of living with plants and animals. However, as they also demonstrate, ridding plant and animal-related matter is intrinsically about the human accommodation of non-human capacities and agencies. Plant matter's capacity for growth means that it continually has the potential to display too much growth, to be straggly, out of control, to become 'wilderness' and to revert to nature. Rather differently, pet animals' insistence on co-fabricating domestic environments in ways that mark their presence mean that pets continually have the capacity to demonstrate too much of their cohabitation in dwelling structures. Clawed furnishings, scratched furniture, ripped-up decorative surfaces and textures, shed hairs and the utilisation of bodily excreta for territorial marking would all be instances of such co-fabrication, and indicative of too much nature present in the interior spaces of living. In their different ways, then, living with plant and animal matter foregrounds domestication as the accommodation of a potentially always excessive nature.

Since living with plant and animal matter is about regulating the potential for excess, it follows that living in such relations is itself a matter of continual vigilance. Although we see this in practices of garden maintenance, for example in Pauline's continual struggle to deal with the privet, and in Andrew's dad's exhortations to never let the lawn get in such a state again, it is in the pet-owning households that vigilance is most clearly displayed. Indeed, in cleaning up bodily leakages, in concealing the signs of too much presence in trace, in restricting their pets' movement within the house, and in throwing out matter with too much pet presence in it, pet owners demonstrate the effectiveness of another's gaze in shaping their lives. This is the gaze of those who choose not to live with non-humans in their midst. In restricting, concealing, disguising, replacing and ridding the traces of their pets' presence in matter, these pet-owning households are not just enacting domestication but are acknowledging the conditions in which nature's presence in domestic space is culturally accommodated; as a regulated, disciplined, subservient and highly scrutinised presence. In acknowledging this gaze through their practice, pet owners show the anxieties and insecurities of living in relations of domestication in a culture which continues to define nature as culture's other.

The practices of garden management and pet regulation revealed in this ethnography emphasise that domestication is a relation of accommodation that is simultaneously a struggle to order excess and about the reproduction of social order. Two issues in the fieldwork make this abundantly clear: the gardens on Wear Road that had reverted to nature and the antagonisms released through attitudes to dog excrement in public space. In the first instance, gardens attached to dwelling structures whose inhabitants had allowed them to revert to nature were read by others as manifestations of 'lack'; as indicative of inhabitants' lack of care, lack of knowledge and lack of social respect. Indeed, the reversion to nature and corresponding loss of domesticated plant matter worked as metaphor: it worked as a comment on those who lived there and, more generally, as a marker of social degeneration on the Rivers estate. In the second case, we see the workings of a counter-tendency: here the sanitisation and purification of the environs of habitation stands as a comment on social improvement. But, in attempting to eliminate dog excrement from various public spaces and placing this matter firmly back in its household of ownership, the poop scoop works to intensify the divisions between dog and non-dog owning households. Since Mary Douglas' *Purity and Danger* (1966), the power of excrement to reveal our keenest social distinctions has been recognised. However, in requiring dog owners to accommodate their pets' bodily waste, society is not just intensifying the domestication of dogs, but is also attempting to domesticate their owners, as the managers of animal waste. Given this double domestication, of people through their dogs, it is perhaps not surprising that the ridding of dog excrement (or not) was the focus of some of the most intense social conflicts in the entire ethnographic fieldwork, spilling over to encompass argument, dispute and full-scale confrontation amongst the people who live in the various areas of South Hightown.

My second main point is domestication's salience to dwelling. The importance of the connections between the domestication of both plants and animals and a settled way of life are, of course, well-established. They mark the transition from nomadic and/or semi-permanent modes of life to the development of permanent settlements; and the rest is history. Nonetheless, what tends to be overlooked in grand narratives such as this is that domestication is a lived relation of cohabitation and inhabitation. It goes on as a continual way of living. And, as this chapter vividly shows, the rhythms of living with and caring for both domesticated plant matter and companion animals are such that we are required to be at home, at least for some of the time. Feeding, cleaning-up after, watering, walking, mowing and weeding require that someone be present every day, and doing these activities, merely to sustain the relations of domestication. That the majority of households participating in this research lived in these relations and performed these activities themselves (rather than paying someone else to do them) is surely significant. Not only does it disclose a cultural normative and a taken-for-granted facet of everyday life in English dwelling structures, but it shows that this is indeed a way of life; one that is remade when we move house (Andrew and Mel, Ginny and Lesley) and when new pets replace those that have died (Pauline). Accommodating nature, then, is one of the key ways through which we make our homes, through working with a material culture that is alive, that stays in this place, that lives through being in this place, and which through this allows us to inhabit this place, as an effect of their habitation.

NOTES

1 Both Ted and June and Linda and Paul regularly purchase gardening magazines, including *Gardeners' World* (a TV tie-in) and *Homes and Gardens* (a more 'aspirational' publication). They also watch the gardening programmes on Friday evenings on BBC 2 television. These media are the primary sources of their gardening knowledge. It is this which works to further differentiate these gardening couples from Geoff and Hilary. Although Hilary, in particular, will buy and read a gardening magazine occasionally, she does so through a professional positioning; to see what ideas in garden design and planting are being promoted and to garner ideas of what she might put together in planting.

2 Harry's continued cultivation of a few sets of onions in the bungalow garden is particularly significant. Having lived all his life in this area of South Hightown, Harry – like many men – used to take part in the annual vegetable and flower shows that were once part of everyday life in this village. For men like Harry, to garden was to grow leeks and onions, as well as other vegetables. As elsewhere in County Durham, the annual vegetable/flower show in South Hightown has long since become history, although both Peggy and Harry continue to tell remarkable stories about 'leek wars' and the preparation of 'magic potions' for cultivating competition standard onions and leeks. Moving to the bungalow, however, meant that Harry no longer had the garden space to devote to extensive vegetable cultivation. Keeping a few sets of onions going in this garden is a trace of a previous life in cultivation, as well as a means to keeping alive the previous social life of onions on the Rivers estate.

3 The exception in lawn management practice is Geoff and Hilary, whose lawn is allowed to grow longer in summer to sustain meadow flowers that the other three households would describe as 'weeds'.

4 The exception here is Peggy and Harry, who use their wheelie bin for getting rid of garden waste and household vegetable matter.

5 So too are the remaining study households, though they are not discussed here.

6 Another indication of Andrew's anxieties in gardening came when I returned to Alternative Terrace in the summer of 2004. Andrew, pointing at the two fruit trees that he had planted the previous year, said, 'Do you think I've got these too close together?'

7 See Chapter 2, note 8.

8 The exception to this practice would appear to be estate car owners, who – at least on the basis of casual observation at the tip – seem to transport excess plant growth in their cars. Estate cars however, are designed around the provision of large interior spaces for the transportation of bulky objects. They separate out zones of human occupancy from these other zones of transportation.

9 The number and spread of companion animals is telling here. Of the sixteen households who participated in the research, seven did not have animals (Peggy and Harry, Betty, Christine and Malcolm, Claire and Nathan, Jo-Anne, Ellie and Steve and Geoff and Hilary). Several, however, had multiple animals (Carol and John, Rob and Sandra, Judy, Linda and Paul, Andrew and Mel and Ginny and Lesley).

10 As an aside, it is important to note that Tess was actually found by Ellie, Rachel and Chloe whilst they were out shopping. She was a stray. The two girls wanted to keep her, but Ellie did not. Offering Tess to her mother was Ellie's way of allowing the girls to have a pet without having 'the hassle of having to care for her'. It allowed her to continue to be the good mother. Pauline, however, saw this as 'a bit of a liberty' on Ellie's part, and a big restriction on her life. Having had her previous dog put down a few years previously, Pauline had been enjoying the reduced ties of living without a dog. Nonetheless, she acquiesced. In part this was, as she admitted to me, about missing living with a dog, but Tess's potential arrival in her house also offered the opportunity to 'be grandma' in a different way. Indeed, Rachel comes to stay at her grandma's to look after Tess and to walk 'her dog' (with Pauline). At the same time, and as part of the bargain struck with her daughter, Pauline has insisted that Ellie pay for any veterinary bills associated with Tess, and that she has her in her house on the weekends when Pauline is not at home. Tess, then, is an example of a companion animal that lives and binds

socially related households, rather than living in just one home. Moreover, the manner of her accommodation is one that foregrounds companion animals' capacity to allow us to enact key social identities, in this case grandma, as well as mother, daughter and granddaughter. Tess's status as a stray is also significant here: it testifies to the importance of domestication to the social lives and indeed existence of dogs.

11 Since I routinely walked Tess at lunch times on the days Pauline was at work, I can testify to Tess's effects on the things in this house. Covering up Tess' misdemeanours by placing them in the wheelie bin, or trying to put them back together again, became a regular part of taking her for a walk, as she chewed-up raffia mats, shoes, the post and seemingly anything else that took her fancy.

12 The placement of dog excrement in the wheelie bin has remarkable affinities with the management of babies' bodily waste through the disposable nappy. Indeed, the poop scoop has obvious parallels with the construction of the disposable nappy, combining a plastic lining with paper inner. Such parallels in matter raise further questions: if poop scoops are the canine equivalent of the disposable nappy, then is the poop scoop further evidence for pets' cultural construction as baby equivalents? That pets are actually far from this should be abundantly clear from this chapter, from the manner of their accommodation.

Chapter 8

Ridding, accommodation and dwelling

The preceding chapters demonstrate that ridding is indeed critical to the practices of everyday life. Along with acts of acquisition, holding, keeping and storing, acts of ridding things are centrally implicated in the fabrication of homes and are integral to the various practices of habitation and inhabitation that occur therein. As we have seen, they are part and parcel of making the toast, storing food, doing the laundry, tidying-up, living with pets, doing the decorating, moving in to a house and being modernised. Furthermore, these acts of ridding are always just going on; they occur across various temporal registers, simultaneously. Not only are they how we make an accommodation accommodating (a home), but they are central too to the state of being at home, to dwelling. In this final chapter, the focus shifts to address the core theoretical concerns of this volume: ridding, its relation to dwelling, and the relation of both to the people and things within the dwelling structure. The chapter is intended as a relatively discrete theoretical position statement which, whilst grounded strongly in the core findings of the ethnography, nonetheless can be read independently of the previous stories but in conjunction with Chapter 1.

There are three core sections to the chapter. In the first, I establish the importance of what I term the 'gap in accommodation' for theorising acts of ridding. In the second, I consider what is actually going on when things are rid through this gap, emphasising that this is about both the intrusion of the representational outside, and using saving and wasting to make present the relations of love, care and devotion that sustain living in relations of cohabitation within dwelling structures. Building on these arguments, and in the third section, I then consider some of the questions which sit at the heart of a dwelling perspective. What makes English dwelling structures unique physical entities is that, like many other buildings but unlike many other physical fabrications, they are things which people move through, not things which we can displace elsewhere by moving along. Neither, at least in the UK, are these dwelling structures that occupants demolish and build again, or which are likely to have been destroyed recently, for example through war or 'natural' disasters such as earthquakes, volcanoes, hurricanes and tsunamis.

Instead, it is the enduring qualities of many UK dwelling structures, often over decades and frequently hundreds of years, which sets them apart, making them classic conduits for people as well as things (Chapter 2). Along with fluctuations in the housing market, it is, however, the capacity of our dwelling structures to accommodate us in ways which are accommodating, rather than their physical longevity, which accounts for our staying in them, over years, rather than moving through them continually. Indeed, such 'stayings' are further confirmed by housing market statistics which show that, whilst around 10% of households move house in any one year, around 50% have not moved in 20 years, with the average stay in any one house being 10–15 years (National Statistics: Social Trends 2002 and 2004). This capacity to accommodate, though, is not guaranteed. Indeed, it is key life events – birth, death, the forming of partnerships and their fissuring – which frequently provide rupture points, when dwelling structures shift from the accommodating to the unaccommodating, placing their inhabitants, as well as things, in the 'gap in accommodation'. However, to make dwelling structures physically absent in the UK requires that it is we who displace ourselves, through moving out, leaving them behind rather than moving them along. As I show, drawing on examples from the ethnography, to leave behind, however, is something that several of the research participants here have opted not to do. Even though their social relations of inhabitation have changed through births and deaths, they have stayed in particular dwelling structures, in some cases engaging in activities of building conversion to forge new accommodations from these dwelling structures. I argue that this signals the continued importance of dwelling for some and the openness of contemporary dwelling structures to building as dwelling. The chapter ends by insisting on the continued importance of notions of dwelling to contemporary research on consumption and the material culture of the home.

Enduringness, transience and the 'gap in accommodation'

As the previous chapters demonstrate, the various practices of everyday life are fundamentally bound up with handling and/or moving the things we have 'to hand' around us. At the most mundane of levels, when the women living on Wear Road dust their collections in their living rooms – as they all do at least twice a week – they pick these pieces of china up, dust them carefully, and then replace them back in their place, on the fireplace, on the mantelshelf, on the window ledge. In doing the laundry, clothes are moved through the house, from bedrooms to laundry baskets, to kitchens and utility rooms, to washing lines and gardens sometimes, and thence back to wardrobes and drawers. Toys migrate from bedrooms to playrooms, to living rooms and back. And then there are the more infrequent movements, which bring things out of their place of storage: 'summer wardrobes' are exchanged for winter ones; barbecues and children's paddling pools emerge from their places of winter hibernation, typically a shed or a garage; motor bikes are unveiled for the summer riding season; or when we rummage around in cupboards for the Polyfilla that we know we have somewhere. The movement of things within the dwelling structure is fundamentally bound up in practices of inhabitation. But many of these practices of inhabitation disrupt the spatial holdings and orderings of things. They move things in and out of cupboards, wardrobes, fridges and freezers, for example. And they do this across a temporal register that ranges from the repetitive everyday opening and shutting of the fridge, through the daily rhythms of waking and opening the wardrobe door to, at the other extreme, the more infrequent moving of people in/out of inhabiting a particular dwelling structure. As I show in this section, this pattern of doing things with and to the things to hand around us works to forge what I term the 'gap in *accommodation*'. I argue here that this 'gap in accommodation' is, in turn, of critical importance to theorising acts of ridding.

As Kevin Hetherington (2004) makes explicit, much existing work on the gap locates it firmly within a social beyond the home and the household, in accounting practices (Munro 1995 and 1998) and in the rituals of first and second burial (Hertz 1960). But the gap is a mutable notion. In Hetherington's work on consumption as disposal, the emphasis is on how the gap works to move things between the physical and representational registers. However, his primary concern is with the work of absence and of the return of the gap. In contrast, my concern here is to locate the gap within dwelling structures and in their inhabitation. At the same time as working with the relations between the physical and representational states, I argue that what goes on in practices of inhabitation in dwelling structures is about people doing things with and to the various things held within dwelling structures. It is these doings, across various temporal registers, which work to open up a gap, in which existing accommodations with things are brought into view, examined and considered.

Let us begin with the two broad temporalities of accommodating things disclosed by the previous chapters, enduringness and transience. Various examples of both abound. The collections highlighted in Chapter 5 are perhaps the most potent instances of enduringness encountered in the ethnography, but so too – less predictably perhaps – is Ted and June's dishwasher (Chapter 6). The things that really endure, then, that we keep, hold on to and which stay with us, enclaved, to the point of exceeding our lives, are those things that we use to narrate a self and a life. Their keeping works to connote a sense of who we are, of our social identities, but works too as a memory device, constituting a past in things for an imagined future, ours and that of the significant others who will live on with our absent presence encoded in these things. In contrast, other things pass through our homes and in and out of our possession. The furniture and furnishings discussed in Chapter 3, the beds and cots of Chapter 4, the appliances of Chapter 6 and, above all, the children's clothing of Chapter 5, are all indicative of the transience of our accommodations with certain things. For sure, transience can be about a temporally restricted staying with things, for example the keeping of baby-related things such as walkers and prams, which lasted for no more than a year or so in all the study households with very young children. But equally, transient accommodations can be relatively long-lived, as with Pauline's microwave, which lived with her for fourteen years before being got rid of. The critical point, however, about transient things is that these are things which never come to be invested with the capacity to narrate a particular self or life. Instead, they remain just things in their staying with us, not things which stay precisely because of their capacity to narrate our selves.

Enduringness and transience are not just effects of the degree to which our selves are present or not in our things, however. Rather, they are temporalities forged additionally through practices of inhabitation with things. For much of everyday life, then, our lives and those of the things we have acquired and appropriated exist in parallel worlds. Accommodated in our dwelling structures, working to make these accommodating to us and places to be at home in, our things may be co-present but they are largely separate from us. We might be wearing one particular set of clothes, for example, but as we do the other clothes in our possession hang in wardrobes and lie folded-up in drawers; they may be tumbling around in a washing machine or flapping in the breeze on a washing line. Whilst children play a computer game or ride their bikes, other things like roller blades or Barbie dolls lie discarded, perhaps in specially purchased storage boxes or, more likely if the households in this ethnography are anything to go by, strewn around wherever they were last put down. And, when we go out to work or to school, to the shops or for a day out, on holiday or to visit others, our things remain, either working away for us – taking and recording phone messages, recording TV programmes, downloading films, keeping ready-made meals frozen – or waiting for us to return, to perhaps put them to use. Much of home-based consumption is comprised of such moments of separation between people and their things. But it is also about moments in which we do things with and to the things we have to hand around us. Usually these doings are thoroughly corporeal moments. We pick up and hold in our grasped hands certain things – a mug with which to make and drink a cup of tea, a screwdriver to begin to assemble a piece of flat-pack furniture, an iron to steam various shirts and tops, a pair of shears to start cutting a privet hedge. Or we merely touch things, momentarily using our finger tips to press the start button on a washing machine, a PC, the TV remote or to depress levers on a toaster. Less frequently, we might marshal our entire bodies in our encounters with certain things, summoning up our strength to lift and remove appliances, kitchen units, pieces of furniture and bathroom suites. Or, no less physically, but far more mutedly, we wear our clothes through our bodies, knowing both through their feel as this relates to the movement of skin with and against cloth. It is through our corporeal engagement with things, then, that we come to be aware of them and to know them. However, our corporeal engagements with things also constitute a gap.

When we handle or touch the things we have 'to hand' around us in our homes, we not only bring them, move them, to hand, but move them into fields of vision. In so doing we bring into being a gap, moving things from the physical state to the representational state. Handling or touching particular things may be about doing things to things, as with dusting and laundering. It might be about use, as in wearing clothes or using a screwdriver to assemble flat-pack furnishing, but it is also, profoundly, a moment of potential scrutiny and appraisal. As we handle, then, we may just handle, doing things with things on autopilot because of their familiarity – not seeing, because our minds are elsewhere. Or, and simultaneously, we may both assess the state things are in and project our selves into our things, exploring their capacity to continue to narrate and express our identities and subjectivities, as well as their apparent value. The 'gap', then, is constituted and traversed in a moment of movement, when the largely separated lives of people and things in the domestic come together as juxtaposed co-presences; and is a moment when the representational outside potentially penetrates the walls of the dwelling structure.

What this begins to suggest is that certain things, simply by virtue of their centrality to particular practices of inhabitation, move into the gap with greater frequency than others. The things we use repeatedly through each day (things like kettles, cooking utensils, phones or TV remotes) and the things we use on a daily basis (clothing, toiletries or bedding, for example) are not just the things that we subject to greater or more intense use than others, but are the things that are handled most frequently too. Open to repeated potential scrutiny, is it any wonder that it is precisely these sorts of things that emerged from the ethnography as amongst the most transient of things in our homes, and as the things which were most likely to be tired of, bored with, frustrated by and consequently jettisoned. In contrast, that which endures without ever being enclaved – notably the content of lofts, garages, sheds and cupboards – does so, I would suggest, precisely because it is rarely handled and as a consequence, rarely even enters the gap. We can see this most clearly in the very moments when such zones are disrupted: for instance, in Christine and Malcolm's excavation of their loft after sixteen years (Chapter 3). Here, the enduringness of a particular accommodation of things was broken. Long forgotten about things were moved out of their place of holding because future events – the insulation of their loft – demanded their movement. More importantly, the very process of movement and handling opened them up to scrutiny, and to questioning their continued accommodation. A similar event was Andrew's excavation of their garage (Chapter 2). Although far more exceptional as events than everyday acts such as tidying or doing the laundry, exactly the same set of processes ensue. Moving things and handling things, then, are not just integral to particular practices of inhabitation. Moving things and handling things bring people and things together, and things into a heightened zone of scrutiny. In being moved, touched and handled, things are positioned to be looked at, felt, smelt, considered and thought about. The movement of things, then, their handling and touching, brings into being not just a gap but a 'gap in accommodation'. This is a gap which foregrounds and allows us to address the continued accommodation of things, or not, within dwelling structures.

The 'gap in accommodation', then, is integral to as well as produced through the various practices of inhabitation. And it is in this gap that we negotiate a staying with things, separating that which is to remain 'to hand' (that which we wish to continue to accommodate) from that which is placed in conduits that displace it elsewhere, making it not to hand. Correspondingly, the 'gap in accommodation' itself accommodates the practices of holding, keeping *and* ridding. But holding, keeping and ridding things are not just thing accommodations. Rather, we use all three of these practices with things to narrate identities and the social relations of (co)habitation, using physical absences in things to make present the social relations of love, care and devotion that sustain living in proximity, together, under one roof. It is to these concerns that I turn in the next section.

Ridding, the idealised self and the social relations of cohabitation

Whilst most previous research on home consumption has emphasised practices of appropriation, the evidence from this ethnography is that ridding, along with holding and keeping, is every bit as much part of identity work as acts of expenditure and acquisition. As I show in this section, the identity work of ridding that goes on in the gap in accommodation is multifaceted, encompassing both narratives of the self in things and key social relations of cohabitation. Furthermore, it is the conduits of ridding, as much as the things themselves, that are used to narrate these identities and relations. I begin with a set of actions taken from preceding chapters which relate to the placement of matter which is troublesome to the narration of the self beyond the threshold. In these instances, ridding is about using physical displacement to move along unwanted meanings in things and to resume narratives of the self. Furthermore, such acts usually place things in conduits that connect with the waste stream. Although grounded in *Purity and Danger* (Douglas 1966), these actions also disclose the workings of the normative, making apparent that such acts of ridding are an accepted part of what ought to be occurring as part of certain practices of habitation, and that these practices are both framed by this normative and constitutive of it. I then move on to examine how other acts of ridding which centre saving and wasting are entwined more in the core social relations of cohabitation within households. Emphasising the work of mothers in saving certain children's things from wasting, and the work of men cohabiting with women in expending and wasting the surplus, I argue that both these acts of ridding are fundamentally acts of love and devotion.

Ridding, the idealised self and the practice of the normative

As highlighted in Chapter 1, much of the literature on home decoration emphasises the importance of the normative in the production of home interiors. Our homes in decoration are considered to be projections of ourselves and expressive of ourselves, albeit that a more accurate reading might be one which highlights either fantasy and the ideal or the significance of compromises and taste conflicts between cohabiting selves (Clarke 2001 and 2002). As the previous empirical chapters demonstrate, this same normative is at work in key moments of inhabitation, notably in moving in (Chapter 2) and in being visited (Chapter 4), and also impinges critically on two key practices of domestication, gardening and living with companion animals (Chapter 7). For the most part then, moving in is accompanied by precisely the sorts of acts detailed here. The ripped-out kitchen and bathroom of Jo-Anne, the jettisoned heating system, windows, tiling and doors of Ginny and Lesley, and the rotten floorboards and old carpets of Andrew and Mel discussed in Chapter 2 are all prime examples of moving-in households' attempts to expunge the traces of previous occupants and occupation. In so doing, households use the practice of the normative to constitute the normative. In expunging traces of previous habitation, we prepare dwelling structures for new accommodations between people and things, thereby ensuring that the dwelling structure mutates from mere accommodation to being accommodating of us and expressive of us. A similar set of processes is disclosed in relation to accommodating the staying-over visitor (Chapter 4), in which the presence of the normative works to generate anxieties – as it does for Pauline and Judy – over the ability of certain of our things to match up to our idealised notion of who we might want to appear to be. As with moving in, the effect of the normative is to expel matter which is deemed incapable of sustaining a particular self narration. Moreover, it also allows for the acquisition of something or things deemed a more appropriate expression of self, thereby enabling the resumption of the narration of the self in things.

Yet, for all these similarities, there is one critical difference between these two practices of habitation and their attendant acts of ridding, which I want to pursue here. Whereas the ridding of moving in is about the removal of the previous inhabitants in taste and things, the acts of visitor-related jettisoning both involve the ridding of things previously chosen by Pauline and Judy, and which had been accommodated within their respective homes for some years. This is altogether more perilous terrain than that of the trace of previous habitation, or indeed than the effects of living with pets and garden growth (Chapter 7), and I will argue that it has very definite effects on the conduits of ridding mobilised by both women. In Chapter 4 we saw how both Judy's bathroom makeover and Pauline's jettisoning of the 'plant-pot mugs' resulted in the routing of the expelled matter directly to the wheelie bin, and therefore into the waste stream. As I emphasised there, both acts are in strong contrast to both Pauline and Judy's usual accommodations with things. Indeed, neither woman regards wasting positively, nor do they throw very much away. As a consequence, Judy's home is full of accumulations of things – in the loft, in the garage, in the bedrooms, in cupboards. In contrast, Pauline continually redirects the things that are routinely being given to her to her extended family or her vast social network of friends, using these things to constitute her relations with people, and their routing to narrate her sense of self. Given this, it is as significant that Pauline does not route the mugs in the same way, as it is that Judy actually throws matter out. That both women do what they do with these things is indicative of the mismatch between the meanings they project into this matter and their narrations of self. This is where the wheelie bin comes in. Capacious and emptied by local authority contractors on a weekly basis, these receptacles allow for quick, easy, fast-fix removal/disposal. But they also remove matter in a manner which is invisible to most others – think of the way in which the lid opens and then shuts, hiding from view that which is being discarded. Wheelie bins, then, are ideal conduits for displacing troublesome things; precisely the sorts of things whose presence in the house discloses a self we might not wish others to see. Whilst the capacity of certain things to continue to be able to narrate the self is brought into question through the workings of the normative in visiting, the expulsions generated through this same normative can seemingly be accommodated only through acts of wasting which allow for the radical and largely invisible separation of people from their things. Whilst burning and burial might once have been how many households managed such troublesome matter, there seems little doubt that in the UK in the early twenty-first century it is wheelie bins and black plastic sacks which are the primary conduits for those previous accommodations which, even in their ridding, even particularly in their ridding, we wish to obscure from others.

As is clear from the foregoing, households draw on various instances of the normative in different practices of habitation, using this normative to expel and reject certain of their things as well as to keep and to hold onto others. The normative allows for potential dis-identifications between people and the things around them, acknowledging, for example, that the patina of things may not always be positive (Judy's bathroom accessories) and that tastes can change (Pauline's mugs). Moreover, it works to normalise the practice of ridding, particularly in relation to certain practices of habitation. So, moving in and being visited both routinise ridding, as a means to accommodate the expressive self and to dispel anxieties about ourselves in things. As we see in the next section, when we look at the social relations of cohabitation, we find the same emphasis on ridding as a means to narrating key social relations and very much the same emphasis on particular conduits as a narration of identity.

Saving and wasting: ridding, love and the social relations of cohabitation

In instance after instance of laundering and tidying-up, two of the key practices discussed in Chapter 5, it is almost invariably women who are also mothers who are moving things – typically children's clothes and toys – into and through the gap in accommodation. And, as we saw there, particularly in relation to younger children's clothing, such matter is frequently released and lost to children through laundry work. What is going on here is central to the work of mothering and to the identity of Mother. Children's clothing is continually monitored – for fit, wear and increasingly style – precisely because to be seen to be clothing a child inadequately or inappropriately is to lay mothers, and it is still mostly mothers, open to charges of inappropriate parenting. Children's wardrobes are constantly under scrutiny, clothing is appraised and negotiated for appropriateness, as all the mothers of girls of five and upwards observed. Correspondingly, the flow of children's clothing in and out of particular homes can be seen to constitute a normative in children's wardrobes, and to encompass clothing styles, ranges and choices, from 'party' and 'smart' to 'school' and 'slobby'. For sure, there is much to be written about this development, but what concerns me here is what happens to the clothes being got rid of, and in particular the routes they follow. Without exception in the ethnography, this released clothing matter went in one of two directions. Either it travelled through particular social networks of mothers to their children, or it was released through institutionalised conduits, typically charity shops and charity doorstep collections. Such practices of release draw on the discourse of the good mother. In ridding children's clothing in these ways, not only is a mother able to represent herself as a caring, appropriate parent, but in offering up these invariably 'good quality' things to other mothers, she is able to sustain a whole host of notions that suffuse contemporary mothering, above all thrift and sacrifice. Indeed, in giving her children's clothing freely, she manages both to imagine herself as giving other mothers – almost invariably imagined to be 'less fortunate' – the capacity to mother appropriately through clothing and to confirm the child as the object of devotion, general and specific (Miller 1998).

Much the same sentiments and motivations are at work, and can be readily observed, in relation to other forms of children's material culture that move into the gap in accommodation, particularly baby-related things (cots, prams, walkers and the panoply of baby toys) and those children's toys that are deemed not for holding over or keeping for a younger child, or as memory devices. What matters for mother after mother is that this matter, stuff which is felt to be no longer appropriate to keep but which at the moment of acquisition resonated with parental love, is rekindled as an object expressive of such love. These love objects, then, are not to be wasted. Why? Because in being wasted – be it through burial in a landfill or through burning in an incinerator – it would be parental love that would be being wasted and not just the object. Furthermore, to waste children's material culture in such a way would be to bring into question the very constitution of the child as an object of devotion by the subject of devotion. Active wasting here would constitute the child figure as one to be denied in things through the destructive loss of things – a manoeuvre which would go to the heart of maternal ambivalence (Parker 1995). When we shift the locus of consumption to within the home, then, we see that it is not just expenditure and shopping which signal the potency of the child as a figure of devotion in contemporary consumer culture, but the avoidance of waste too. In saving the children's material culture that enters the gap in accommodation from being wasted, mothers are not just highlighting the continued importance of thrift within contemporary mothering, or even constituting a moral economy of mothers, but are continuing to affirm their devotion to the child God. Moreover, they are using the conduits of ridding to signal their love.

The continual circulation of children's material culture in, out and through households and its placement in conduits which save it from wasting is one means through which social identities of cohabitation are narrated. Involving mainly mothers and children, they are possibly the primary means by which we use the out-placement of things to make present our closest social relations. But there are other ways in which ridding works to sustain relations of cohabitation. Visible only in the interstices of Chapters 2, 3 and 7, these mainly involve the work of men. To begin to open this up, I want to highlight what happens when accumulations of things are moved into the gap in accommodation, rather than singular objects or a few related objects such as Judy's bathroom accessories or Pauline's mugs. Predictably, most of these occurred in relation to the modernisation work on Wear Road (Chapter 3), but there are others too. One of these was when I helped Pauline clear out her outbuildings, in preparation for their partial renovation. Another occurred just after the period of ethnographic fieldwork, when Judy cleared out her garage for the first time in seventeen years, an act precipitated by her need to clear the space to effect the replacement of the rotten garage doors. In all these instances, households resort to one of three routes to deal with such accumulations in matter: having sorted that which is to be re-accommodated from that which is to be discarded, they shove the discards into the back of the car and transport them to 'the tip'. Alternatively, as Christine and Malcolm did, they might hire a skip or, as Pauline did in relation to the outbuildings and Andrew in relation to the garden waste (Chapter 7), they resort to the informal economy, paying someone else to cart away matter deemed too messy to go in a car. Immediately, then, we see how excess gets to be cast as waste. But what is of even more significance is how excess is managed within the household, and the transformations wrought to the excess of inhabitation once it enters the gap in accommodation.

To take the transformations first: for the most part, accumulations are regarded as holdings by households. These accumulations have often been kept and held-over for their imagined capacity to 'come in useful some time' or because they have been forgotten about – hence the accumulation amongst other things of half-used tins of gloss paint, of bits of string, of a few roofing slates, a few bricks and some nearly empty bags of cement in Pauline's outbuildings. Holdings, however, are not immune to transformations in their materiality. Left untouched by human hands for periods of years, things may indeed start being appropriated by other non-human agencies – take for example the pigeon that had taken over and died in Christine's old fur coat or the mice which got to Peggy's daughter's wedding dress. Or, things may start to change their properties. Paint that was kept turns out to have hardened and solidified; fabric begins to rot; water may encroach on the space of holding and begin to accelerate rusting in things. So, what emerges when these accumulations are unearthed is very often a different materiality to that which was placed in holding and which is remembered as in holding, if indeed it is remembered. The temporalities of back-stage accommodations then often work to transform things from the imaginary potential of the holding to excess – a dead and decomposing pigeon in fur, for example – or at the very least to the category of the surplus. Indeed, when moved into the gap in accommodation – as with Pauline's outbuildings' contents, Christine and Malcolm's loft contents and Judy's garage contents – much of this surplus discloses itself to be not just surplus to individual households but beyond their capacities to imagine as capable of re-contexualisation. In such instances, to route things through conduits that connect to waste management seems the appropriate course of action. Moreover, because of the sheer enormity of this surplus in matter it is more capacious receptacles than the wheelie bin which are called upon as conduits – hence the importance in these circumstances of the skip and the tip.

As important, though, is how the majority of households institute the routes out for this surplus. Throughout the ethnography, at least in households with live-in male partners, the tip journey was invariably constituted as men's work. There are various possible explanations for this clear gender division of labour, including both the socialities of most civic-amenity sites

– largely orchestrated by small groups of men whom the majority of the population seem to regard as in some way either dubious or 'dodgy' – and the continued association of very heavy physical work with men. Almost certainly, both have a degree of purchase as explanations, but what I prefer to emphasise is that, whilst they may have complied in doing this work, these men, to a man, did not regard this task with any degree of pleasure. Indeed, some, like Rob and Andrew, absolutely loathed it. Yet they continued to regard it as something that just had to be done, and by them. The task could be put off perhaps, but it certainly could not be avoided. To understand this, I think we have to return to the relation between expenditure and love and devotion within households living in social relations of cohabitation.

What I want to suggest is that there is a very definite correspondence between what is going on when women use shopping expenditure to consti-tute children as objects of devotion and men's compliance in acts of wasting. Specifically, I want to argue that wasting is another act of expenditure, this time of the surplus, and that it too signifies devotion, but this time of men. That wasting is very much about the expenditure of the surplus is highlight-ed by the anthropological literature on sacrifice, and in Bataille's writings on waste and excess.[1] The excess generated by households, however, is not the same thing as the surplus of sacrifice, which is the excess generated by the productive economy. Rather, this is a surplus generated within and through household's practices of habitation and inhabitation. What links this surplus to the surplus of sacrifice, however, is that it has to be expended. We can see this when we observe how, once disclosed as the surplus, it becomes seem-ingly imperative for households to remove it. It cannot remain, precisely, I think, because its presence works as a block to future imagined acts of expenditure through acquisition. To expend the surplus, then, is simultane-ously to facilitate the acquisition, appropriation and accommodation of the new.

That men are the subjects of devotion in wasting was disclosed in several moments of the ethnography, but here I will highlight only three. The first of these occurred during one particularly fraught moment of modernisation in Peggy and Harry's bungalow. At her wits' end with living in turmoil and without cooking facilities or seating other than plastic garden chairs, Peggy marched into the living room carrying a dralon foot rest, and declared that she was just 'sick of this thing as well'. She did this as Harry was on his hands and knees with me on the living room floor, inspecting the damage that the workmen had just done to the TV and video stand. Harry had started making comments about touching up the stand; a stance which infuriated Peggy. Not only did she want the damaged stand out of the bungalow, but she wanted the foot rest out too. The normally placid Harry retorted: 'If you didn't keep buying this stuff woman, I wouldn't be having to get rid of it!!' before march-ing off to his greenhouse. Long after things had calmed down, this was a phrase which niggled away in my mind. Without a car, and reliant on their large family, on car-boot sales, and on their and a neighbour's wheelie bins as conduits for ridding, Harry had erupted at this point precisely because the household's surplus had become excessive, casting real doubt on his capac-ity to expend it swiftly. What his retort also acknowledged, however, was the intensity of the connections between wasting and acquisition. Peggy's intense investments in consumer culture and in the home as an expression of self mean that shopping is critical to narrating her sense of self. Once connected up to Harry's ridding activities, we can see that this is a self that can only be narrated through Harry's wasting of the surplus. Indeed, expending the surplus is the only means by which this couple can continue to accommodate the flow of the new into the house. In wasting the surplus, then, Harry is accommodating to living with Peggy in things. To waste here is an act of love, grounded in the accommodations of cohabitation.

Peggy and Harry provide an important counter to the tendency to regard acts of wasting as exclusively destructive and as indicative of negative emotions, for instance of hate, jealousy or revenge. For sure, we do use wasting things to 'trash the ex'; children will smash the favourite toy of the current best friend; and many will break things as substitutes for inflicting violence against the person, but – even in its most excessive forms – wasting can be positive and expressive of love. That this is so is further confirmed by two of the most poignant moments in the ethnography, in which the absence of wasting within two households started to disclose itself as resonant of both loss and an absence of living with men as subjects of devotion. Predictably, perhaps, given that she is the oldest female participant in the ethnography and a widow, it is Betty's household which disclosed such points most clearly. Early on in the fieldwork, soon after meeting Betty, I was asking her about the things she had recorded in her diary. I was puzzled, because Betty seemed to have got rid of an awful lot of things in the two weeks since I had seen her last, including a three-piece suite, three washing machines, two cookers, a carpet and two fridges. Yet the rooms in her bungalow looked much the same in things to me as when I had last visited her. As we talked about this list of recorded things, it transpired that these were the things that Betty could remember having got rid of in the previous years. In contrast, through the period of the ethnography only one thing – the washing machine discussed in Chapter 6 – exited the bungalow. This same pattern of staying with things is something that many of the older female residents of The Rivers estate talked about with me, at the Environment Day and at community coffee mornings. Although not participating as households, these older women – all of them widows – told me stories which narrated themselves as 'hoarders', compared to the wasting of their daughters and daughters-in-law. Although typical of generation talk in its explicit critique of the younger generation's attitude to things, the real work of this talk is to mask the stilling of things in the homes of these older widows. Things accumulate in these homes, for all these women continue to shop; things move into the gap in accommodation, for practices of habitation are still going on; but what rarely happens is for things to be released from the gap, other than the 'memory stuff' that it is important to pass on to significant others (Marcoux 2001). In Betty's case, much of this is bound up in her memorialising of certain of the things of her late husband. Of possibly greater importance though, is that her social relations of inhabitation are enacted through his absent presence. Bert – like virtually all the men on The Rivers estate that I encountered – did the work of wasting the surplus in their household; in accumulating things, then, Betty activates his ghost. Betty's holding and keeping of things works to make Bert present by leaving the work of expending the surplus undone.

Although separated, not widowed, forty years younger than Betty, and living with her child rather than alone, Jo-Anne's relations of inhabitation contain a similar absent presence. One day, when I was talking about the outbuildings on Alternative Terrace with Pauline, Jo-Anne joined us and confided to me that one of the reasons why she had not got rid of the previous contents of her kitchen and bathroom was precisely because of her lack of 'a man in my life'. She later repeated this in another recorded conversation, so I have no reason to doubt that these indeed are her sentiments. Cast out of her house, yet displaced only as far as her house's outbuildings, the continued accommodation of her kitchen and bathroom discards works to signal her idealised social relations of inhabitation. Here, the task of wasting the surplus is being held over for an imagined future partner, to connote his love and devotion to Jo-Anne. The absence of wasting here, then, whilst not making present a particular ghost, works to accommodate an imagined, desired future presence, and allows Jo-Anne to narrate her current life as a single parent as finite and transient. I can think of no clearer demonstrations of wasting's connections to love than the current accommodations in things of Betty and Jo-Anne, in which wasting's denial works to memorialise and project men as subjects of devotion and to mark these women's current social relations of habitation as ones of absence and loss.

Dwelling structures, accommodation and dwelling

The previous section demonstrates conclusively that ridding is not just about the displacement of things rendered troublesome through the workings of the representational outside, but that it is simultaneously about dwelling. Ridding is grounded in the social relations of cohabitation between people, of living with related others in proximity, under one roof. Moving things through the gap in accommodation, making them absent from the dwelling structure in particular ways, is critical to the articulation and making present of love relations, just as holding on to certain other things can signify the absence or loss of love objects. To think about ridding, then, is simultaneously to raise questions about cohabitation, about living in particular dwelling structures in particular social relations, and about articulating these relations through what we do with the things to hand around us. Ridding, then, is fundamentally about being at home amongst and with others; it is about dwelling. It is to this broader question that I turn in this section.

In the previous chapters the emphasis is very much on practices of inhabitation in which people move things into the gap in accommodation (Chapters 2–5); on things which move into the gap by virtue of their capacities to fail to perform particular activities well enough (Chapter 6); and on the capacity of animate non-human things to push matter into the gap (Chapter 7). Indicative of the disclosures and absences of an ethnography in which none of the study households actually moved out of a dwelling structure (see Chapter 2), this emphasis obscures the fact that people too are accommodated by dwelling structures. Like things, we move through these structures in practices of habitation; exiting the door on a daily basis if we are healthy and in employment, returning to eat, to relax, to do domestic work, to play, to care for children and to sleep. The temporalities of our exits and returns may stretch, for example if we work away from home or when we go on holiday, but we return nonetheless, to be re-accommodated in the dwelling structure. And for many households, particularly those comprising socially related individuals, this is how we go on, over temporalities that extend to years and decades, precisely because the dwelling structure is so accommodating of us and where we feel at home. But the dwelling structure is not always this. Its capacity to be accommodating may be brought into question, through for instance the workings of a housing market which imagines the attractions of another, higher value property in the catchment area of a specific secondary school, and which normalises the practice of 'trading up'. Albeit that the evidence for the importance of such rational motivations for moving house is incontrovertible, such accounts frame moving as an event to be explained by forces external to the household. They do not admit that the events which move us through and out of dwelling structures are frequently the very events that constitute dwelling itself, specifically birth and death.[2] In what follows, I draw first on two of the households in the ethnography to show how birth has the capacity to move dwelling structures from the accommodating to the more problematic category of accommodation, and how – rather than moving house – in both cases households worked out new accommodations with their homes, through building. I then go on to look at those households where death in relations of cohabitation has either occurred or is talked about and openly anticipated. The two households concerned disclose two contrasting accommodations to death: whilst one has lived on in the same dwelling structure, the other has used moving house to try to forget, at least in part, the relations of living with dying.

Let us begin with two of the households with young families – Sandra and Rob and Ellie and Steve. As we saw in Chapter 4, Sandra feels that they are bursting out of their home. It is Alice's birth which has brought this to a head. As Sandra said to me, 'When it was just Josh, Rob and me, we were OK', but – as we saw in Chapter 4 – in order to accommodate Alice and Alice's things in a way which demonstrates the appropriate degree of parental love and devotion, the couple have had to convert what was their junk room into a nursery/bedroom. Because they live here, in this particular house, and because it is this house to which Sandra returned having given birth to Alice, they have had to engage in a set of activities – demolition and conversion – which are not so far removed from the act of building itself. It is a similar story with Ellie and Steve. Here the birth of Chloe – the couple's second child – prior to the fieldwork led to a substantial interior re-build and conversion of the loft area of their house to accommodate two bedrooms for the two girls, as well as a new bathroom. Now, what is so interesting about both these households, at least in a theoretical sense, is that they did not move house to accommodate birth events, but rather rebuilt their homes to accommodate their growing families. As I argue now, in both cases this is not an act of economic rationality but is rather embedded in dwelling itself.

   In Chapter 4 we saw that Rob himself was born in the house in which he lives with Sandra (his wife), their two children and their animals. Furthermore, he lived in this house as a child and as a young adult. His father, too, from whom Rob purchased this house, lived in the same dwelling structure for several decades, and he still lives in South Hightown. In a very real sense, then, this terraced cottage is a family dwelling structure in the Heideggerian sense, lived in by generations of the same patrilineal family. Talking with Sandra and Rob, separately and together, it is clear that it is this which works to hold this family in this dwelling structure. They are held here by the strength of dwelling across the generations, in this house, in this street and in this place. Indeed, although there is some talk between the couple about what might happen when Rob's dad dies – in the sense that this event is seen to free the couple up to move in future – my sense is that the attachments of dwelling are already being woven in relation to the couple's children. All the time Rob's dad is still alive, Rob says, he will not move from South Hightown, and living in South Hightown for him – at least in the now - seems to be about living in this house, in this street and not in another house or another street. But Josh, their eldest child, is now attending the local village primary school, as his dad did before him, and his dad before that, and Alice now sleeps in the room in which her dad slept and played as a young child. To move house, then, and to move beyond South Hightown, would rupture this sense of generational attachment to place and to the dwelling structure that is home. For Sandra, however, for whom the house has no such attachments and many frustrations, precisely because of its history, this is an accommodation that she just has to make in order to live with Rob. Moving house for this couple, then, is not currently an option, not because they cannot afford to move house – they can – but because of the complex positioning of this particular house within Rob's family's dwelling and within his memory.

   In contrast to Sandra and Rob, Ellie and Steve's rebuilding acts are about Ellie's dwelling rather more than Steve's. The sense of dwelling that emerges here, however, is not grounded in a dwelling structure that has been lived in by generations of one family. Rather, it is located in the psychological desire for security, in which the home constitutes the space for a self to be. During one visit to see Ellie, she talked a great deal to me, entirely unprompted, about what she described as her insecurities and how she saw these relating to both her parents' relationship and hers with Steve. Pauline and Keith's separation and living-together-apart is something which both preys on her mind and which has had effects on her housing decisions. Ellie knows that even though she is very happy with Steve, she may well not stay living with him. Her parents' history of cohabitation and separation, her professional career, her relationship history and the relationship histories of her friends and her brother all tell her this. As a result, the house the couple live in is actually Ellie's property. So, when it came to accommodating their growing family, Ellie had to choose: either she had to buy another house with Steve or rebuild her home. In choosing the latter, Ellie showed just how potent the imagined future in dwelling can be and the intensity of her psychological investments in this particular house. This house – Ellie's house – is her security in future dwelling; there for her and her children as an insurance against the possible separation of Steve and her. Albeit that he is the children's father, and that he lives in this house, Steve never achieves the state of dwelling here, precisely because Ellie's investments in this dwelling structure preclude it. For her to dwell here requires that Steve does not, a situation which led Steve to purchase his own house during the ethnography – which he currently rents out. This too is his insurance, against a possible future when he is no longer accommodated within the current dwelling structure.

Births constitute key moments in dwelling; they bring our bodies into the world. But as we see from the above instances, there is no guarantee that moving house will follow. Instead, room conversions can be used to come to new accommodations with dwelling structures, and as we have seen, these particular accommodations are fundamentally about dwelling itself. The dwelling of some, then, is disclosed in the birth that frames the capacity of another, their child, to inhabit a particular body and to live in the world. It is a similar story with respect to deaths.

Two distinct tendencies emerged within the ethnography in relation to death and dwelling structures. On the one hand, there are those such as Betty and the other widowed women I met in South Hightown, who continue to live on in the same dwelling structure they inhabited with their late husbands. Frequently allied to the keeping of particular effects – notably ashes and other mementos (Hallam and Hockey 2001) – living on in the space of cohabitation is a means both to preserve the absent presence of cohabitation and of memorialising loss in dwelling. It activates the ghost of the dead. In contrast, for others the response to living with death was very different. In the course of many of our many conversations, Peggy talked with me repeatedly about two key events in her life, the death of her parents and also about her and Harry's future deaths. The death of her mother – a few years after her father's – was the event which precipitated Peggy and Harry's moving from their own house to a council-owned bungalow. Peggy explained this to me, emphasising that she could not continue to live in a house that was still inhabited by the ghosts of her sick parents. Its accommodation of them both through long periods of terminal illness, and Peggy's emotional investments in their care within her home, had worked to transform her home from a place of pride to a place of painful memory. Moving house was the only way in which she could come to a degree of accommodation with this trace, by making herself absent from this dwelling structure through moving along. When I went back to see Peggy several months after the fieldwork, she spoke a lot about her own anticipated death but also about Harry's, saying that if Harry died first she would 'Go back home; there's nothing for me here.' I asked Peggy what she meant by this. She replied that 'home' was the village of her birth and childhood, not this place to which she had moved when she married Harry and in which she has lived for the past thirty-five years. Ostensibly, Peggy's dwelling history looks like a clear example of enduringness. Not only have she and Harry lived together in the same place for thirty-five years, but they have lived on the same street all this time. Peggy, however, regards this as no more than an accommodation. Like the much younger Sandra and Steve, for her cohabitation has required her to accommodate to another's dwelling. But, for her to dwell alone seems to require that she returns to the place she feels to be home, accommodating to death by moving along.

Much as with birth, death has the capacity to disclose both living as dwelling and living as accommodation. Moving out or staying in the dwelling structure are both responses to birth and death events, but when staying occurs it intimates that dwelling is potentially going on, at least for someone who inhabits the dwelling structure. For sure, it may be that staying is just easier, less effort and a means to carry on with the day-to-day practices of everyday life in a routine, unexamined way, whereas moving house – however short the distance – works to disrupt and rupture at least some of these rhythms and securities. But staying is also about the emotional securities that living in a particular dwelling structure continues to confer, at least for some. We can see this with Ellie, with Rob, with Betty. And there are others in the ethnography who also talk in the same way – like Pauline, who talks about her house as a place which she's not leaving 'until I'm carried out in me box', and Judy, who talks more elliptically about it taking 'a very great deal to get me to move from here'. Some of the dwelling structures in this ethnography, then, are very much places of dwelling. They have been rebuilt to accommodate births and have the capacity to absorb the absent presence of death, and they are where some of their inhabitants at least feel most at home, comfortable and at peace. Importantly, this is irrespective of the fabric of the structure itself. It could be a suburban 'box' (like Judy's), a nineteenth-century terraced cottage (Pauline, Rob, Ellie) or a one-bedroom council bungalow (Betty). Equally, though, the very same dwelling structures can be just an accommodation for cohabiting others. Indeed, what emerges from this ethnography is that whilst contemporary dwelling structures have the potential for dwelling, the social relations of cohabitation can work to preclude this, resting instead on the capacity of others who live with them to live through accommodation.

Consumption, material culture and dwelling

As will be evident from the previous section, to regard the contemporary moment as one in which we have lost the capacity to dwell would be inappropriate. Rather, even in ordinary households such as those participating in this ethnography, we can still find dwelling in the Heideggerian sense, as a precursor to building. Even in its commoditised form, then, housing has the capacity to absorb the building that connotes dwelling, in the form of loft conversions and extensions particularly. Moreover, and as we have seen, in South Hightown at least, dwelling in the sense of being at home in place has not disappeared. Indeed, here – and in sharp contradistinction to some of the prevailing theoretical representations of modernity – we can still easily find dwelling structures that have been lived in by generations of one family, and streets inhabited by generations of families, admittedly living in juxtaposition to others whose lives have been geographically more extensive and mobile.

For the majority of UK householders however, the connection between building and dwelling has been severed. Although the building of extensions and loft conversions continues apace, the workings of the UK housing market ensure that many more UK householders move each year rather than stay to build. As I argued in Chapter 1, though, whilst this might look like an end to dwelling, it is not. Rather, and as this volume clearly demonstrates, what has occurred is a shift in the locus of dwelling, from building to the activities of dwelling, and specifically to doing things with and to the things to hand around us. Being 'at home', then, is achieved through living amongst certain things and doing things with and to these things. Some of these things are those memorialised and enclaved things which have featured so strongly in material culture studies over recent years. But being 'at home' is also achieved through what is done with and to ordinary everyday consumer objects. At one level, the presence (and absence) of these objects in our homes enables the narration of the self we wish to be seen to be. At another, though, as the ethnographic stories of previous chapters show, being 'at home' is fundamentally about various practices of inhabitation. These practices range across temporal registers that range from moving in/out of a dwelling structure at one extreme, to the daily need for human sleep or the repetitive changing and laundering of a young baby's clothes at the other. But all these practices are doing things with and to the things we have to hand around us in dwelling structures, which includes getting rid of them. And, as I have argued here, it is through these practices that we constitute accommodating dwelling structures, shifting an accommodation to a home. Moreover, it is through these practices of inhabitation that things themselves move into what I have termed the 'gap in accommodation'. And it is in the gap produced by handling and doing things with and to ordinary consumer objects that we negotiate the staying, holding, keeping and ridding of things. For me, then, ridding is part of dwelling. Yet ridding is simultaneously about saving and wasting and the connections of both to love, devotion and the relations of living in cohabitation within households. In shifting consumption research from sites of exchange back into the home, consumption has in a sense both come home and been reconfigured. What I hope to have achieved here is to demonstrate just how important both dwelling and living with ordinary everyday things actually are to the advancement of work on the material culture of the home.

NOTES

1 See Bataille (1989), Hubert and Mauss (1964). Miller (1998) provides a good review of this literature, as a backdrop for his reading of shopping as sacrifice in London.

2 This is not to say that dwelling is closed off by birth and death, in the manner of the phenomenological sense of being in the world. But it is to insist on the significance of birth and death to any sense of human inhabitation. To inhabit rests on bringing into the world a particular body in which to live in the world, whilst death moves that body along, simultaneously bringing into becoming the absent presence of having lived. The other key event which moves us through dwelling structures is divorce and/or separation.

Appendix

Location of fieldwork: North-east England ('South Hightown' – a former coal-mining village in County Durham, and suburban Newcastle).

Number of households: 16
Number of participants: 38
Number of adults: 28 (17 women, 11 men)
Number of children: 10

Ages of participants:

< 18	18–25	26–35	36–45	46–55	56–65	66–75	> 75
10	–	8	7	5	3	8	–

Ethnicity:

White British: 38

Social class of households (by main earner):

I	II	IIIN	IIIM	IV	V
1	5	4	3	3	–

Education (by highest qualification):

none	GCSE/OL	AL	NVQ	HNC	Diploma	UG degree	Higher degree
10	3	–	3	1	1	9	1

Dwelling type:

Pre 1939–1945		Post 1945	
Small terrace	3	Small terrace	
Medium terrace	2	Medium terrace	
Large terrace	1	Large terrace	
Small semi		Small semi	4
Medium semi		Medium semi	1
Large semi		Large semi	1
Medium detached		Medium detached	
Large detached	1	Large detached	
Bungalow		Bungalow	3

Housing tenure:

Owner occupiers: 10
Council tenants: 6

Length of occupation:

< 6 months	6–12 months	1–2 years	3–5 years	5–10 years	11–15 years	16–20 years	> 21 years
1	2	–	5	2	5	–	1

Bibliography

Amit, V. (ed.) (2000), *Constructing the Field: Ethnographic Fieldwork in the Contemporary World*. London: Routledge.

Anderson, K. (2003), 'White natures: Sydney's Royal Agricultural Show in post humanist perspective', *Transactions Institute of British Geographers* 28: 422–41.

Armstrong, K. (2000), *Our Village: Memories of the Durham Mining Communities*. Seaham: The People's History Ltd.

Appadurai, A. (ed.) (1986), *The Social Life of Things: Commodities in Cultural Perspective*. Cambridge: Cambridge University Press.

Atkinson, I. (2001), *Life and Tradition in Northumberland and Durham*. Otely: Smith Settle.

Attfield, J. (2000), *Wild Things: The Material Culture of Everyday Life*. Oxford: Berg.

Aull Davis, C. (1999), *Reflexive Ethnography: a Guide to Researching Selves and Others*. London: Routledge.

Banim, A. and Guy, E. (eds) (2003), *Through the Wardrobe: Women's Relationship to their Clothes*. Oxford: Berg.

Barr, S. (2004), 'What we buy, what we throw away and how we use our voice, sustainable household waste management in the UK', *Sustainable Development* 12 (1): 32–44.

Barr, S., Gilg, A. and Ford, N. (2001), 'A conceptual framework for understanding and analysing attitudes towards household-waste management', *Environment and Planning A* 33 (11): 2025–48.

Bataille, G. (1989), *The Accursed Share, Volume I*. New York: Zone Books.

Bauman, Z. (2002), *Liquid Modernity*. Cambridge: Polity Press.

Belk, R. (1995), *Collecting in a Consumer Society*. London: Routledge.

Bell, D., Caplan, P. and Karim, W. J. (eds) (1993), *Gendered Fields: Women, Men and Ethnography*. London: Routledge.

Bennett, K., Beynon, H. and Hudson, R. (2000), *Coalfields Regeneration: Dealing with the Consequences of Industrial Decline*. Bristol: Policy.

Beynon, H. (ed.) (1984), *Digging Deeper: Issues in the Miners' Strike*. London: Verso.

Beynon, H., Cox, A. and Hudson, R. (2000), *Digging up Trouble: the Environment, Protest and Opencast Coal Mining*. London: Rivers Oram.

Birdwell-Pheasant, D. and Lawrence-Zúñiga, D. (1999), *House Life: Space, Place and Family in Europe*. Oxford: Berg.

Bhatti, M. and Church, A. (2001), 'Cultivating natures: homes and gardens in late modernity', *Sociology* 35: 365–83.

Boldero, J. (1995), 'The prediction of household recycling of newspapers – the role of attitudes, intentions and situational factors', *Journal of Applied Social Psychology* 25 (5): 440–62.

Bowlby. R. (2000), *Carried Away*. London: Faber and Faber.

Brook, I. (2003), 'Making here like there: place attachment, displacement and the urge to garden', *Ethics, Place and Environment* 6: 227–34.

Buchli. V. (ed.) (2002), *The Material Culture Reader*. Oxford: Berg.

Buchli, V. and Lucas, G. (2000), 'Children, gender and the material culture of domestic abandonment in the late 20th century', in J. Sofaer-Derevenski (ed.), *Children and Material Culture*. London: Routledge.

Buchli, V. and Lucas, G. (2001), *Archaeologies of the Contemporary Past*. London: Routledge.

Bulmer, M. (ed.) (1978), *Mining and Social Change: Durham County in the 20th century*. London: Croom Helm.

Chapman, D. and Hockey, J. (eds) (1999), *Ideal Homes?* London: Routledge.

Chevalier, S. (1998), 'From woollen carpet to grass carpet: bridging house and garden in and English suburb', in D. Miller (ed.), *Material Cultures*. London: UCL Press.

Chappells, H. and Shove, E. (1999), 'The dustbin: a study of domestic waste, household practices and utility services', *International Planning Studies* 4: 267–80.

Cieraad, I. (ed.) (1999), *At Home: An Anthropology of Domestic Space*. Syracuse: Syracuse University Press.

Clark, A. (ed.) (2002), *Mining Memories: Stories of the Northumberland and Durham Coalfields*. Seaham: People's History.

Clarke, A. (1998), 'Window shopping at home: classified, catalogues and new consumer skills', in D. Miller (ed.), *Material Cultures*, pp 73–99. London: UCL Press.

Clarke, A. (1999), *Tupperware: the Promise of Plastic in 1950s America*. Washington and London: Smithsonian Institution Press.

Clarke, A. (2000), '"Mother swapping": the trafficking of nearly new children's wear', in P. Jackson, M. Lowe, D. Miller and F. Mort (eds.), *Commercial Cultures: Economies, Practices, Spaces*, pp. 85–100. Oxford: Berg.

Clarke, A. (2001), 'The aesthetics of social aspiration', in D. Miller (ed.), *Home Possessions*, pp. 23–46. Oxford: Berg.

Clarke, A. (2002), 'Taste wars and design dilemmas: aesthetic practice in the home', in C. Painter (ed.), *Contemporary Art and the Home*, pp. 131–52.

Oxford: Berg.

Clifford, J. (1997), *Routes*. Cambridge, CA: Harvard University Press.

Cockburn, C. (1985), *Machinery of Dominance: Women, Men and Technical Know How*. London: Pluto Press.

Coffey, A. (1999), *The Ethnographic Self*. London: Sage.

Colloredo-Mansfeld, R. (2003), 'Introduction: matter unbound', *Journal of Material Culture* 8: 245–54.

Cooper, T. (2003), 'Durable consumption: reflections on product life cycles and the throwaway society'. Paper presented at Product Life and the Throwaway Society Workshop (Sheffield Hallam University, Centre for Sustainable Consumption), 21 May 2003.

Cooper, T. and Mayers, K. (2000), *Prospects for household appliances, The E-Scope Report*. Halifax: Urban Mines.

Cowan, R. S. (1983), *More Work for Mother: the Ironies of Household Technology from the Open Hearth to the Microwave*. New York, Basic Books.

Csikszentmihalyi, M. and Rochberg-Halton, E. (1981), *The Meaning of Things: Domestic Symbols and the Self*. Cambridge: Cambridge University Press.

Cwerner, S. and Metcalfe, A. (2003), 'Storage and clutter: discourses and practices of order in the domestic world', *Journal of Design History* 16: 229–40.

Dahab, D., Gentry, J. and Su, W. (1995), 'New ways to research non-recyclers: an extension of the model of reasoned action to recycling behaviours', *Advances in Consumer Research* 22: 251–6.

Dant, T. (1999), *Material Culture in the Social World: Values, Activities, Lifestyles*. Buckingham: Open University Press.

de Certeau, M., Giard, L. and Mayol, P. (1998), *The Practice of Everyday Life, Volume II*. Minneapolis: University of Minnesota Press.

DoE (1990), *This Common Inheritance: Britain's Environmental Strategy*. London: HMSO.

DoE and Welsh Office (1995), *Making Waste Work: a Strategy for Sustainable Waste Management in England and Wales*. London: HMSO.

DoE Transport and the Regions (2000), *Waste Strategy 2000 for England and Wales*. London: HMSO.

Douglas, M. (1966), *Purity and Danger: an Analysis of the Concepts of Pollution and Taboo*. London: Routledge.

Dwyer, C. and Jackson, P. (2003), 'Commodifying difference: selling EASTern fashion', *Environment and Planning D: Society and Space* 21: 269–91.

Ellis, R. and Haywood, A. (2004), 'Virtual radiophile? The changing collecting practices of the vintage radio community in an Internet era', *Chimera Working Paper* 2004 (13), August 2004.

Emery, A., Griffiths, A. and Williams, A. (2003), 'An in depth study of the effects of socio-economic conditions on household waste recycling practices', *Waste Management and Research* 21 (3): 180–90.

Entwistle, J. (2002), 'The aesthetic economy: the production of value in the field of fashion modelling', *Journal of Consumer Culture* 2: 317–39.

Farrell Krell, D. (ed.) (1978), *Basic Writings: Martin Heidegger*. London: Routledge.

Fisher, T. and Shipton, J. (2003), 'In and out of the twilight zone: understanding packaging re-use'. Paper presented at Product Life and the Throwaway Society Workshop (Sheffield Hallam University, Centre for Sustainable Consumption), 21 May 2003.

Freeman, H. (2002), 'A family and its rubbish – an everyday story of unnecessary waste', *The Guardian*, 28 December 2002.

Freidberg, S. (2003), 'Cleaning up down South: supermarkets, ethical trade and African horticulture', *Social and Cultural Geography* 4: 27–43.

Freidberg, S. (2004), 'The ethical complex of corporate food power', *Environment and Planning D: Society and Space* 22: 513–31.

Garber, M. (1992), 'Overcoming 'auction block': stories masquerading as objects', *Critical Quarterly* 34 (4): 74–96.

Garvey, P. (2001), 'Organised disorder: moving furniture in Norwegian homes', in D. Miller (ed.), *Home Possessions*, pp. 47–68. Oxford: Berg.

Gereffi, G., Korzeniewicz, M. and Korzeniewicz, R. (eds) (1994), *Commodity Chains and Global Capitalism*. Connecticut: Greenwood.

Gershuny, J. (1978), *After Industrial Society: the Emerging Self-Service Economy*. London, Macmillan.

Gregson, N. and Crewe, L. (1997), 'Performance and possession: rethinking the act of purchase in the light of the car boot sale', *Journal of Material Culture* 2: 241–63.

Gregson, N., Crewe, L. and Longstaff, B. (1997), 'Excluded spaces of regulation: car boot sales as an enterprise culture out of control?', *Environment and Planning A* 29: 1717–37.

Gregson, N. and Crewe, L. (1998), 'Dusting down Second-hand Rose: gendered identities and the world of second-hand goods in the space of the car boot sale', *Gender, Place and Culture* 5: 77–100.

Gregson, N., Crewe, L. and Brooks, K. (2000), 'Narratives of consumption and the body in the space of the charity shop', in P. Jackson, L. Crewe and K. Brooks (eds), *Commercial Cultures: Economies, Practices, Spaces*, pp. 101–22. Oxford: Berg.

Gregson, N., Crewe, L. and Brooks, K. (2002a), 'Discourse, displacement and retail practice: some pointers from the charity retail project', *Environment and Planning A* 34: 1661 – 83.

Gregson, N., Crewe, L. and Brooks, K. (2002b), 'Shopping, space and practice', *Environment and Planning D: Society and Space* 20: 597 – 617.

Gregson, N. and Crewe, L. (2003), *Second-hand Cultures*. Oxford: Berg.

Gregson, N. and Beale, V. (2004). 'Wardrobe matter: the sorting, displacement and circulation of women's clothing', *Geoforum* 35: 689 – 700.

Gregson, N., Metcalfe, A. and Crewe, L. (in press) 'Identity, mobility and the throwaway society', *Environment and Planning D: Society and Space* (forthcoming).

Gullestad, M. (1984), *Kitchen Table Society: A Case Study of the Family Life and Friendships of Young Working Class Mothers in Urban Norway*. Oslo: Universitetsforlaget.

Gullestad, M. (1993), 'Home decoration as popular culture: constructing homes, genders and classes in Norway', in T. del Valle (ed.), *Gendered Anthropology*, pp. 128–61. London: Routledge.

Gupta, A. and Ferguson, J. (eds.) (1997), *Anthropological Locations: Boundaries and Grounds of a Field Science*. Berkeley, CA: University of California Press.

Hallam, E. and Hockey, J. (2001), *Death, Memory and Material Culture*. Oxford: Berg.

Hartwick, E. (1998), 'Geographies of consumption: a commodity chain approach', *Environment and Planning D: Society and Space* 16: 423–37.

Hartwick, E. (2000), 'Towards a geographical politics of consumption', *Environment and Planning A* 32: 1177–92.

Harvey, D. (1989), *The Condition of Postmodernity*. Oxford: Basil Blackwell.

Hawkins, G. (2000), 'Plastic bags: living with rubbish', *International Journal of Cultural Studies* 4: 5–23.

Hawkins, G. and Muecke, S. (eds) (2003), *Culture and Waste: The Creation and Destruction of Value*. Lanham, Maryland: Rowman and Littlefield.

Heidegger, M. (1978) [1954], 'Building, dwelling, thinking', in D. Farrell Krell (ed.), *Basic Writings: Martin Heidegger*, pp. 347–63. London: Routledge.

Held, D., McGrew, A., Goldblatt, D. and Perraton, J. (1999), *Global Transformations*. Cambridge: Polity Press.

Hertz, R.(1960), *Death and the Right Hand*. New York: Free Press.

Hetherington, K. (2004), 'Secondhandedness: consumption, disposal and absent presence', *Environment and Planning D: Society and Space* 22: 157–73.

Highmore, B. (2002), *Everyday Life and Cultural Theory: an Introduction*. London: Routledge.

Hirsch, E. (1992), 'The long term and the short term of domestic consumption: an ethnographic case study', in R. Silverstone and E. Hirsch (eds), *Consuming Technologies: Media and Information in Domestic Spaces*, pp. 208–26. London: Routledge.

Hitchings, R. (2003), 'People, plants and performance: on actor network theory and the material pleasures of the private garden', *Social and Cultural Geography* 4: 99–113.

Hoskins, J. (1998), *Biographical Objects*. London: Routledge.

Hubert, H and Mauss, M. (1964). *Sacrifice: Its nature and Functions*. Chicago: University of Chicago Press.

Hubbard, P. and Lilley, K. (2004), 'Pacemaking the modern city: the urban politics of speed and slowness', *Environment and Planning D: Society and Space* 22: 273–94.

Hudson, M. (1994), *Coming Back Brockens: a Year in a Mining Village*. London: Cape.

Hudson, R. (1989), *Wrecking a Region*. London: Pion.

Hughes, A. (2000), 'Retailers, knowledges and changing commodity networks: the case of the cut flower trade', *Geoforum* 31: 175–90.

Hughes, A. and Reimer, S. (eds) (2003), *Geographies of Commodity Chains*. London: Pearson.

Ingold, T. (2000), *The Perception of the Environment: Essays in Livelihood, Dwelling and Skill*, London: Routledge.

Jackson, P. (1999), 'Commodity cultures: the traffic in things', *Transactions Institute of British Geographers* 24: 95–108.

Jackson, P. (2004), 'Local consumption cultures in a globalising world', *Transactions Institute of British Geographers* 29: 165–78.

Jackson, P. and Thrift, N. (1995), 'Geographies of consumption', in D. Miller (ed.), *Acknowledging Consumption*, pp. 204–37. London: Routledge.

Jackson, P., Perez del Aguila, R., Clarke, I., Hallsworth, A., de Kervenoael, R. and Kirkup, M. (2006), 'Retail restructuring and consumer choice 2: understanding consumer choice at the household level', *Environment and Planning A* 38: 47–67.

James A., Hockey, J. and Dawson, A. (eds) (1997), *After Writing Culture: Epistemology and Praxis in Contemporary Anthropology*. London: Routledge.

Kopytoff, I. (1986), 'The cultural biography of things: commodification as a process'. in A. Appadurai (ed.), *The Social Life of Things*, pp. 64–94. Cambridge: Cambridge University Press.

Kwint, M., Breward, C. and Aynsley, J. (eds) (1999), *Material Memories: Design and Evocation*. Oxford: Berg.

Laporte, D. (2002), *History of Shit*. Cambridge, MA: The MIT Press.

Layne, L. (1999), 'He was a real baby with baby things: a material culture of personhood, parenthood and pregnancy loss', in H. Ragoné and W. Twine (eds), *Ideologies and Technologies of Motherhood*. London: Routledge.

Leslie, D. and Reimer, S. (1999), 'Spatializing commodity chains', *Progress in Human Geography* 23: 401–20.

Leslie, D. and Reimer, S. (2003), 'Fashioning furniture: restructuring the furniture commodity chain', *Area* 35: 427–37.

Livingstone, S. (1992), 'The meaning of domestic technologies: a personal construct analysis of familial gender relations', in R. Silverstone and E. Hirst (eds), *Consuming Technologies: Media and Information in Domestic Spaces*, pp. 113–30. London: Routledge.

Lucas, G. (2002), 'Disposability and dispossession in the twentieth century', *Journal of Material Culture* 7: 5–22.

Macdonald, S. (1997), *Reimagining Culture: Histories, Identities and the Gaelic*

Renaissance. Oxford: Berg.

Macdonald, S. (2002), *Behind the Scenes at the Science Museum*. Oxford: Berg.

Madigan, R. and Munro, M (1996), '"House beautiful": styles and consumption in the home', *Sociology* 30 (1): 41–57.

Massey, D. (1993), 'Power geometry and a progressive sense of place', in J. Bird et. al. (eds), *Mapping the Futures: Local Cultures, Global Change*, pp. 59–69. London: Routledge.

Mara, C. (1998), 'Divestments', in K. Dunseath (ed.), *A Second Skin: Women Write about their Clothes*, pp. 57–60. London: The Women's Press.

Marcoux, J.-S. (2001), 'The refurbishment of memory', in D. Miller (ed.), *Home Possessions*, pp. 69–86. Oxford: Berg.

McDonald, S. and Ball, R. (1998), 'Public participation in plastics recycling schemes', *Resources Conservation and Recycling* 22 (3–4): 123–41.

McDonald, S. and Oates, C. (2003), 'Reasons for non-participation in a kerbside recycling scheme', *Resources Conservation and Recycling* 39 (4): 369–85.

McDowell, L. and Massey, D. (1984), 'A Woman's Place', in D. Massey and J. Allen (eds), *Geography Matters*. Cambridge: Cambridge University Press.

McKendrick, N. (1959/60), 'Josiah Wedgwood: an eighteenth century entrepreneur in salesmanship and marketing techniques', *Economic History Review* 12: 408–33.

McKendrick, N., Brewer, J. and Plumb, J. (eds) (1983), *The Birth of a Consumer Society: the Commercialisation of the Eighteenth Century*. London: Hutchinson.

Mee, N., Clewes, D., Phillips, D. and Read, A. (2004), 'Effective implementation of a marketing communications strategy for kerbside recycling: a case study from Rushcliffe, UK', *Resources Conservation and Recycling* 42 (1): 1–26.

Miller, D. (1987), *Material Culture and Mass Consumption*. Oxford: Blackwell.

Miller, D. (1988), 'Appropriating the state on the council estate', *Man* 23: 353–72.

Miller, D. (1997), 'Consumption and its consequences', in H. Mackay (ed.), *Consumption and Everyday Life*, pp. 14–48. London: Sage.

Miller, D. (1998), *A Theory of Shopping*. Cambridge: Polity.

Miller, D., Jackson, P., Thrift, N., Holbrook, B. and Rowlands, M. (1998), *Shopping, Place and Identity*. London: Routledge.

Miller, D. (2001a), 'Possessions', in D. Miller (ed.), *Home Possessions*, pp. 107–22. Oxford: Berg.

Miller, D. (ed.) (2001b), *Home Possessions*. Oxford: Berg.

Miller, D. (2001c), *The Dialectics of Shopping*. Chicago: The University of Chicago Press.

Miller, D. (2002a), 'Consumption', in V. Buchli (ed.), *The Material Culture Reader*, pp. 237–43. Oxford: Berg.

Miller, D. (2002b), 'Accommodating', in C. Painter (ed.), *Contemporary Art and the Home*, pp. 115–30. Oxford: Berg.

Milligan, C., Gattrell, A. and Bingley, A. (2004), '"Cultivating health": therapeutic landscapes and older people in Northern England', *Social and Cultural Geography* 58: 1781–93.

Mintel (2003), *DIY Review – UK*. http://reports.mintel.com/sinatra/mintel/my_infro/expand (accessed 16 July 2004).

MORI (2002), *Public Attitudes Towards Recycling and Waste Management*. Research study conducted for Strategy Unit, Cabinet Office (September 2002). Report available at http://www.strategy-gov.uk/2002/waste/downloads/mori/pdf (accessed 30 October 2003).

Munro, R. (1995), 'Disposal of the meal', in D. Marshall (ed.), Food Choice and the Food Consumer, pp. 313 – 25. Glasgow: Blackie.

Munro, R. (1998), 'Disposal of the X gap: the production and consumption of accounting research and practical accounting systems', Advances in Public Interest Accounting 7: 139–59.

National Statistics (2002), Social Trends Volume 32. http://www.statistics.gov.uk

National Statistics (2004), Social Trends Volume 34. http://www/statistics.gov.uk

Nayak, A. (2003), Race, Place and Globalisation: Youth Culture in a Changing World. Oxford: Berg.

Norris, L (2004a), 'Creative entrepreneurs: the recycling of second hand Indian clothing', in A. Palmer and H. Clark (eds), *Old Clothes, New Looks: Second Hand Fashion*. Oxford, Berg.

Norris, L. (2004b), 'Shedding skins: the materiality of divestment in India', *Journal of Material Culture* 9: 59–71.

Obara, L. (2006) *Is Waste Minimisation a Challenge Too Far? The Experience of Household Waste Management and Purchasing in the UK*. Centre for Business Relationships, Accountability, Sustainability and Society. Working Paper Series No. 29: Cardiff University.

O'Brien, M. (1999), 'Rubbish power: towards a sociology of the rubbish society', in J. Hearn and S. Roseneil (eds), *Consuming Cultures*, pp. 262–77. Basingstoke: Macmillan.

Okely, J. (1996), *Own or Other Culture*. London: Routledge.

Okely J. and Callaway, H. (eds) (1992), *Anthropology and Autobiography*. London: Routledge.

Pahl, R. (1984), *Divisions of Labour*. Oxford: Basil Blackwell.

Painter, C. (ed.) (2002), *Contemporary Art in the Home*. Oxford: Berg.

Palmer, A. and Clark, H. (eds) (2004), *Old Clothes, New Looks: Second Hand Fashion*. Oxford: Berg.

Parker, R. (1995), *Torn in Two: the Experience of Maternal Ambivalence*. London: Virago.

Parfitt, J., Lovett, A. and Sunnenberg, G. (2001), 'A classification of local authority waste collection and recycling strategies in England and Wales', *Resources Conservation and Recycling* 32 (3–4): 239–57.

Pattison, G. (2004), 'Planning for decline: the D village policy of County Durham, UK', *Planning Perspectives* 19: 311–32.

Pearce, S. (1995), *On Collecting*. London: Routledge.

Pearce, S. (1998), *Collecting in Contemporary Practice*. London: Sage.

Perrin, D. and Barton, J. (2001), 'Issues associated with transforming household attitudes and opinions into materials recovery: a review of two kerbside recycling schemes', *Resources Conservation and Recycling* 33(1): 61–74.

Pink, S. (2000), 'Informants who "come home"', in V. Amit (ed.), *Constructing the Field: Ethnographic Fieldwork in the Contemporary World*, pp. 96–119. London: Routledge.

Pink, S. (2004), *Home Truths: Gender, Domestic Objects and Everyday Life*. Oxford: Berg.

Price, J. (2001), 'The landfill directive and the challenge ahead: demands and pressures on the UK householder', *Resources Conservation and Recycling* 32 (3–4): 333–48.

Raikes, P., Jensen, M. and Ponte, S. (2000), 'Global commodity chain analysis and the French filière approach: comparison and critique', *Economy and Society* 29: 390–417.

Rathje, W. and Murphy, C. (2001), *Rubbish: An Archaeology of Garbage*. Tuscon: University of Arizona Press.

Rose, G. (1997), 'Situated knowledges: positionality, reflexivities and other tactics', *Progress in Human Geography* 21: 305–20.

Scanlan, J. (2004), *On Garbage*. London: Reaktion Books.

Sennett, R. (2003), *Respect: the Formation of Character in an Age of Inequality*. London: Penguin Books.

Shove, E. (2003), *Comfort, Cleanliness and Convenience: the Social Organisaton of Normality*. Oxford: Berg.

Shove, E. and Southerton, D. (2001), 'Defrosting the freezer: from novelty to convenience: a narrative of normalisation', Journal of Material Culture 5: 301–19.

Skeggs, B. (1997), *Formations of Class and Gender: Becoming Respectable*. London: Sage.

Strasser, S. (2000), *Waste and Want: A Social History of Trash*. New York: Owl Books.

Strategy Unit (2002), *Waste Not Want Not*. http://www.number-10.gov.uk/su/waste/report (accessed 30 October 2003).

Storr, M. (2004), *Latex and Lingerie: Shopping for Pleasure at Ann Summers Parties*. Oxford: Berg.

Thrift, N. (2003), 'Practising ethics', in M. Pryke, G. Rose and S. Whatmore (eds), *Using Social Theory: Thinking through Research*, pp. 105–21. London: Sage.

Thomas, N. (1991), *Entangled Objects: Exchange, Material Culture and Colonialism in the Pacific*. Cambridge MA: Harvard University Press.

Thompson, M. (1979), *Rubbish Theory: the Creation and Destruction of Value*. Oxford: Oxford University Press.

Tonglet, M., Phillips, P. and Read, A. (2004), 'Using the theory of planned behaviour to investigate the determinants of recycling behaviour: a case study from Brixworth, UK', *Resources Conservation and Recycling* 41 (3): 191–214.

Tonglet, M., Phillips, P. and Bates, M. (2004), 'Determining the drivers for householder pro-environmental behaviour: waste minimisation compared to recycling', *Resources Conservation and Recycling* 42 (1): 27–48.

Tranberg Hansen, K. (2000), *Salaula: The World of Second-hand Clothing and Zambia*. Chicago: University of Chicago Press.

Urry, J. (2002), 'Mobility and proximity', *Sociology* 36: 255–74.

Urry, J. (2004), 'Connections', *Environment and Planning D: Society and Space* 22: 27–37.

Valentine, G. (1997), 'A safe place to grow up? Parenting, perceptions of children's safety and the rural idyll', *Journal of Rural Studies* 13: 137–48.

Warde, A. (2005), 'Consumption and theories of practice', *Journal of Consumer Culture* 5: 131–53.

Wardhaugh, J. (1999), 'The unaccommodated woman: home, homelessness and identity', *Sociological Review* 47: 91–109.

Weiner, A. (1992), *Inalienable Possessions: the Paradox of Keeping-while-Giving*, Berkeley CA: University of California Press.

Williams, P., Hubbard, P., Clark, D. and Berkeley, N. (2001), 'Consumption, exclusion and emotion: the social geographies of shopping', *Social and Cultural Geography* 2: 203–20.

Williamson B. (1982), *Class, Culture and Community*. London: Routledge.

Young, D. (2001), 'The life and death of cars: private vehicles on the Pitjantjatjara Lands, South Australia', in D. Miller (ed.), *Car Cultures*, pp. 35–57. Oxford: Berg.

Young, D. (2004), 'The material value of color: the estate agent's tale', *Home Cultures* 1: 5–22.

Index